MW00659423

Nataraj Books
7073-75 Brookfield Plaza
Springfield, VA 22150
Phone (703) 455-4996

MUSIC MAKERS

Living Legends of Indian Classical Music

MUSIC MAKERS

Living Legends of Indian Classical Music

ASHOK ROY

Rupa & Co

Grateful acknowledgement to:

Shri Harish Kapadia
Smt. Kasturi Chaurasia
Shri Lalgudi Krishnan
Smt. Madhura Jasraj
Smt. Mayuri Sharma
Shri Mohan Ramani
Shri. P.G. Burde
Shri Rattan Mohan Sharma
Dr. Saraswati
Ms. Shamira
Dr. Soma Ghosh
Shri S. Radhakrishnan
Smt. Subhalakshmi Khan
Smt. Sukanya Shankar
Ms Terry Galindo

Technical Credits:

Art & Design Execution:
Bapu Patil, Kishore Eshwar, T.S. Rasheed

Technical support:
Advertising Avenues, Graphic Vision,
Liberty Graphics, Kshipra Patel, Kshitij Nagwekar
Single tone photographs in the 'Living Memories' section are from the personal collection of the participating maestros.

Colour photographs are by the author.

Some colour pictures of M.S. Subbulakshmi have been specially re-created from available black 'n' white printed material. Courtesy: Shri Atma Nathan.

Conceived and designed for the publisher by
Inner Voice
E-mail : ivoice@vsnl.com

Text Copyright © ***Ashok Roy*** 2004
Colour Photographs Copyright © ***Ashok Roy*** 2004

Published in 2004 by
Rupa & Co
7/16 Ansari Road, Daryagunj
New Delhi 110 002

Sales Centres:
• Allahabad • Bangalore • Chandigarh
• Chennai • Hyderabad • Jaipur
• Kathmandu • Kolkata • Ludhiana
• Mumbai • Pune

All rights reserved.
No part of this publication may be reproduced, stored in a retrieval system, or transmitted in any form or by any means, electronic, mechanical, photocopying, recording or otherwise, without the prior permission of the publishers.

Printed in India by Gopsons Papers Ltd., Noida

C O N T E N T S

Amjad Ali Khan 10
Bhimsen Joshi 24
Bismillah Khan 40
Gangubai Hangal 56
Hariprasad Chaurasia 70
Jasraj 84
Kishan Maharaj 98
Kishori Amonkar 112
Lalgudi Jayaraman 128
M. Balamuralikrishna 142
M. S. Subbulakshmi 156
N. Rajam 170
N. Ramani 184
Ram Narayan 198
Ravi Shankar 214
Semmangudi Srinivasa Iyer 234
Shiv Kumar Sharma 246
T.H.Vinayakram 264
Umayalpuram K. Sivaraman 280
Zakir Hussain 298
Zia Fariduddin Dagar 318

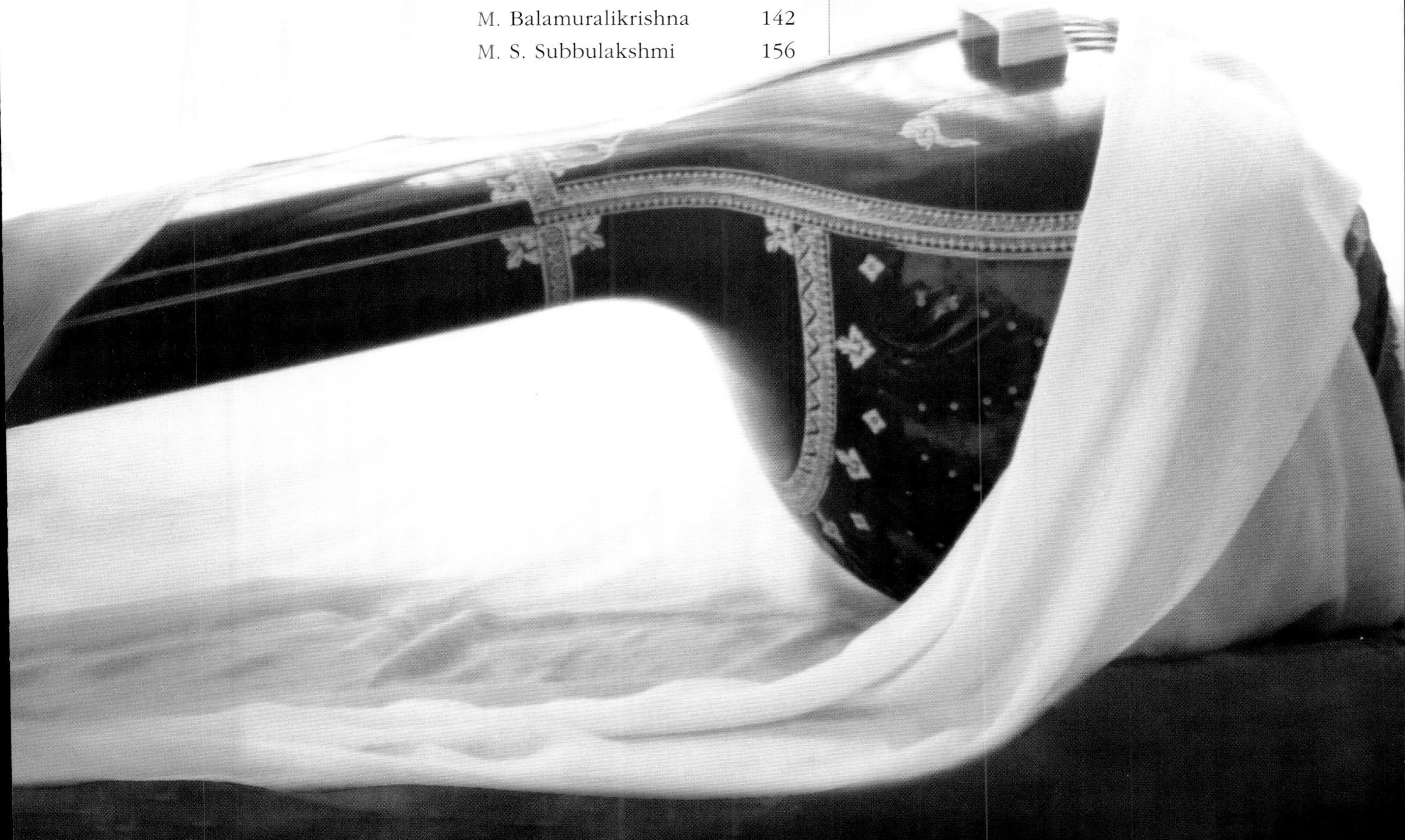

Music Makers

PROLOGUE

If in the beginning there was the word, such a word had to be divinely musical.

In the collective psyche of India, however, what dwells as the origin of the universe is the mystical word Om. And our efforts at comprehending this grand cosmic suggestion is instantly rewarded when we let this spectacular entity enter our mind as sound. When sound speaks to our soul directly and instantaneously, it leaves no doubt that this indeed is true. The Om was, and is, the original 'happening'.

Even today, when we think of Om and let it reverberate into our inner space, we realize that, in all its power and glory, the origin of the universe was musical. The Om is not just sound, it is music. Endless, fathomless, enormous cosmic music.

It is understandable, therefore, that we came to embrace music as an omnipresent, all-nurturing entity since the dawn of the order and logic of music. Thoughts found speech in tune with our vocal chords.

We listened with awe and gratitude to Mother Nature who, accompanied by the dynamic cycle of seasons, provided a constant musical background to the rocking cradle of human evolution. We noticed with recurring wonderment the melodic whistling of languid breeze through hollow bamboo trees...percussive rumblings of simmering volcanoes...pregnant pauses of silence alternating between eloquent breakers lashing the seashores...soothing notes of cascading waterfalls...musical swaying of trees against the aggressive wind...the crescendo of a thunderbolt...and of course, the melodic ecstasy of the falling rain...

With the tuning of our hearts and the maturing of our minds, the heavens began to drift into our grasp. The gods we romanced inspired us to be musical. The celestial Gandharvas and Kinnaras visited us with their heavenly melodies. The sage Narada strummed his Veena and sang praises of his Lord as he roamed the three worlds. And a deep thirst must have haunted our souls when we came to believe that Lord Shiva too sang in glorious isolation in his abode at mount Kailash.

Lav and Kush, the young sons of Rama sang ballads from Ramayana even as they were part of the epic itself. Scriptures moved along musical paths. The hermitages reverberated with the tuneful chanting of the Sam Veda. Wandering mendicants roamed the dust roads with music on their lips. Invoking the blessings of goddess Saraswati, dance, drama, poetry and verse began to celebrate their intense relationship with music.

And then, it was time for that legendary close encounter with heavenly music. The dark enchanter Krishna walked the earth, and played on the mortal heartstrings of the Gopis of Vrindavan with his magical flute. As if, through Krishna's mysterious and playful design, the thunderous power of Om momentarily mellowed into melody. The mortal eye had suddenly glimpsed the cosmic, and its vision had been exulted and expanded forever.

As we began to consciously relate the premise of music in nature, with the promise of music within our spirit, the heritage of Indian music began to take longer strides. As changing seasons affected everyone in the emerging society, and changing moods inspired every individual to self-expression, folk music became the most popular form of relaxation, narration and celebration.

From the songs of harvest to the ballads of valour, from mythical epics to the secular rituals, from lyrical love stories to the tales of conflict, music blended into our way of life. Even the roar of the Punchajanya conch-shell of Krishna, while fanning the fighting spirit in the devastating battle of Kurukshetra, must have had a musical ring to its echo.

Singing legends left their voices resonating in the expanding space of history. From Mira Bai to Kabeer, from Tansen to Tyagaraja, from Narsi Mehta to Sri Chaitanya...from Amir Khusru to Baiju Bawra...saints and scholars left a rippling effect across the length and the breadth of this chosen land of devotion and spirituality.

Today we suspect that everything in the pristine and orderly world is musical. Silence too can be musical. Just as the mother's rhythmic heartbeats are a rocking cradle to the unborn baby, her thoughts and reveries might be the baby's first lullaby. It is just as well, therefore, that moods, emotions and our awareness of time, space and spirit have a direct and compelling relation to the music we create. Both, in spontaneity and within emergent frameworks.

A disciplined inquiry into the nature and appeal of primitive folk music, the music of the soil, the water and the wind, is what is believed to have formed the bedrock of the ragas and the raginis of Indian classical music. Each raga, soaked in the elements of nature, and bathed in intuition and spirituality, dances into existence like a flame every time it is stirred by the vocal chords and shaped by the singer's breath. Just as the rose, which receives sustenance from the plant rooted in the soil, has its own interaction with sunlight and the wind as it blooms. And while each rose is identifiable as a rose, no two roses can be expected to be exactly identical. Similarly, when a raga wafts into existence, it may be rooted within its accepted form and dimensions and even grammar, but the swaras, the shrutis, the style, the mood and the emotions will always give it a unique identity as it rises and merges into time and space...like a moment gone by, never to be repeated or revisited. Words, notes or notations can scarcely capture or convey the colour and essence of Indian music.

Between themselves, the Hindustani style and the Carnatic system of classical Indian music, enshrine an entire world of musicality. As the great North-South divide, they seem to stand apart in fierce individualistic pride and prejudice, reluctant to exchange notes. Yet, to the probing ear, they merge reverentially in the higher or deeper realms of musical appreciation.

While Western classical music offers complete and definitive creations where notes relate to one another in composed consonance and structured harmony, Indian classical music, whether Hindustani or Carnatic, is an intuitive, spontaneous and spiritual outpouring from an inner fountain of melody.

The Carnatic tradition presents fully composed musical creations, or kritis, which like the Western sonata, move along established structural nuances, to elaborate the raga in all its formal and emotional content. The complete picture of the raga remains imprinted in the original and individual composition of the composer. Every new concert therefore, is as much a tribute to the original composer of the kriti, as it is an inviting challenge to the talent and maturity of the current singer.

The Hindustani recital, showing only peripheral adherence to definite or traditional compositions, is always a unique rendition of the raga. Retaining a basic measure of conformity with the structure and movement of the raga, the tala, and the oral tradition of a bandish or a lyrical identity, each recital is always a fresh and unique creation born to the moment and dissolving into the ever flowing river of time.

The early treatise and traditions of Indian music could not flow smoothly along the boulevards of history because Sanskrit, the root language of learning, had to weather political censure. Musical lineage then had to sustain itself through oral and highly secluded, if not secretive, modes of instruction. The Guru-Shishya Parampara, or the preceptor-disciple tradition, was rejuvenated in this environment, and music families or gharanas began their intricate journey through turbulent social, feudal and political influences.

The gharanas, through their legitimate pride and possessive passion for their distinctive style and repertoire of ragas and nuances, flourished in clusters, preserving and enhancing the music flowing from gurus to disciples. The absence of intermingling or cross border osmosis among diverse gharanas has somewhat stifled some musical flourish in certain cases. But this very syndrome, by and large, has also contributed to preserving the character and purity of Indian music during the British rule.

Finally, going beyond social, cultural or historical context, Indian music's most distinctive character lies in its being intuitive and spiritual. The individual musician, whether vocalist or instrumentalist, is the nucleus of this divine art form. It is he, who having mastered the art and craft through years of sadhana and sacrifice, and having earned the blessings of his guru, surrenders to the sweep of spontaneity, and soars above the realms of expectation, every time he sings. The wind beneath his wings being his own individual genius. And in that journey and quest, also lie the joy and liberation of the world that listens.

Precisely the reason why exploring the profiles of some of the living legends of Indian music might be a rewarding experience to even the most casual browser of the following pages.

After all, like the pied piper, it is only the music makers who have the charisma and magnetism to lead us deep into the energized field of Indian music...

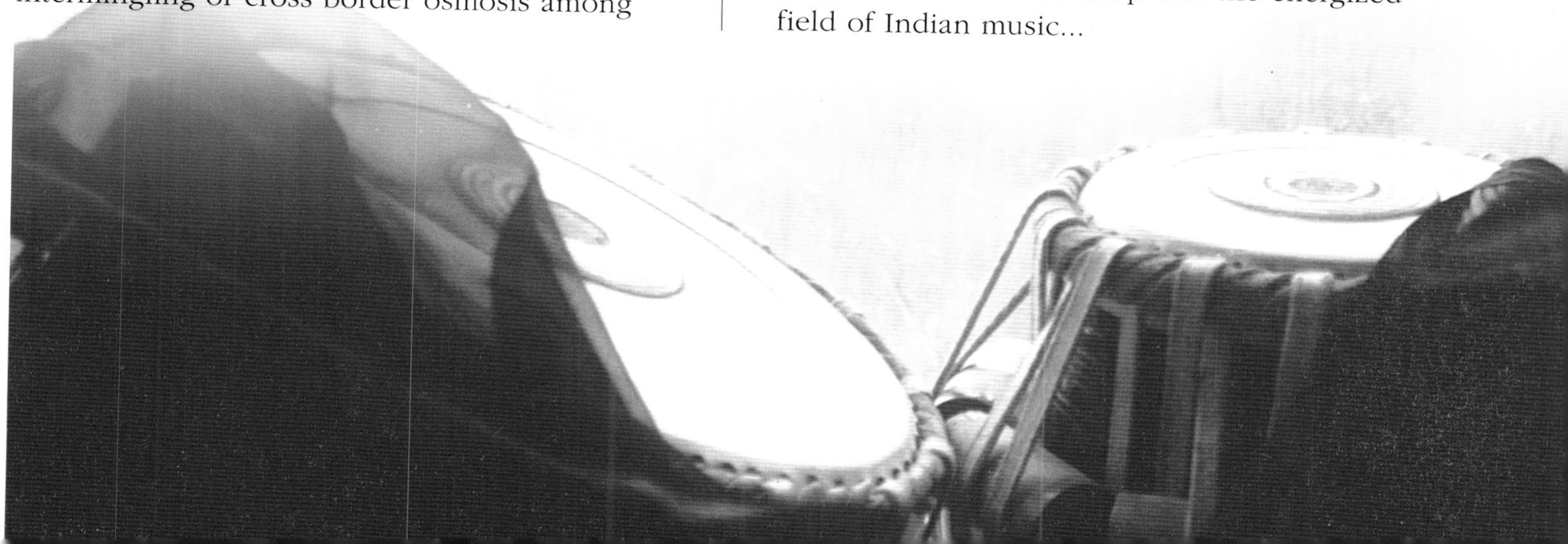

AMJAD ALI
KHAN

All those fables we've heard about legendary music makers from those royal courts of the golden eras appear totally credible today when we set eyes upon Ustad Amjad Ali Khan, the *Monarch of the Sarod*. He is the handsome embodiment of all that's regal and radiant about Indian classical music.

Khan saheb's musical genius is inherited from a glorious lineage and some of it is directly acquired from Haafiz Ali Khan, his father and *ustad,* who played the Sarod with such dexterity and dedication, that he was often revered as the *Prophet of the Sarod*.

Ustad Haafiz Ali Khan's single-minded involvement with his music is legendary. Right after a formal award ceremony at the Rashtrapati Bhavan, India's first President Dr Rajendra Prasad was getting acquainted with this regal personality in a traditional sherwani and turban, to whom he had just handed over the national honour of Padma Bhushan. In the course of polite conversation, the president asked Khan saheb if he could be of any service to him, or help solve any problem he might have. Haafiz Ali Khan replied that he had no personal problem, but simply requested the President to save *Darbari Kanada* from the danger it faced! Dr Rajendra Prasad's genial face must have betrayed some confusion, when Khan saheb explained quite passionately that people were taking undue liberties with the rendition of Miyan Tansen's Raga Darbari, and destroying its sanctity and purity. He, as the president and *badshah* of the country, should be able to do something about it! The president then went on to ask the reassured Khan saheb if he could also grant him any personal favours. Although it would have been both prudent and facile to ask for a government house or any other presidential favour, Ustad Haafiz Ali Khan said with polite gratitude, that he had nothing more to ask for, except the permission to retreat from that august gathering, because it was time for his *namaz*...A young Amjad Ali following hurriedly after his father's long strides, might have been a trifle overwhelmed by the situation to immediately realize that here was another lesson from his guru, albeit spontaneous, that there's nothing more important in this world than your music and your god.

A moving performance: with Vijay Ghate

Not that young Amjad Ali needed any reiteration about the role music had to play in his life. Being sensitive, even at a tender age he was quite aware of his calling in this world. As performer and teacher, Ustad Haafiz Ali Khan had himself done justice to the illustrious ancestry of the Senia-Bangash *gharana* he represented, but unlike the immediate successors of his peers and contemporaries, his progenies or disciples had not earned that kind of eminence. Being born to his father rather unexpectedly in the autumn of his life, young Amjad could sense that a void in his father's heart was gradually being filled with the emergent promise of genius he held out for his father and *ustad*. Although Amjad did not get to see his father's younger days of performance, he strove to get the most out of his father's teachings and philosophy under the *guru-shishya parampara,* in order to fulfill the 'prophet's' final prophesy for the music world.

The sarod had thus become his dear friend and sole playmate at a very tender age, and music, his only passion. There were no conscious choices to be made about one's career or future; a clear destiny held him close and led him by those very hands that had already begun to strum out beautiful music from the glittering instrument.

Many pleasures and exploits of a normal childhood were left standing at a distance, perhaps gaping in silent admiration at the way the austere discipline and application through the long hours of *talim* and *riyaaz* were shaping and polishing the young music maker. Even before he entered his teens, Amjad Ali began to perform on stage and even tour the far corners of the country. His charming, young looks and budding stage presence were in perfect contrast with his growing musical maturity, and the two combined to make a memorable impact on audiences wherever he went.

Soon Amjad Ali Khan became a dazzling name to grace major concerts and music festivals in India and even beyond its shores. Ustad Haafiz Ali Khan had at last realized the dream of seeing his son take over the strings, as it were, of both his instrument and his musical lineage into that prophesied land of true greatness. Before he retreated from the platform

he shared with his son, as his hearing had begun to fade away, he had heard and treasured the lingering sound of thundering applause.

Just a short span of formative years under the umbrella of rich tradition had played its role perfectly. A deep understanding and respect for the essence and philosophy of Indian classical music, as manifest in the personal life in the form of three cardinal aspects of his god, guru, and art, had begun to bestow upon Amjad Ali Khan the well-rounded musical personality of a stalwart. His regal bearing, his *tameez-tahzeeb,* his musical introspection, made him a complete performer, a coveted ustad and a much admired ambassador for India's art and culture, through the continuing and flowering tradition of classical music. While most of this music's illustrious exponents for centuries had to be content with pleasing just their royal patrons, the entire expanding world was now becoming the grand stage for Indian classical music. And a frontrunner among its exponents was Amjad Ali Khan.

Revolutionizing the art of sarod playing, a young Amjad Ali had introduced the *Ekehra taans,* and the *Khayal* and *Thumri gayaki* styles on the sarod way back in the early fifties. And his introspection and creativity have never waned. New creative expressions, some in the form of unexplored *ragas* and *raginis* were drawn to him in moments of intense musical *samadhi*. Surfacing from the ocean of endless repertoire of Indian classical musicality, they lingered on, as if dancing around on nimble feet, and asking him in seductive whispers, 'wouldn't you embrace us, embellish us, and give us a name? Or would you send us back into obscurity and oblivion?' Somehow they seemed to know, Amjad Ali Khan was one of those rare musicians who could give due respect and credence to seeds of creative possibility. Despite his dedication to discovering the undiscovered, he was committed to preserving the sanctity of traditional ragas. For the first time, ragas like *Saraswati, Hansdhwani, Bhupali, Abhogi, Bhopal Todi, and Hari Kauns* were heard. For both the old and new, he emphasized the importance of playing musical compositions in their entirety, including the *sthaye* and the *antara*.

Amjad Ali Khan also stressed the salience and vitality of rhythm in his performances. Senior most masters of percussion had always eagerly accompanied a young Amjad Ali. And interestingly enough, countless renowned tabla players of today remember being introduced by the young Khan saheb. Legendary masters of other instruments felt honoured to share the stage and play duet or *jugalbandi* with him. This included music stalwarts from both Hindustani and Carnatic systems. And some, even from the West.

But perhaps the sweetest *jugalbandi* of his life has been the romantic overture between dance and music. His frank admiration of the elevating beauty and riveting talent of the classical danseuse Subhalakshmi Barooah, after a brief romantic pursuit around concert circuits, culminated in one of the most successful and blessed marriages in music lore. The exemplary grooming of young Amaan Ali Bangash and Ayaan Ali Bangash into multifaceted personalities and promising music makers of the emerging era, has equal contributions from both their loving parents.

The confluence of Subhalakshmi and Amjad Ali Khan continues into many other spheres of musical and cultural significance. The much-awaited Ustad Haafiz Ali Khan Awards ceremony, which is held annually in India and Europe, and honours both Indian and Western classical music, is one such example of the ripple effect of the family's deep commitment and respect for the rich tradition of musical integrity and achievement. Every year, some of the truly worthy music makers are sought out, some from temporary oblivion, and lovingly felicitated by an eminent panel headed by the Khan couple.

Amjad Ali himself has already been honoured with innumerable titles and awards, including India's Padma Vibhushan, Crystal Award by the World Economic Forum, UNICEF'S national ambassadorship, inclusion in the International Directory of Distinguished Leadership, honorary doctorate from University of York, Deshikauttam from Shantiniketan and the Gandhi Medal from UNESCO. The legacy of solo all-night concerts was initiated and lovingly sustained by Khan saheb's efforts over several performances in major cities since 1971. The latest in that string was a unique and memorable concert in Calcutta in 2003, where the entire night was made memorable for the packed audience by three succeeding solo sarod recitals by young Ayaan, Amaan and Khan saheb himself! In the international sphere, one of his most acclaimed collaborations was his music composition titled, 'Tribute to Hong Kong', performed by the Hong Kong Philharmonic Orchestra, conducted by Fu Ku Mora.

Amjad Ali Khan's dedication towards grooming and inspiring young learners and performers of music has been exemplary. Most of his disciples today are performing artists and are taking the message of Indian classical music all over the world. This interest in teaching has made Amjad Ali take up honorary professorship at Universities of York, North Eastern, Washington and New Mexico. In 1988, he hosted and presented forty sarod players from all schools of music to take part in the first ever

'Sarod Festival'.

Khan saheb wears his achievements and titles lightly, quite like his famous charming smile. Enriched with the right musical sensibility, his philosophy of life forbids him to strike any harsh note of conceit or arrogance. Even his letter paper does not flaunt an *'Ustad';* it simply reads: Amjad Ali Khan. A blend of dignity, poise and humility in a setting of magnificence is Amjad Ali's hallmark, and it is equally evident even in the ambience he helps create. One living example of it is the grand Sarod Ghar museum at his ancestral home, which lovingly houses a stunning collection of musical instruments, gleaming majestically, and radiating memories of the masters of yore who had once made them resonate with life!

Indeed, the most coveted awards he treasures in nostalgic pride are some melodious memories frozen in the realm of legend. He lovingly remembers that evening in Kashmir when the legendary queen of light classical music, Begum Akhtar, breaking established norms of concert decorum, insisted on taking the stage *before* a much younger Amjad. With a serious sense of purpose, she had to literally win a playful scuffle and run to the stage, leaving behind a bewildered Amjad torn between sweet embarrassment and welling pride. And after her own riveting performance was over, she sat at the forefront of the huge and appreciative audience to endorse the rare tribute she had already paid to the young wizard of pure classical music.

Similarly, once earlier in Benaras in a nightlong concert, Amjad had to take the stage at 3 O'clock in the night before a huge audience, who had already witnessed the magic of the legendary dancer Birju Maharaj accompanied by a prodigious Zakir Hussain, and the atmosphere was still fragrant with Pandit Bhimsen Joshi's magnificent *Darbari* and his popular *bhajan* 'Jo bhaje Hari ko sada...'. Amjad was left asking himself as to what sublime music could he possibly produce at such a time and place! Finally, invoking the blessings of his guru and all the revered music saints of India, as he always does before a

Presiding over a recent Ustad Haafiz Ali Khan Award ceremony. Seen with wife Subhalakshmi and music stalwarts Abdul Halim Jaffer Khan, Niaz Ahmad Khan, Prabha Atre and Zakir Hussain

concert, Amjad ventured into the self-discovered raga, Lalita Dhwani, and was able to ascend a level blessed with divine inspiration! Ustad Bismillah Khan, who sat in the audience, later confessed that he was pulled in two different directions: whether to go for his early morning *namaaz,* or continue basking in the ethereal spell created by Amjad's sarod. Until he realized there was no real difference between the two and he continued to sit till the end, and embraced young Amjad Ali with his characteristic passion.

No titles or awards can ever match these rare moments of tribute to one's music. And there are so many of them already, which keep flooding back. The spontaneous praises from Roshan Ara Begum, the daughter of the great Abdul Karim Khan saheb, after that memorable concert in Pakistan...the lingering embrace of Lord Yehudi Menuhin after exchanging notes at a seminar on the finer points of Western and Indian classical music...singing a new inspired raga at the *samadhi* of the saint musician Tyagaraja...the marathon all-night concert where he was accompanied by three legendary tabla players, one following another...

So many honours, so many worthy disciples, such treasures of acquired and intuitive knowledge, such rare meetings and divine blessings...yet, steeped in humility, the *Ustad* admits that when he sits in the audience he is still a student, a receiver, seeking and applauding the worthy in everyone's art. Just as he is able to empathize with the sufferings of humankind spread across the planet, and share the concerns born of the violence and intolerance strewn around everyday life...he prays through his music for that day when the spirit of peace and harmony shall strike the right chord in everyone's heart...

It is indeed impossible to capture the essence of such an exemplary musician in a frozen statement, but to select just one scene from the etchings of time, one could turn to that electric ambience of the packed Carnegie Hall hosting a concert to celebrate fifty years of India's Independence...where, not the conclusion of the recital, but the mere entry of the majestic figure of Ustad Amjad Ali Khan inspired the eminent audience to a thunderous standing ovation! An eloquent moment of pride when the *Monarch of the Sarod* had yet again taken a bow to conquer the heart of his musical empire.

Even today, when he says that life's just begun, and there's so much to explore and achieve, one realizes that a young leader's role is never an easy one to play: it has to hold in its sweep the essence of the present, and the promise of the future...And if anyone can do it with both dignity and dexterity, it is *Khan saheb* Amjad Ali Khan.

Living Memories...

Performing with his legendary father Ustad Haafiz Ali Khan

With wife Subhalakshmi, and sons Amaan & Ayaan

In love with sarod at a young age

Three generations, steeped in music

With Lata Mangeshkar and Atal Behari Vajpayee

With president Bill Clinton...

Mr. & Mrs. Khan with Prince Charles & Lady Diana

Another electrifying performance

The ustad takes a bow

Q. If Subhalakshmi-ji gave up her dance career to do complete justice to her role as wife and mother...how do you feel about it as a husband?

A. *I think I have mentioned this even earlier, especially in the launch functions of the book about me written by Amaan and Ayaan. Their mother's contribution in their life is much more than mine; she is their first guru. In fact, all mothers are their children's first guru. We keep saying 'Bharat Mata', but women in this country are often abused, outraged, oppressed and even burnt to death. This pains me beyond measure. That's why it was a special moment for me when I composed raag Subhalakshmi as a tribute to my wife, and played it to an audience of 2,500 people. I meant it as a tribute to all those great women who sacrifice their promising careers for the sake of their home, husband, children and their future. Subhalakshmi's contribution in my life is enormous, and I sincerely feel she deserves much more respect than I do. In fact had she not been married to me, she would perhaps have been the greatest dancer in the country.*

Q. Besides the sarod, which is your favourite instrument?

A. *Besides the sarod I love vocal music. In fact, I am always trying to sing through my instrument. I also understand and explore the finer points of other instruments.*

Sitar and tabla are instruments I have played. And I believe every instrument, flute, sarangi, esraj, santoor, jaltarang, even the keyboard have their individual flavour and fragrance, colour and context...But sarod is my life's companion; I love it and I worship it! I wish, one day, the entire world understands and appreciates what the sarod is saying and how it is saying it...

Q. Do you believe it is necessary to be deeply spiritual in order to be a good Indian classical musician?

A. *Music and spirituality are inseparable. Spirituality, religion, faith, trust, compassion, love, romance...are the base of Indian classical music. But the spiritual aspect is more in pure sound. Because music has to be experienced and felt, there's nothing to 'understand' in music. Music is like fragrance, colour, air, water, fire...which have no discrimination or religion. They are always selflessly at the service of the entire world. By watching the elements I feel I am connected to every faith, every soul on earth...*

Q. What is your impression of Western classical music?

A. *It has a great tradition too, and I have great regard for it. I love the effect of the symphony, I*

admire the discipline. I have heard Beethoven, Bach, Mozart, Tchaikovsky...Western classical music is the creation of three participants: composer, conductor and performer/s. They write music, they read music, and it's quite remarkable. Over a hundred musicians combine with great discipline, talent and harmony to create a great piece of music. While on the Indian classical scene, a large gathering of musicians might just create confusion and cacophony. Because, Indian classical music is the creation of individuals, born of the moment, inspired by his heart, mind and soul...

Q. How do you relate to Carnatic music?

A. *I have great regard for their philosophy of music: every kriti resonates with devotion. Once I played a raga composed by Tyagaraja himself, named Shri Ranjani, where, in the kriti, he is asking, " O, my Lord, is it ever possible that in this lifetime I can fully understand the depth and meaning of all the seven swaras..."*

Carnatic music has a great tradition, many great masters and a great many young talents today, who ensure a great future. But in the context of Carnatic music I must once again speak of something I have always felt. This nomenclature of Carnatic and Hindustani is not justified. Karnataka is not separate from the country Hindustan, but is a part of it.

I therefore strongly feel, and many of our stalwarts from the south agree with me that, our two systems and traditions of classical music should be referred to as Indian classical music of the north, and Indian classical music of the south. This will, to a large extent, destroy the perceived divide, and promote mutual admiration and understanding between the two great musical traditions of India.

Q. If you believe in rebirth, what do you think you were in your previous birth?

What would you like to be if you take rebirth?

A. *I always say that Indian classical music is a long and endless journey. We need to be totally dedicated to our art, God and guru. I do not know what I was earlier, but surely I must have been in search of musical expression for many lives...so God has given me the sarod. Maybe I used to play some other instrument, or maybe, yes, I do feel I used to sing...and today I am singing my song through my sarod. And, god willing, if I am born again, maybe my unfinished journey of music will then attain completion...Because every raga is an ocean...Yaman or Darbari or Shuddha Kalyan...one lifetime is not enough to fully explore a raga. So I would like to be born as a classical musician and I would like to be born in Gwalior, which is the birthplace of Miyan Tansen and my ancestors...and I would love to be dedicated to the service of music every time I return to this world...*

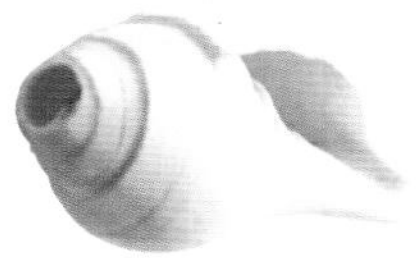

BHIMSEN JOSHI

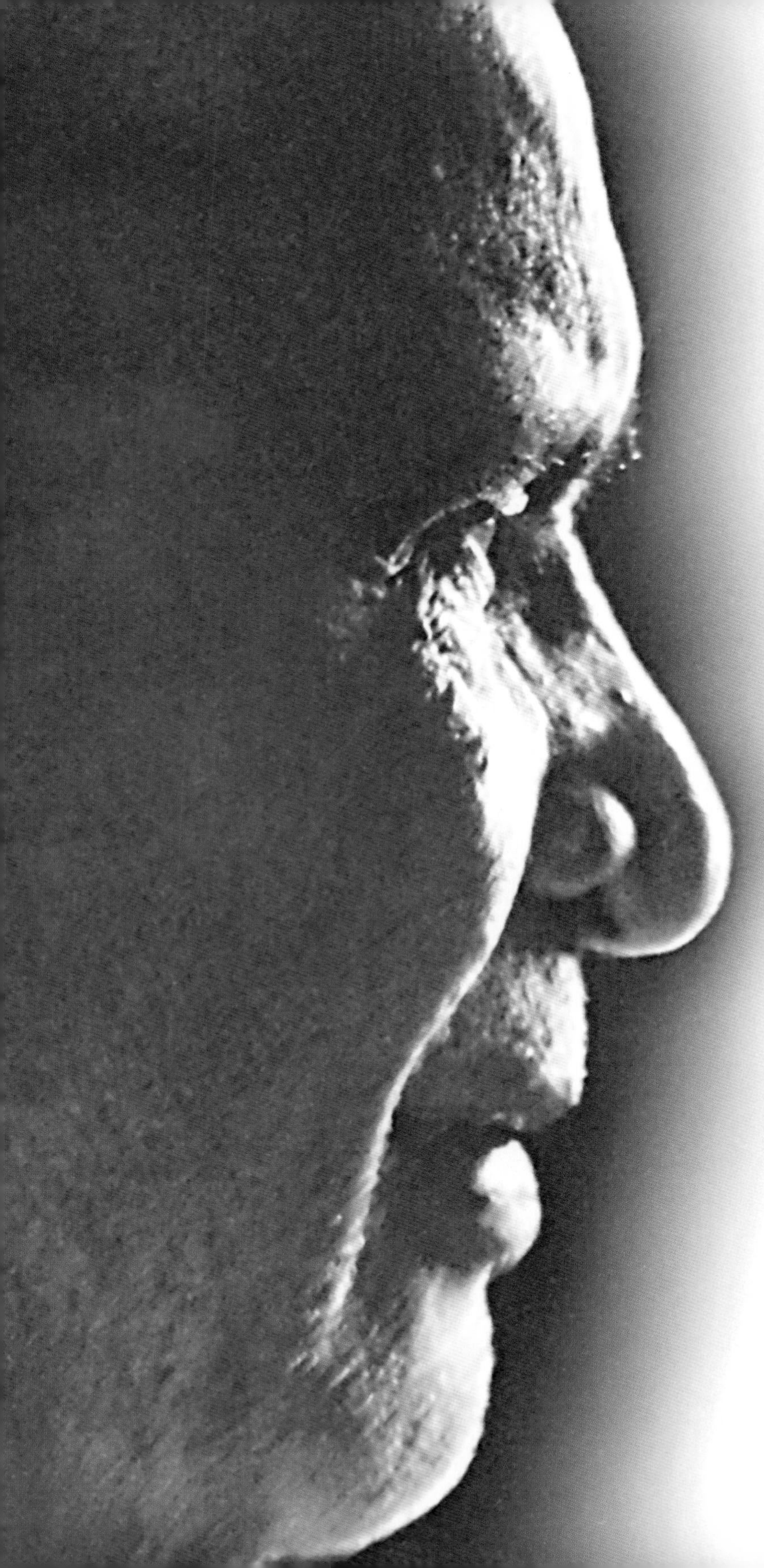

A small group of cultured, middle-class citizens was out on an afternoon stroll along a broad, dusty road in the historic town of Bijapur. As the gentlemen approached a *masjid* in their path, one of them noticed a young, ten-year old boy lying exhausted near the main entrance. When they drew closer, the others too noticed the boy, as he sat up suddenly and began to sing. Although his dusty, road-soiled clothes could not completely obscure his social background, his singing in a starved voice was much more of a revelation.

Unable to pass him by without appeasing their curiosity, the gentlemen subjected the tramp-like child singer to some incisive interrogation. Straight, monosyllabic answers soon revealed that he was indeed the beloved son of respectable, middle class parents and had run away from his home in Karnataka a couple of months ago, had travelled through many places like Bombay and Pune and had reached this place in blind pursuit of his goal in life. Shaken and stirred, the cultured and amicable group leader asked, "And what's that goal?" The answer was crystal clear, "To learn music." Someone else then asked in the tentative tone of an autograph seeker, "What's your name?" The answer echoed, "Bhimsen Gururaj Joshi."

That wasn't really the first time young Bhimsen had left home without telling anyone. Nor did it prove to be the last. When he was merely five, he had quietly followed the intriguing strains of a music band, which was passing through the lane where he lived. The orchestral group had reached its destination and had even discharged its contractual duties and dispersed, when the host noticed a lone little child sleeping there. He lovingly carried the sleeping boy to the security of the nearest police station from where Bhimsen's anxious father was thankfully able to retrieve his missing son. It was then decided that henceforth a sticker bearing his name and address be stuck on his person to facilitate anyone who happened to find a lost-in-music 'Bhimu' and would be kind enough to contact his father, the principal of Bagalkot school.

Bhimsen's passage to Bijapur itself wasn't a stray incident of childish impulse. The compassionate gentlemen who found him in front of the mosque notified his family and the prodigal son was duly collected and taken home, thus ending a two-and-a-half month long period of parental trauma. But Bhimsen's vision and goal had obviously eluded him, and soon he was dreaming of another escapade in pursuit of music.

Of course it wasn't just *any music*. He had already heard the kind of music, which gave him a glimpse of the melodic ethereal world, the *Gandharva lok*. To Bhimsen's music-obsessed vision, it was the beginning of a bright rainbow that faded enticingly into the horizon of his future. The words were *'Piya bin nahin aawat chaine'* and the magical voice was that of Ustad Abdul Karim Khan. "This is it!" Bhimsen must have muttered having found his focus, "This is how I want to sing..."

His father was out of town, and feigning sudden anger towards his loving mother over something as trivial as a mere spoonful of *ghee* at mealtime, Bhimsen ran away from home yet again. Into the distant open arms of the goddess of music—*his* kind of music.

Travelling ticket-less by train, and earning random cash and kindness by singing to passengers and pedestrians, an eleven-year-old Bhimsen eventually reached Gwalior, which, he had heard, was a major seat of classical music. Searching for the abodes of music stalwarts, he landed up in the presence of the famous Rajabhaiya Poonchwale, who, after a brief hearing, agreed to teach him. Bhimsen soon realized that this wasn't exactly the music he wanted to learn, but continued for some time, simply because the arrangement there provided the crucial security of one free meal a day. He learnt that Ustad Haafiz Ali Khan was a wonderful human being and among the top names in classical music. Bhimsen impressed him too and began to learn earnestly from him. Haafiz Ali Khan lovingly guided young Bhimsen into the oceanic depths of one single elaborate raga: *Marwa*. Bhimsen gratefully remembers it even today and also endorses the belief that Marwa is that one single raga, the mastery over which gives the learner the feel and confidence to sing any raga with *Èlan*.

Soon *Khan saheb* had to embark on another of his frequent concert tours, leaving a restless Bhimsen in quest for his next source of learning. This time's escapade took him from Pune to Gwalior, to Kharagpur to Calcutta to Delhi, finally reaching Jalandhar in the Punjab. Along this difficult and circuitous path he impressed diverse music gurus, yet couldn't really learn much because some asked for money which he could not afford and others could not offer the kind of music he really longed to learn.

He was all of twelve years when he finally appeared in front of Mangatram Acharya in Jalandhar. Although Mangatram-ji was an exponent of the *Dhrupad* style, Bhimsen instinctively felt at home under his wings. He found a roof over his head, and for the first time in months, an assurance of adequate food. He plunged into an austere daily regimen as if with vengeance. Getting up early and bathing in cold water, even in the bone-chilling winter of Jalandhar, and then completing a strenuous physical workout that would humble a wrestler, Bhimsen would eat lots of nourishing food and put in long hours of learning and *riyaaz* throughout the day. Pleasing his guru with his talent and dedication, young Bhimsen became an indispensable figure also in the famous Hariballav Music festival, where he sat with the tanpura behind almost every star musician who came from all over India to grace the occasion. Listening to this diverse galaxy of music greats his horizon suddenly expanded and his inner yearning to find *his* kind of music and his ultimate guru reached its crescendo.

One of the invitees to the festival, Vinayakrao Patwardhan advised an eager Bhimsen that his ideal guru would be none other than Rambhau Kundgolkar, popularly known as Sawai Gandharva. Interestingly, Sawai Gandharva was a disciple of Ustad Abdul Karim Khan whose recording of *'Piya bin nahin aawat chaine'* had virtually thrown Bhimsen into the orbit of this relentless musical quest. And it was stark irony that, considering the time and distance already covered by Bhimsen across the country, his 'ideal' guru's abode, Kundgol, was almost next door to the home he left behind. Two turbulent rivers of emotion, finding the same direction, merged into one another, and Bhimsen returned home, embraced his long-lost family members, and wept. His life-hardened and weather-beaten frame appeared tall and tough beyond expectation. His voice too had just received that jab of adolescence, yet his weeping must have been music to his parent's ears...

Without risking any delay, Gururaj Joshi took his son to Sawai Gandharva's abode. The Kirana *gharana* maestro gave Bhimsen a good, long hearing and was impressed. The guru, however, told Bhimsen that he would teach him only if he were willing to *forget* most of what he had already imbibed till then. Sawai Gandharva needed a blank sheet to begin imprinting one of the most exemplary chapters in *guru-shishya* tradition in music, and Bhimsen, having finally arrived at the doorway of destiny, readily agreed.

Bhimsen's courageous quest and adventures until now were by no means wasted. Apart from seeing life in the streets, and the entire spectrum of human nature, his eclectic side had constantly assimilated the best of everything that confronted him. Besides, he could now complement his steely resolve with robust health and a capacity for great physical endurance. In the *gurukul* way of life, Bhimsen

Bhimsen at the Enayat Khan Award ceremony, with celebrated instrumentalists Ali Akbar Khan and Vilayat Khan

now made himself available for household duties for his guru, which involved among other things, carrying water from a distant river in large pitchers thrice a day. In youthful enthusiasm, his young shoulders absorbed all that strain for years and the resultant pain was to surface only much later in life. When his father Gururaj chanced to see this in one of his visits to his son's new home, Bhimsen quietly reassured him, saying, he was happy with his life there.

The happiness, however, was short lived. Without preamble or assigning reason, Bhimsen was suddenly sent back home: Sawai Gandharva couldn't teach him anymore! An anxious Gururaj thought of seeking some other guru for his son, but Bhimsen told him that he would not like to deviate from the Kirana *gharana* teachings. So he began a lone *yagna* whereby, through sheer introspection and diligence he began to elaborate upon and refine whatever he had picked up directly and indirectly from his master. Alongside relentless practice, he collected a couple of accompanists and began to present his music to random audiences, creating quite a stir in the neighbourhood.

The veena-playing saint Shri Raghavendra Swamy had been the spiritual guru of the Joshi family. His *samadhi* was in Mantralay, at the banks of the river Tunga. With his father Gururaj and a few accompanists, Bhimsen went there with the desire to pay a musical homage to the music-loving saint. With the permission and blessings of the presiding swami-ji, the small group followed a blissful musical routine for a couple of months beside the holy river. It is believed that every night Bhimsen would get musical instructions in his sleep and would give vocal expression to it the next day, to the delight of the modest audiences that gathered there. Some locals even reported that every evening a black dog would appear from nowhere and would sit near Bhimsen while he sang rich, spiritual music. At any rate, everyone enjoyed a shared feeling of being blessed, during those two months at the auspicious abode of Raghavendra Swamy and it was a rejuvenated Bhimsen who returned home and immersed himself in inspired and arduous *riyaaz*. Soon again, along with his adventurous accompanists, a sixteen-year old Bhimsen set out on an exploratory tour of the southern states and gained further experience in audience rapport and concert confidence.

The next logical step was to appear on radio, and with great expectation Bhimsen ventured into the bustling city of Bombay in search of a struggler's haven. Struggle he did in extreme measure, sharing a room with ten other fortune seekers, and catching up with his *riyaaz* only at the oddest of places and hours. Finally, the audition with the radio station went off well, but the news of being selected took its own sweet time to come.

In the meanwhile, Bhimsen made another

impulsive move. He began to land up at as many concerts of Sawai Gandharva as he could possibly get wind of, hovering around at a safe distance so that he could listen to his guru's recitals without being seen. Every new raga he heard in this manner would then be immediately internalized and mastered through long and lonely hours of self-willed practice. This extraordinary mode of relationship continued for a while until one fine day he received a summon from Sawai Gandharva to return to Kundgol. The gesture was as sudden and unexplained as the earlier shock of being sent back home! Stunned and thrilled, Bhimsen rushed to the abode of his dreams, at the feet of his enigmatic *guru*.

Presumably, the earlier routine of household duties was waiting for him, but the difference this time was remarkable. Sawai Gandharva began to teach his young disciple with tremendous ardour and insight. Bhimsen didn't know then, that while he kept spying upon his guru's recitals at various concerts, some of his well-wishers had quietly conspired a reciprocal gesture, whereby Sawai Gandharva himself was made to listen to one of Bhimsen's inspired public performances. Although neither side directly revealed its secret, it is quite possible that this could partially explain the newfound zeal with which the *guru-shishya* bonding began to fructify.

For three concentrated years, Bhimsen followed a stringent musical regimen. The day began with two hours of yoga-mantra *sadhana* at dawn. Then, interspersed with mundane daily chores, would unfold three extensive sessions of *taalim* and *riyaaz* till nightfall. *Todi* in the morning, *Multani* in the afternoon and *Pooria* in the evening; nothing else, and nothing less. The expanse, depth and the very persona of ragas that the masters of the art talk about, will find ample endorsement here. Three years of total immersion into just three fundamental ragas, and not a single wasted moment! In fact, even today, over six decades into his illustrious career, *Todi, Multani* and *Pooria* still feature among Bhimsen's favourite ragas.

Time passed quickly in a state of eager assimilation and entranced *sadhana* until Sawai Gandharva's ever-delicate health deteriorated further to a crippling state. It was now apparent to Bhimsen that it was this health problem—

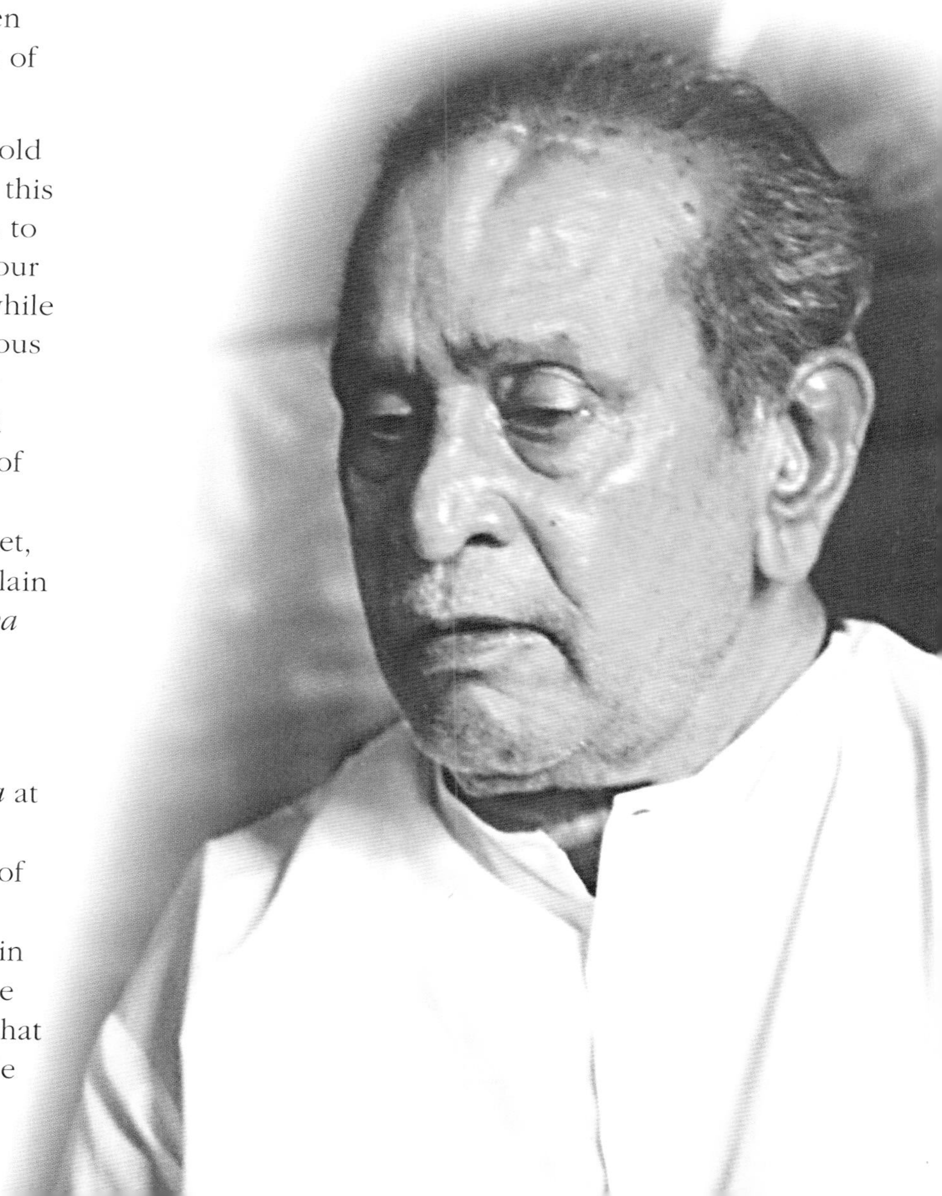

acute hypertension on that occasion—that had earlier prompted his guru to send him back home. This time, however, instead of distancing, it resulted in a tighter embrace. With a manifest sense of tearing urgency, Sawai Gandharva began to shower his choicest musical gems on his favourite disciple, until one fateful day, confronting further deterioration of health he whispered to Bhimsen that the moment had come for him to become his formal, *ganda bundh shishya,* and step out into the outer world holding aloft the glorious flag of the Kirana gharana...Bhimsen was still in his teens when he received with both hands the sacred bestowal of this great honour and responsibility.

Talking of lineage, Ustad Abdul Karim Khan's blessings too must have silently merged with that of Sawai Gandharva when Bhimsen's *ganda bandhan* ceremony was being solemnized. Even critics agree that such glorious continuity has not been matched by too many instances even in the vast and rich tradition of Indian classical music. Yet, this impassioned loyalty to the *gharana* has never restricted Bhimsen's reach and admiration towards talent from all quarters. The highly successful and respected 'Sawai Gandharva'annual music festival at Pune, where Pandit Bhimsen plays host with great enthusiasm, grace and humility, is a spectacular testimony to his universality.

Bhimsen, to begin with, was blessed with an inborn talent and thirst for the highest kind of music. His voice, even in the early days, was often compared to the 'Roman pillar'. It must have been the strength, clarity and structural perfection of those ornate columns that inspired such imagery. And like the flowing antiquity of architecture, the unfolding musical maturity of Bhimsen has further justified this comparison, which goes to show that monumental achievements in music are eminently possible if you have a Roman column of a voice to build on. But Bhimsen didn't merely possess the voice, more importantly, he allowed himself to be *possessed* by music. Totally focused on his life's calling, he strove to make the most of the best and the worst of life's surprises. He surely had music as the motivator while investing in himself physically through strenuous exercise; and even when it came to hard labour, he made it work in his favour. Thus ensuring lasting command over robust good health, superhuman stamina, and amazing breath control. There are people who still reminisce about a marathon concert where they heard a young Bhimsen Joshi sing for twelve hours at a stretch, punctuated with just two brief coffee breaks!

Sawai Gandharva's open arm attitude to eclecticism, endorsed his disciple's lifelong quest for the best in music. Bhimsen's pride of belonging to the *Kirana Gharana*, quite generously, included the wisdom of seeking and assimilating the rare and good points of singers from other lineages as well. Bhimsen himself acknowledges the influence of Bal Gandharva, Kesarbai, Bade Ghulam Ali Khan and Amir Khan on his musical sensibility.

Similarly, Bhimsen was enamoured by Mushtak Hussain Khan's *gayaki* and the appeal of lighter classical music of Rasoolanbai of Benaras and Siddheshwari Devi and Begum Akhtar of Lucknow. Brushing aside a more lucrative prospect of steady programmes in Bombay, he undertook the uncertain journey eastward, to Rampur. Living with Ustad Mushtak Hussain Khan in a spirit of dedicated service for six months, Bhimsen was taught just one raga: *Nat Malhar*. His next musical pilgrimage, to Lucknow, was much more rewarding because that's where he met and heard many music greats like Bismillah Khan, apart from the thumri exponents he specifically wanted to hear to his heart's content. The darkening clouds of the Second World War ended his happy Lucknow phase and he returned to Bombay. The struggle continued in a *vilambit* pace until that momentous event in Poona, where, in celebration of Sawai Gandharva's sixtieth birth anniversary, Bhimsen dazzled the star-studded gathering with his first major public performance! And soon enough the entire Maharashtra sat up and took note of this twenty four-year-old torchbearer of the *Kirana Gharana*.

Bhimsen's next achievement was to make inroads into the southern parts of the country,

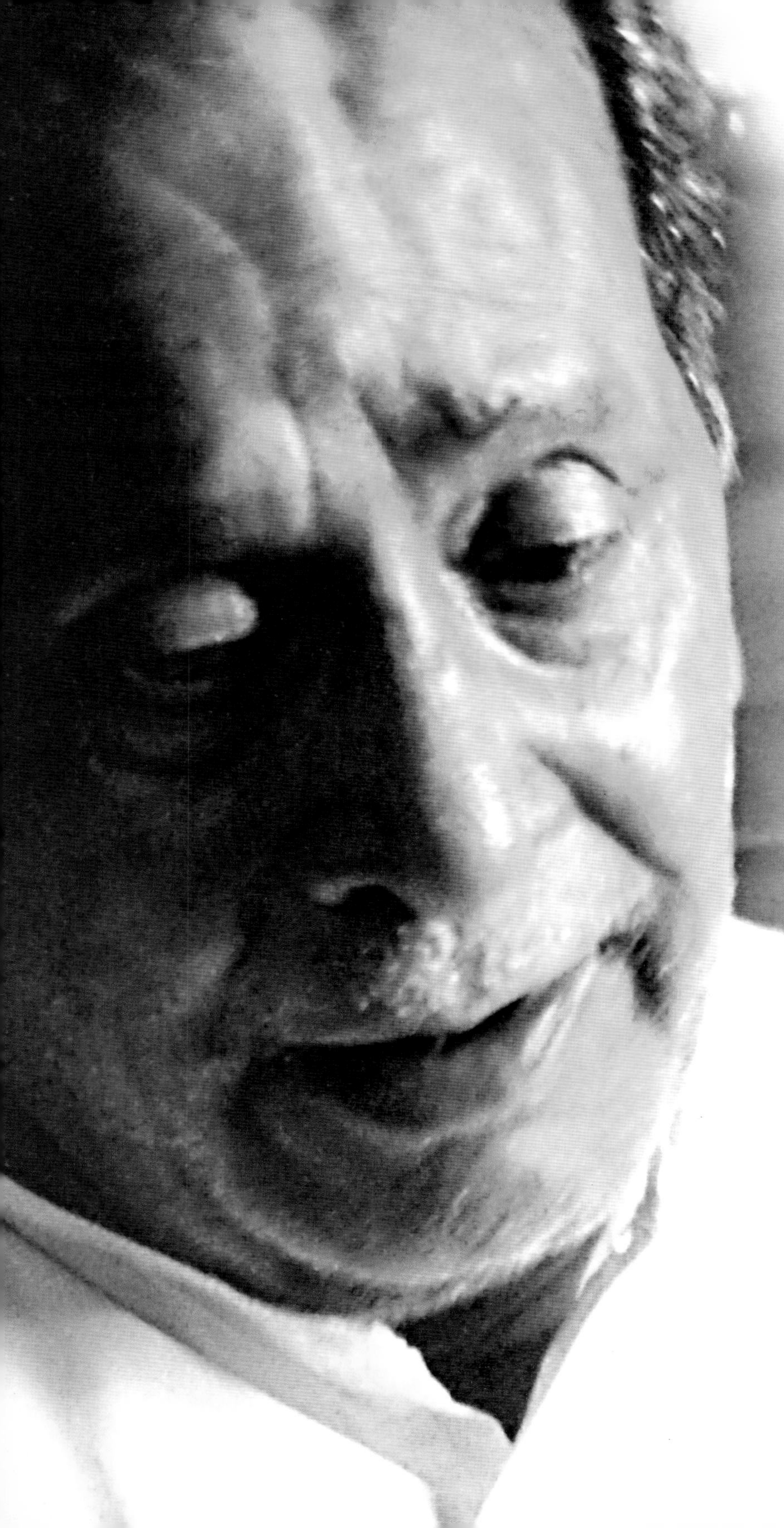

carving out a place for himself in the hearts of the people who did not have much exposure to north Indian music. The magnetic appeal of Bhimsen's singing got many faces from the *Carnatic* music world to turn northward as well.

After the south was adequately stirred, Bhimsen's burgeoning stature invaded the classical music circles of eastern India. Soon the music lovers of Calcutta were singing his praises in unison. A series of frequent concerts made Bhimsen a household name and a much-applauded artiste on the classical music platform. Radio broadcasts, recorded albums, and public concerts all over India began to resonate with the clarity and dexterity of his powerful and unadulterated masculine voice. Extra speakers had to be placed outside packed auditoria to appease charged audiences who refused to be left out. Newspapers have even reported that, once during a nightlong concert in Calcutta, dejected admirers had banged their heads and wept openly, when an inebriated Bhimsen Joshi was unable to take the stage...

After India was conquered, it was the overseas concerts that felt the impact of Bhimsen's musical genius. The West was already waking up gradually to classical music from India, but it was only the instrumentalists who held the magic wand till then. The voice of Bhimsen began to shatter the verbal barrier and make vocal classical music a serious contender for the mind share of the Western audiences. Beginning with his maiden trip to Afghanistan, Bhimsen Joshi by now has showered his music on well over twenty countries and has accepted repeated invitations to more than fifty cities of the world. Once at a European venue, he had to keep returning to the stage as many as fifteen times in gracious response to the waves of thundering applause after his recital.

To be able to enhance any composition with just the right touch of classicality has always come easily and instinctively to Bhimsen. Like a magic wand, this has been lovingly wielded over huge audiences who have not necessarily been familiar with hardcore classical music. This explains the huge and historic success of his *'Sant Vani'* programmes, inspired by the great Indian saint poets, where the right chemistry between devotional zeal and classical appeal has repeatedly drawn and mesmerized the simple folks in very large numbers. This same quality has also been on display in the rousing collage on national television *'Mile sur mera tumhara...'* where a glimpse of vintage Bhimsen, more than anyone else, has been indelibly imprinted on the hearts of millions of Indians.

Even the most flattering adulation, however, has never tainted his aura of simplicity and humility. It will be a fair speculation to say that no soul has ever felt any hostility towards Bhimsen and neither has Bhimsen ever hurt a man or beast. The world knows that most music makers are highly emotional if not downright volatile people. But Bhimsen has been able to sublimate his baser instincts to such an extent that even the vagaries of a singer's mood do not curb his ability or eagerness to give off his best to every music loving audience—wherever, whenever.

'Teertha Vitthal, Kshetra Vitthal'...Wherever Bhimsen has arrived along the path of his musical pilgrimage, he has cast a spiritual spell over the audience. Deep faith and devotion to God have always cloaked Bhimsen like a pristine shawl. In an eventful life, full of strife and turmoil, this has been his invisible armour. A natural winner, he has risen above all situations without moral or emotional compromise...At various stages of his life he has successfully confronted the wrath of elements and the pangs of poverty...He may have embraced an addictive indulgence like alcohol, but he has also been able to crush it under the enormous power of will...He has found love in two great women and made them co-exist with dignity and harmony, as wife and mother of his worthy children...Even at a highly vulnerable age he has taken a bone-breaking fall in his stride...He has battled with brain tumour and a temporary loss of memory and musicality, only to triumph over it all...and to the delight of millions of music lovers, he has regained much of his old form as the colossal Bhimsen of mythological stature, striding the arena of Indian classical music...

Yet again, when our eyes well up with tears of joyous emotion as he sings *'Jo bhaje Hari ko sada'*, the difference between 'Hari' and 'music' seems to blur like everything else in sight. And in that frozen moment of realization, only the voice of Bhimsen Joshi resonates...like a silver chord between heaven and earth.

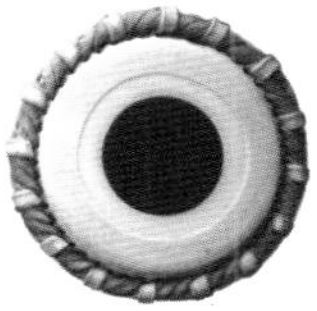

Living Memories...

The handsome maestro

Tuning the taanpura

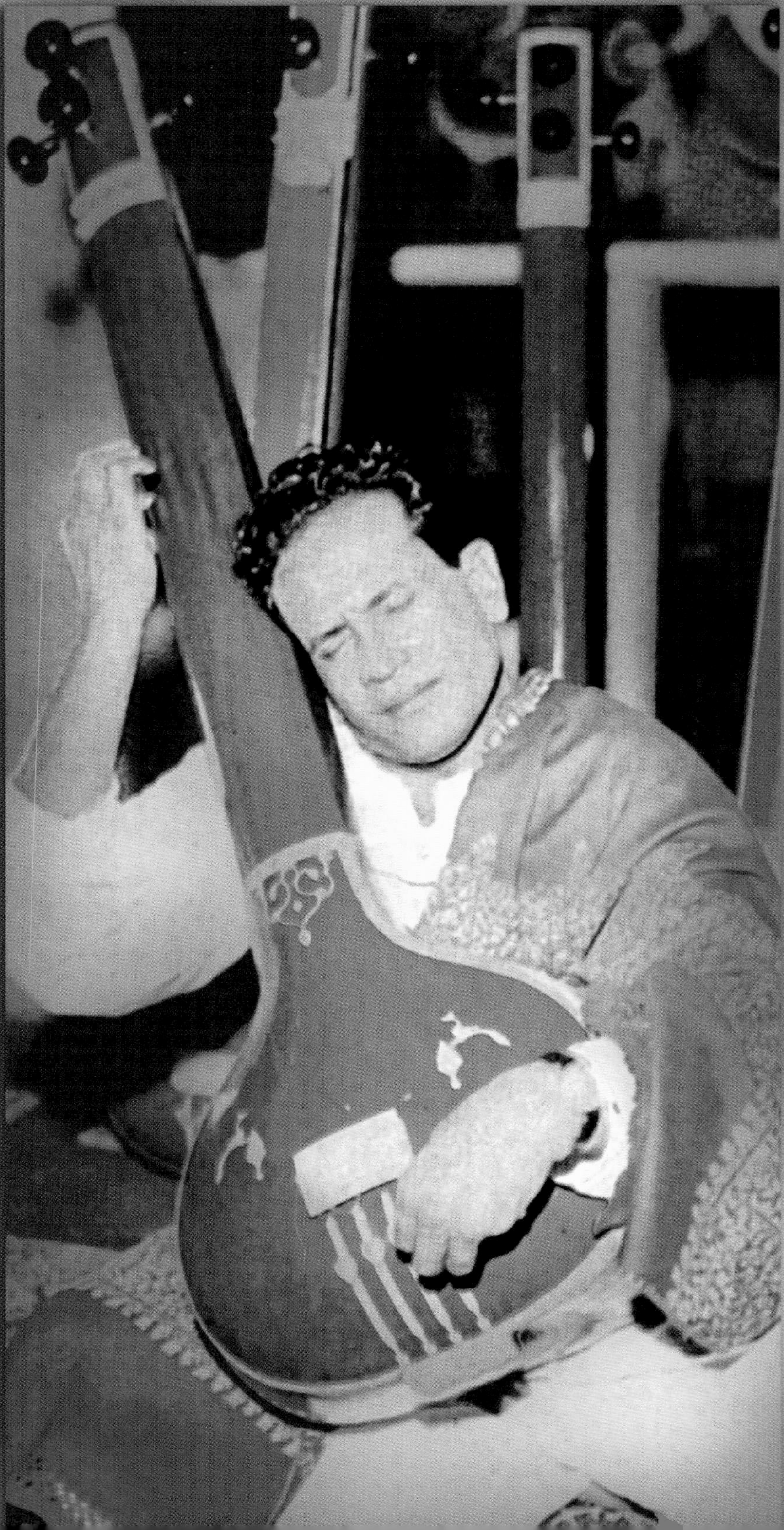

Lost in music

With Jasraj

At home with his musical lineage

At a recent performance

In full flow

With singer wife Vatsala

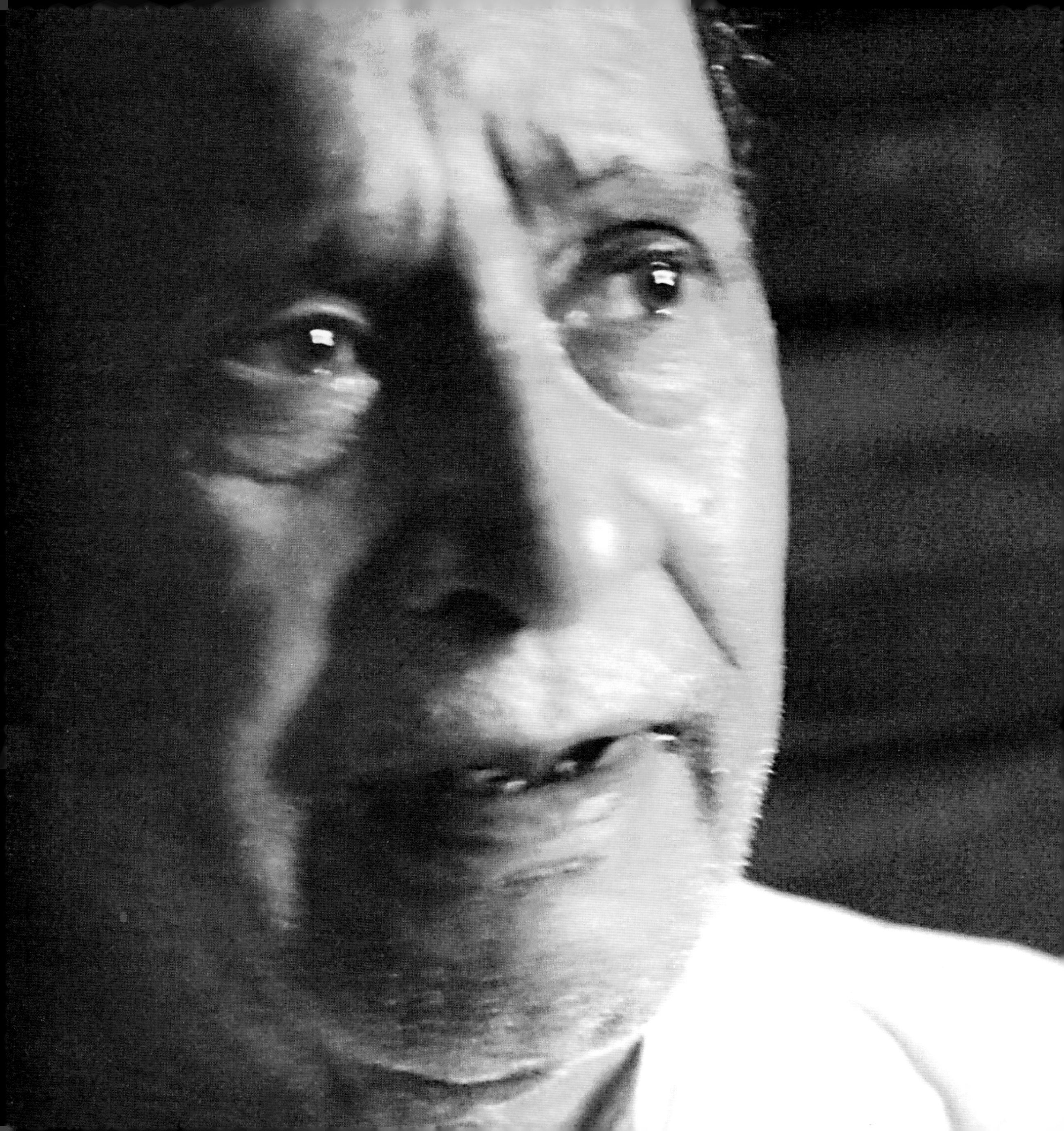

Direct answers: Straight from the heart...

Q. You left home for the love of music and today you are permanently enshrined in the hearts of music lovers. How do you look back at this journey?

A. *With gratitude towards God, the music lovers and above all, towards my guru.*

Whatever I have been able to achieve is due to the graciousness of my guru.

Q. Isn't it then just a matter of good fortune to find a worthy guru?

A. *The disciple has to himself decide what kind of a guru he wants, and then go out and look for him.*

Q. Some people criticize those who claim to create new ragas...

A. *There's nothing wrong with an inspired creation; I have myself created ragas like Lalit-Bhatiyar, Marwa-Shree...but yes, traditional ragas have a greater appeal.*

Q. How do you decide which raga you'd sing on a particular occasion? Is it preplanned?

A. *Before ascending the stage when I touch the tanpura, that's when I decide which raga to sing. In festivals etc. one has to also consider what the preceding artists have sung...*

Q. How do you relate to Carnatic music?

A. *Very well. (Smiles) I am myself from Karnataka! And yes, there are many truly great musicians in the Carnatic music world. In fact, even Abdul Karim Khan saheb had cut at least four south Indian records.*

Q. Is a deep sense of spirituality a prerequisite for Indian classical musicians?

A. *Of course. Finally, everyone has to go towards God. Like even the most errant child cries out for his mother when in distress.*

Q. Is there an essential difference between a vocalist and an instrumentalist?

A. *Not really. An instrumentalist also keeps singing in his mind. Except, he doesn't 'voice' it. His instrument is his chosen medium.*

Q. Have you observed the current generation of young singers? What do you think of them?

A. *There are many who are smart and talented. But very few are able to touch you here! (Touches his heart)*

Q. What's your advice to them?

A. *Work hard. And be honest with yourself and your music.*

Q. How do you ensure successful public performances time after time?

A. *Learn to please your inner self with what you sing. The outer world of audiences will automatically love it.*

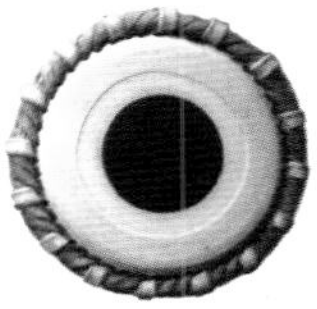

BISMILLAH KHAN

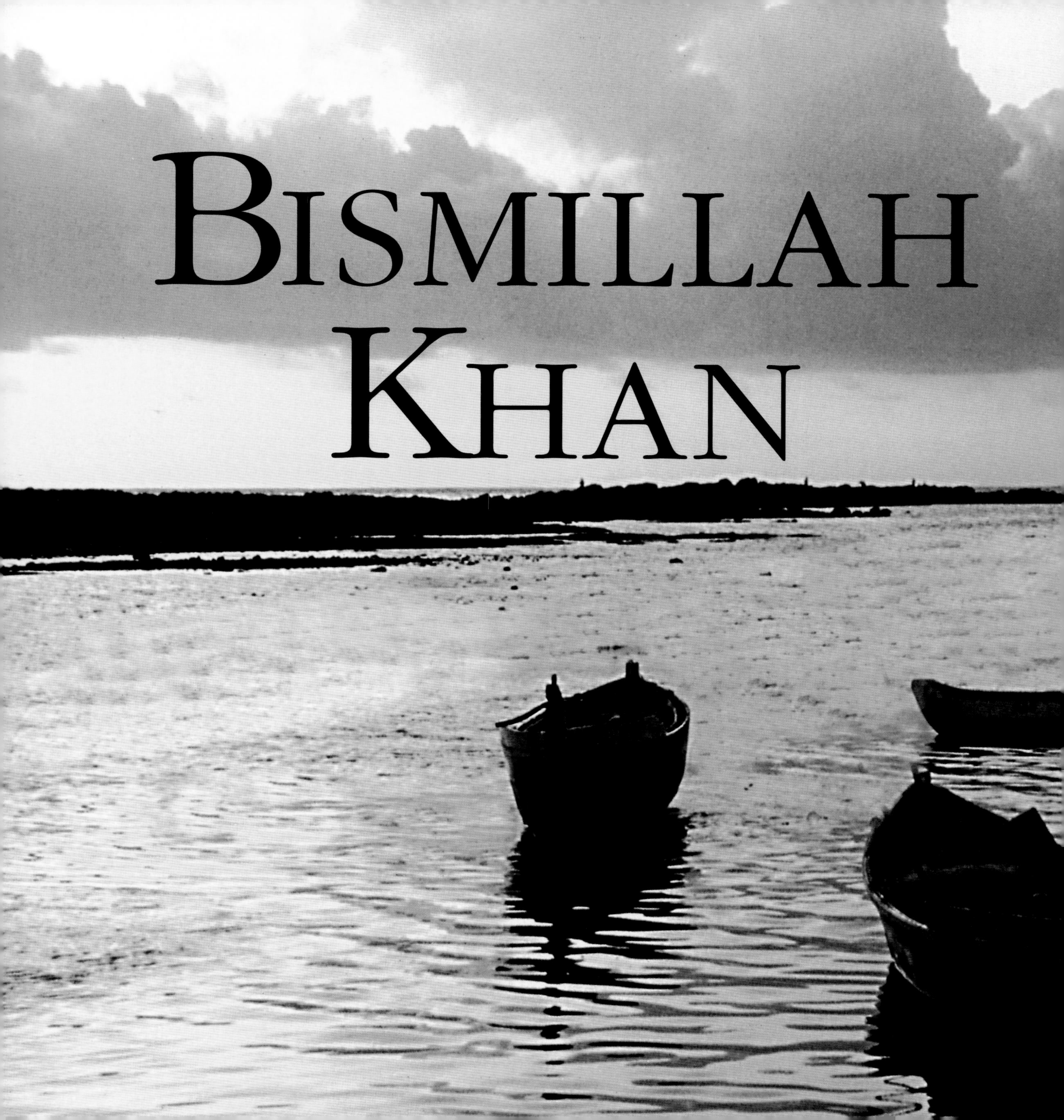

The shehnai of Ustad Bismillah Khan is never a casual experience. Nor is it an instrument of mild arousal. From the maestro's opening whisper into the complex flute, from the very first note of *shadaj* that breaks into the atmosphere, he commands the listeners' captive attention. First, his music seems to cascade over your senses, the crystal clarity of every note washing away your audience vanity. As all your resistance melts down to blissful surrender, you are cleansed and made sacred to receive his music. And then, before you know it, you become the shehnai on the lips of reality. And the music of the moment becomes the very breath of your life.

Yet again, words may have just proved inadequate in describing the music of Ustad Bismillah Khan! But if it has aroused enough yearning to know how Khan saheb himself was sculpted by the power of his divine music, we need to go back towards the beginning of the last century.

Twenty-first March, 1916. It was an enchanted morning of spring in the small princely state of Dumraon, in Bihar. State musicians, *shehnai-nawaz* Rasool Bux Khan and his worthy son Paigambar Bux were getting ready to leave for their morning ritual of playing shehnai at the Bihari temple in the royal palace. They probably had Vasant Bahar on their minds when the cry of *pancham* from a newborn voice rang in their ears! Paigambar Bux's wife Mitthan Begum had just delivered a baby! The happy news brought a spontaneous *'Bismillah!'* to the auspicious lips of the devout grandfather.

The history of the musical family in which Bismillah Khan was born is synchronous with the evolution of the shehnai itself! And as if that was not enough, his maternal ancestry too was dedicated to the melodious notes of the shehnai. And as for the environmental influence, the grand stage was already set in Kashi, the Eastern world's cradle of wisdom, art and music, since the Vedic times...

At age three, Bismillah's mother took him along to his maternal uncle's place at Benaras. The occasion was that of celebrating Id, but once young Bismillah set foot in that three storied house, its air and ambience seemed to embrace him with far reaching effects. There was his elder maternal uncle Vilayat Hussain practising his shehnai in one room, and his younger maternal uncle Ali Bux playing his shehnai in another corner, and the little boy began to nod rhythmically to the tunes, as if in acceptance of the warm invitation to be part of that lineage! Ali Bux even predicted to his sister that her little boy would definitely become a great *shehnai-nawaz* one day.

Young Bismillah remained at his uncle's place and began to soak in the music all around, as he grew up to be a quiet, lovable boy. He did not have much time for games or studies, as his heart was tuned to the music of the ether. The eternal city of Benaras cast a veil of magic all around his vision, lit with the kaleidoscopic wonders of adolescence.

Ali Bux's professional duties began with playing devotion-soaked shehnai, every morning at the Vishnu temple of Varanasi. Then, having welcomed the rising sun with the notes of a morning raga, he would walk up to the famous Balaji temple. There, ensconced in a room reserved for him, Ali Bux would pour his heart out in a long and arduous practice of shehnai. And all through this unbroken period of *sadhana,* young Bismillah would sit watching him, motionless, and breathless in anticipation. When would his 'Chhote Mamu' accept him as his *shagird?*

The day was preordained, so it had to come. At first it was just half an hour of *talim* every morning. Then gradually it got extended as little Bismillah realized that it wasn't easy to emulate the fluent melodies that poured out of his Mamu's shehnai so effortlessly. Shehnai was a difficult instrument, and his *ustad* was a hard taskmaster. A strict and regimented routine of *riyaaz* dispelled all the surface romanticism and awakened young Bismillah to the enormity of the task he had undertaken. He had to endure mocking smiles from other youngsters at home when his instrument produced all kinds of weird sounds under pressure. Only his guru's reassurance and his own sense of destiny kept him going through those initial months of desperate toil.

One fine day, the young disciple sought permission from his guru to practice at the special room in the Balaji temple. Hesitant at first, Ali Bux agreed to grant him the privilege. After his *sandhyarti* and the evening shehnai recital at the Jadaun temple, on an auspicious day, he personally escorted his nephew to his spiritual den at the Balaji Temple, and got him initiated into the vibrations of that seat of *sadhana.* A significant stage of Bismillah's grooming began there as he got used to bolting the door from inside and practising for four to five hours every day, exiled from the rest of the world. Not too far outside, the wavelets on the Ganges danced in melodic appreciation of his ascetic mode of *sadhana.*

Almost a year passed in this manner and Bismillah began to notice a qualitative difference in his music. He gained unprecedented facility with his instrument and began to *enjoy* the ragas he chose to explore. He would get totally absorbed in his own music. He told his Mamu about the strange elation he felt during his evening *riyaaz,* and his Mamu cautioned him not to speak about such things to anyone.

As the summer months approached, young Bismillah went for a visit to his grandfather's place at Dumraon. There, with pride and anticipation, the youngster displayed his newly acquired craft to his elders. His grandfather wasn't impressed with Bismillah's mellow style of playing. "You belong to a great lineage of shehnai players," said his grandfather, "learn to roar like a lion!" The old man took his grandson's shehnai and showed him exactly what he meant. Bismillah was stunned by the power and volume unleashed from his own familiar instrument! The rest of his stay at Dumraon was filled with vigorous exercise, long distance running and a special diet of milk and *badaam*. Within a week he noticed a new vigour and richness in the tonal quality of his shehnai as his breath improved in strides.

Back in Benaras, Bismillah's *talim* and *riyaaz* went on a roll. He grew introspective and tried to integrate the qualities of three great shehnai masters in himself. The intricate technique of *layakari* and *taan* of his older uncle, the clear, robust stamina of his grandfather, and of course, the delicate mellifluous wizardry of his Chhote Mamu, his formal *ustad*. It was like a *sangam,* a confluence of styles. But was it the right thing to do? Or should he move along the simple path shown by his *ustad* alone? As he was delving deeper into this question in a meditative trance, he suddenly felt the light of open space within that closed room of the Balaji temple. His eyes rested on a pair of feet, pink and lotus-like, and traversed upwards to take in the translucent form of a tall, handsome yogi, standing before him with a staff and a *kamandal* in his hands! Smiling benignly, the holy man asked him to play on. But young Bismillah was too stunned to respond! His arms, his instrument, were not in his control anymore. The yogi broke into a hearty laugh and made a benediction in his booming voice! "You will create bliss!" he said, and vanished as suddenly as he had appeared! Unbolting the door, Bismillah ran out into the open but there was no trace of that tall saffron clad figure! His own utter remorse at not being able to play the shehnai for the holy visitor was compounded by the hard slap he received from Ali Bux as he narrated the incident. Such secrets were not meant to be shared with anyone, not even his guru! What if such miracles never happened again! The *ustad* had every right to be upset with his adolescent *shagird,* especially when he had anticipated such a thing and had advised him to be discreet...

More such miracles must have happened to Bismillah Khan later in life, but with his vowed reticence, no details are available to the world. The effects of it could be seen in his music though. His shehnai was beginning to acquire the required impact, the *assar,* as if unseen horizons were fading in before him.

The early flush of youth had its impact on his impressionable innocence. Those were the days of the magic of bioscope, and screen enchantresses like Madhuri and Sulochana quickened his breath! He took great pains to collect the gate money from multiple sources, and jostled with ordinary mortals to capture his seat in theatres. Real life for him, however, was bathed in the purity of music. The passions and sentiments thereof were meaningful only to the extent of aiding him in his musical maturity.

Without their knowledge, the famous courtesans of Benaras, mainly the great exponents of classical music, enriched Bismillah Khan's musical repertoire and sensibility. On his way back from the Balaji temple, many hours were spent in intoxicated listening at the narrow, winding lane of Dalmandi, where the professional singing women lived in close proximity and rivalry of one another. If there were the strains of a *chhota khayal* wafting out of the *kotha* of Rasoolan Bai, there was the legendary Vidyadhari singing a poignant Behag in the next house, unveiling the mystery of the raga in her lilting rendition. Reclining against the staircase walls of these colourful abodes of dance and music, young Bismillah would absorb the

With his favourite vocalist Soma Ghosh

musical nuances, the *bhav* and the *rasa,* and sublimate them in his mind. A few paces of brisk walk would envelop him with Rajeshwari's *dadra,* enriched by the immaculate sangat of the sarangi maestro Gopal Mishra...followed by the allure of Motibai's *thumri,* accompanied by the inimitable Anokhe Lal's tabla...Bismillah's enthralled walk would culminate at the canopy of *thumri* legend Siddheshwari Devi's residence, unless of course his dear older brother Shamsuddin intercepted him and nudged him homewards, whispering a short lecture on the pitfalls of early youth. Reaching home with an embarrassed smile, Bismillah would have to give him ample proof of his perfectly honourable intentions by reproducing each and every exquisite and priceless *bandish* he had picked up, literally, by the wayside!

One fateful day in 1930, when his ustad was getting ready to leave for the famous Allahabad Music Conference, a tearful fourteen-year old Bismillah pleaded with him to be taken along. Ali Bux couldn't deny providence for too long. When the organizer's car rolled in to fetch him, he gave his nephew the nod. A similar nod on the performing stage that evening, brought on that historic moment when, for the very first time, Bismillah Khan's shehnai was exposed to a live audience. After a moody *alaap* in Raga Kedar, Ali Bux improvised on a rare *bandish.* As he nodded to his young *shagird,* Bismillah reproduced it flawlessly, with an added dimension that was rare for any young musician! *Aaftaab-e-Mausiqui,* the radiant 'Sun of Music', Ustad Faiyaz Khan was in the audience seated with other eminent stalwarts of that time. His spontaneous *'wah wah'* filled the air! After the performance, while congratulating Ali Bux backstage, he advised him to protectively nurture the young *shagird,* whose shehnai already showed the qualities of verbal articulation! Then, turning to young Bismillah, he showered him with some precious words of encouragement!

Faiyaz Khan's blessings and the first glimpse of the real world of celebrated performers inspired Bismillah to invest a lot more depth and expanse in his musical maturity. Layer upon layer, he imbibed the essence of the best of music that appealed to his own flowering sensibility. It was an era of great musicians, who lived and breathed divine music. Abdul Karim Khan's sonorous voice with its spiritual appeal was beautifully simulated by Bismillah's shehnai. Young Bismillah was also deeply influenced by Faiyaz Khan's powerful voice and rendition, his *pukar,* his *meend*...Omkarnath Thakur's *Desi Todi,* Haafiz Ali Khan's majestic *Darbari,* Enayat Khan and his magical *Jai Jaivanti*...

Before he could cross sixteen, Bismillah was coaxed into marriage. The elders of the traditional joint family chose his elder *mamu's* daughter as a ready match for young Bismillah. A natural stream of relatively unattached family life began to flow parallel to his devoted pursuit of music. So consumed was he by the magic of music, that even on the second night following his *niqah,* faint strains of a Begum Akhtar *ghazal* in Raga *Jogia Bhairavi* wafting in from a distant gramophone, held more appeal for him than the immediate charm of his bejewelled bride! Blessed with nine children, Bismillah Khan's conjugal life ran its ordained course for half a century. But, as he himself would put it, that's another story!

By the time he was twenty-one, Bismillah had already won a few gold medals in All India Music Conferences. But his heralded arrival and growth in the higher spheres of classical music began on 16 April 1938, with his performance at the historic launch of All India Radio Lucknow. The radio opened up a new highway for his musical journey.

Bismillah Khan & Party. Supported by Nazim Hussain on the tabla and Naiyar Hussain on the shehnai

After the sudden death of his *ustad,* Ali Bux, in 1940, Bismillah wept for days, sometimes through his shehnai, sometimes openly, like a child. It took him months to reintegrate himself and convert that grief and bereavement into steely resolve to do his *ustad* proud.

With ascetic concentration he caressed his shehnai, and the collective sighs of the great shehnai exponents over the years seemed to hover around his ears. From its tribal and folk origins, the shehnai had managed to reach the temple premises, but the society at large still did not accord it the status it deserved. It was still relegated to the *nahabatkhanas* and the peripheries of class and aristocracy. The instrument longed for dignity and status, and Bismillah Khan was determined to free it from the stifling image it had to endure so far. At his favourite temple and mosque, he prayed for its liberation. And simultaneously, he concentrated on investing the instrument with qualities and possibilities hitherto unexplored. He assimilated some special qualities of stringed instruments; strove to include the *jod* and the *jhaala* in his range. All the crafty nuances and the subtle artistry, which were not deemed possible in shehnai before, were lovingly and adroitly woven into his playing technique. The versatility of the grand old ustad Allauddin Khan inspired his daily *riyaaz.* His treatment of the ragas bore reference to the *layakari, tehai* and *pukar* of *Ustad* Faiyaz Khan, who had once praised

his *'kahan'* when he was just a lad of fourteen. Bismillah Khan's microtonal accuracy began to dance with nimble feet and great flourish along the entire spectrum of his improvisation. All the *bhava* and the *rasa,* the emotions and the passions of the courtesans that had been stamped on his adolescent heart, now found a release, a sublime expression in his music. His expanding repertoire now had the feel of purity and perfection. It had integrated his religious fervour, his personal spirituality, and his pure and unwavering love for his ancestral shehnai! He had finally arrived in the classical music scene of India holding aloft his instrument with an air of triumph and dignity! The *shehnai nawaz* and his shehnai, both had claimed their long deserved position on the grand arena of classical music.

The symbolic culmination of it all was witnessed at the dawn of India's independence! Khan saheb Bismillah Khan became the first free Indian to greet the entire nation through the auspicious notes of his shehnai from the ramparts of the historic Red Fort! A galaxy of prominent Indians, including the architects of India's freedom struggle and her destiny, was poised in rapt attention, listening to the moving music of a future *Bharat Ratna!*

As his family grew, Bismillah Khan strove to keep pace with his burgeoning fame and hectic concert schedules. As all major awards and honours kept coming his way, Bismillah was once again bereaved on the personal front. His intimate friend and elder brother, Shamsuddin's shehnai fell silent forever. His childhood spates of seclusion and detachment seemed to return, claiming most of his precious free moments. The enchanted world never learned to allow him enough serenity and seclusion even to this day...

The venerable Benaras Hindu University

honoured the school dropout with a Doctorate of Letters for his mastery of music...The connoisseur king, Zahir Shah of Afghanistan, showered the simple fakir with precious jewels and Persian carpets...The glamour world of films too spread the red carpet for the humble wizard, as his shehnai was invited to resonate throughout the popular film Goonj Utthi Shehnai introducing the movie-going multitudes to the classical magic of the long neglected instrument...The innocent, childlike quality that one may always detect in the twinkling eyes and the open smile of the ageing *ustad* till today, has its secret grounded in his true affection for man and God. He has no use for the hollow trappings of lifestyle, glamour or fame. He loves his Benaras, his *shivalay,* his *masjid,* the ghats of the Ganges. No lure of the outer world can fan any other desire in him. When he had to go for the prestigious Edinburgh Festival and the Commonwealth Arts Festival in 1965, he traded his acute fear of flying with the assurance of a pilgrimage to Mecca and Madina. Every year on the eighth day of Muharram, the devout *Shia* Muslim leads a procession of common citizens through the narrow, serpentine lanes of Benaras, blowing into a special silver shehnai, sending clear signals to the most orthodox *mullas* and *maulvis,* that music is not taboo, but an integral and intimate part of life and expression...He leads the group without a pause until it reaches the *rawzaa* of the martyr Imam Hussain. Sitting cross-legged like a forlorn fakir on the dusty ground, this rare minstrel then plays his shehnai for hours...while his tears flow like the Ganges in divine commemoration.

A logical extension of his honest and guileless behaviour can be seen in his one to one interaction with his audience. When he was invited, as the first Indian ever, to perform at the Lincoln Centre Hall in America, the effect of his electrifying performance was so intense on the huge audience that he had to take as many as seven curtain calls! And at the end of it, when there was an overwhelming demand for a few spoken words from the instrumentalist, his candid confession over the microphone was that wise men did not speak much, and besides, after such an exhausting performance, he was thirsting for a cup of tea! The entire audience greeted the warm human side of the gifted musician once again with resounding applause.

Over his long and rewarding musical odyssey, Khan saheb has heartily praised and inspired other talents around him. No one has ever felt intimidated or slighted by his lofty stature. He has lovingly engaged himself in

duets or *jugalbandis* with artistes junior to him. The masterly sitar of Vilayat Khan and Halim Zafar Khan, the enticing vocals of Girija Devi, the eloquent violin of N Rajam and VG Jog, have all enjoyed their fleeting relationship with the frolicking notes of shehnai from the jovial maestro.

No one can get a true measure of the enormous riches of Indian classical music without listening to the shehnai of Ustad Bismillah Khan! As an extension of his voice, his persona, his spirituality, his very soul, Khan saheb can wield his instrument like a magic wand. His music can simultaneously bring tears to the eyes while it can choke the heart with untold ecstasy! Inheriting an ordinary instrument with a limited range, Bismillah Khan has taken his shehnai along with him to great heights of audience adoration by infusing in it the entire range of possibilities of classical music. The impact of his style has been so great that he does not need to impress the audience with complicated ragas or creative acrobatics. As advised by his beloved Mamu, Ustad Ali Bux, he plays simple and known ragas like *Bageshri, Behag, Khamaj, Malkauns, Kedar* with honesty and sincerity, appealing more to the heart than the mind. And the power it wields over his audiences has been demonstrated in innumerable performances all over the world.

In the contemporary world of music where most stalwarts at the pinnacle of their career lead a jet-set, glamorous life, Ustad Bismillah Khan stands apart with his simple, austere and ascetic lifestyle. With his hermit like detachment and sublime musical contentment, he appears to be among the richest of them all. Today, with a number of diverse financial responsibilities on his shoulders, it would be understandable if he prayed to his God for worldly riches. But, as it had happened with a distressed Swami Vivekananda in front of the idol of Goddess Kali, Khan saheb too will ask his *Khuda* for nothing more than just that one thing he has always asked for: May the Almighty continue to bless him with music that is true and blissful! To the ascetic Bimillah Khan there's nothing else worth asking for from the emperor of the universe!

When future generations of men and women will visit the eternal city of Benaras, and be intrigued by some seemingly ethereal strains of shehnai floating around the ghats of the Ganga and the meandering lanes around the Kashi Vishwanath temple, some old local *sadhu* with matted hair and ash smeared body might whisper to them that actually there's no one playing that music! It is the moving spirit of the city that bemoans a void from time to time. And if his listeners looked incredulous, he might just conjure a glimpse into the legend of *shehnai-nawaz* Ustad Bismillah Khan. With a mysterious glint in his eye, he would explain that Baba Vishwanath was so happy and suffused with the daily offerings of shehnai made to him that he wanted the entire world to listen to that ethereal music. And a devout Muslim, who saw the presence of God in all human beings, was blessed to fulfill that divine wish...

Perhaps his informed audience would once again look around eagerly to spot the source of that unreal music. The twinkling wavelets of the flowing Ganges would be all that would meet their eyes.

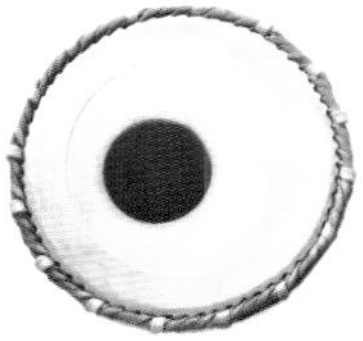

Living Memories...

Lost in divine thought

'Ba-Assar' music

Poised in musical ecstasy

In jugalbandi with N Rajam

The articulate maestro

With a hot ' Chai ka pyala'

In younger days

In jugalbandi with favourite vocalist Soma Ghosh, and supported by the ever-dependable Naiyar Hussain on shehnai

Q. Everyone has heard that story about the music loving business tycoon who pleaded with you to migrate to America...

A. *It was preposterous! How could I stay away from my beloved Benaras? I teasingly told him that I shall consider it only if you could transport my shivalay, my masjid and my Ganga to America...(smiles).*

Q. It is said, there's often a vocalist hidden in every instrumentalist. You too love to sing quite often, don't you?

A. *One complements the other. My mamu, my guru, used to say, singing was the best way to grasp a tune! 'Gaaoge, to sur pakdoge!'*

Q. What's the best way of doing riyaaz?

A. *The guru should decide what's best suited for his individual student. But generally speaking, first try to gain genuine mastery over just four ragas. One each, for the morning, afternoon, evening and the night. With that strong grounding, other ragas can be approached easily. Dedicated hard work and constant practice, of course, are a must.*

Q. Your parents had named you Qamruddin ?

A. *Yes, it rhymed with my dear older brother Shamsuddin. Apart from playing the shehnai together, we were very close from childhood onwards. His untimely death had left me very lonely for a long while.*

Q. What would you advise the younger generation of aspiring musicians?

A. *Just aspiring is not enough. You should aspire for true music, and not for the money, fame or glamour that it can earn you. You should have the earnest desire and a matching devotion towards learning. I remember how my first disciple used to stay with me in the Gurukul tradition, and learn from me at odd hours, sometimes staying awake till late in the night...that's the kind of commitment one expects...*

Q. Are you talking about Jagdish Prasad-ji?

A. *Yes. He was very young when he first came to me from a small village. Today, his talented daughter Bageshwari is learning the shehnai from me...*

Q. A female shehnai player?

A. *Why not? Music does not discriminate between man and woman. It only responds to true devotion.*

Q. You already have many talented children, including the young tabla-nawaz Nazim Hussain. What prompted you to adopt Dr Soma Ghosh as your daughter? Is it just her wonderful singing?

A. *I heard her singing at a function just before my turn came to perform. I was very impressed with her talent and the 'Benaras Ang' that she sang that evening. In fact, it even got me a little worried about my own performance, since it is not easy to wipe off the lingering effects of that magical Benarasi style...However, as we met, she called me Baba, I called her Beti. It was as simple and genuine as that. I am looking forward to such rare young talents like her to take our musical legacy forward...*

Q. The gifted scholar, musician and dancer Rita Ganguli writes in her insightful book about you that you've always asked just one thing of your Khuda. That your music should be 'ba-assar'. What is this assar you speak of?

A. *It is the ultimate effect of 'sachcha sur'. My music should be able to move the mortal soul with the bliss of the divine! That's all I have always desired. And this assar comes to you only after you surrender your ego with genuine humility. Otherwise, you can always learn the art, but the assar will elude you.*

Q. You also told her the secret of practising just one strain, one chosen bandish, at precisely the same time every day, without fail...

A. *Yes, it helps in making you a true musician. It takes you closer to that assar...*

GANGUBAI
HANGAL

She is an heiress to a fading tradition where a woman's fulfillment in life was in devoting her entire being and all her waking hours to the service of a resident god. Time and tide may have conspired to taint that sacred lineage with some social stigma, but with a lifelong shower of pure music, Gangubai Hangal has washed it clean, and has sculpted her own pristine self-portrait of a musical deity. Music has been the wind beneath her wings, carrying her beyond the confines of her background. Music has also been her life-breath sweeping her robust, melodious voice above all manmade boundaries...

Gangubai Hangal was born in 1913 in Karnataka, to a lineage of courageous women. Her mother, Ambabai, like her grandmother, was totally devoted to God and music. Their musical tradition was classical Carnatic and it was only natural, that a very young 'Gangu' was duly and easily introduced to basic *swar gyan* by her loving mother. What she did not understand easily, however, was why their pursuit of music would draw such contrasting reactions from the immediate Brahmin neighbourhood. On the one hand, their talent would be appreciated at social ceremonies, yet, on the other hand, empty tin canisters would be beaten religiously to drown her daily *riyaaz* of music.

Household radios those days were loud, and gramophones were proudly played to attract the public to the music stores and even tea-stalls. While learning formal Carnatic music from her mother early in the morning, young Gangubai had the rest of the day to respond to the diverse strains of Hindustani music floating all around. Abdul Karim Khan...Narayanrao Vyas...Zohrabai Agrawali...Hirabai Badodekar...celebrated singers of that era began to make inroads into her musical mind and her leanings towards the north Indian style of music soon reached a point of no return. Escorted by whoever was available, an adolescent Gangubai began to

visit the nearest music shop in Dharwar, to sit and listen to all the new records that arrived from time to time.

Ambabai herself was famous for her repertoire of light classical *javali* and *kirtana* compositions. She tried hard to pass on some of her treasures to her daughter, but Gangubai was too young perhaps to imbibe the difficult *talas* of those Carnatic compositions. Her mother used to back her quite literally by stroking her back, while young Gangu made her spirited efforts, but her rhythm would go astray the moment her mother's hand was off her back! Soon, Ambabai reconciled to the fact that her gifted daughter was destined to tread the exotic path of Hindustani classical music. There was Hulugoor Krishnachari, a disciple of the great Abdul Karim Khan of the Kirana gharana, who had started a music class in Hubli, and Ambabai decided to send Gangubai there to begin her first formal lessons in Hindustani classical music.

Music circles and concert organizers were rare in Hubli those days. But both Ambabai and young Gangu used to get invitations to sing at social ceremonies. Marriages, births, promotions, anniversaries...no occasion to celebrate would be complete without a touch of appropriate live music. The money offered was not much, but it was precious. Perhaps the only ammunition against the spectre of poverty that waited outside their doorstep like a patient wolf.

Despite her financial state, Ambabai's abode was an open house for music makers and aficionados alike. She was well versed in Sanskrit and Kannada compositions. It is believed that Ustad Abdul Karim Khan had learnt a few of his favourite Carnatic songs from Ambabai. A woman of vision, when Ambabai realized that young Gangu was seriously getting immersed in

Hindustani classical music, she made a rather poignant sacrifice for the sake of her daughter. Almost overnight, she gave up singing completely, just to make sure that the conflicting strains of Carnatic music in the house did not lead to contamination or confusion in the budding vocalist who chose the Hindustani classical style for her career. When Gangubai protested and expressed a wish to learn her mother's music also, Ambabai explained to her that Carnatic music was part of family treasure, and she could always learn it later. Right now, it was important to surrender wholeheartedly to the music she had chosen. The 'later', however, was never to come. Nor was Ambabai destined to witness the ultimate fruition of her daughter's flowering talent. Before Gangubai could enter her twenties, Ambabai left this world after a sudden illness.

Music may come naturally to some chosen favourites of god; to some others it is a resolute, active pursuit. To Gangubai, it has always been like a *yagna havan,* a ceremonial fire to be kept alive with the coarse firewood of worldly sacrifices along with the perfumed offerings of her soulful devotion to music.

To begin with, she had to come to terms with the very status of musicians amidst her social settings. In her private thoughts, she had to rescue music from the quicksand of social doubt and disdain, and place it reverentially in the deep sanctum of her heart. That resolved, she chose to distance herself from the palpable influence of her direct inheritance of Carnatic music, and embrace an alien style. Her mother's sacrifice and blessings ensured that her pursuit of Hindustani classical music did not have to take a rebellious path.

Gangubai's voice too was not as awe-inspiring as the world would encounter later. She had begun singing when even the tanpura was taller than her petite frame, and the drone of that humble four-stringed instrument would almost drown her feeble voice. It needed some relentless *riyaaz* and energy-sapping full-throated efforts to gradually invest her voice with the kind of power that would raise it above the thunderous applause her melody would attract in concerts.

Yet, anxiety was a chronic malady. When she was learning from her guru, her throat had begun to give her trouble. No doctor could prescribe a proper treatment, and some advised the removal of her tonsils. But no one could confidently predict what effect that might have on her voice quality. Finally, a small but delicate operation by a music loving surgeon saved her voice, and later, some further treatment by the same doctor got rid of her throat problems and helped her voice gain some rare power.

Another contributing factor to Gangubai's lifelong struggle with adversities was her location. Indeed, her budding talent had earned her the attention and respect of the record companies and the radio stations even before her tutelage under her main guru had formally begun. But then, every recording those days would entail a tiring train journey, some frantic scouting for escorts, and prolonged absence from pressing household matters, which she could ill afford.

Gangubai's father had always remained a distant entity, and her loving mother too left her bereft before she could really find her feet in this big bad world, leaving her no brother or sister to share the grief. Thus, Gangubai's own emotional vulnerability and an inherited sense of social isolation were the other negatives in her life. Something she had to constantly subdue with the positive strength of spirit gained from her growth and maturity as a musician.

Music itself could have been a balm for her worldly wounds of sorrow. But she has honestly confessed that it wasn't so. First of all, it wasn't always easy to concentrate on her music practice, her daily *riyaaz,* when her mind was grappling with the worries of running the house. With many mouths to feed in the extended family, poverty was a constant threat. The man in her life could have brought some relief, but her destiny, perhaps had plotted otherwise. Gurunath Kowalagi was a good man. He gave her emotional mooring, he gave her talented children, but financially he could never become the provider of security or solace. All his sincere efforts and business ventures were fated to fail, repeatedly wiping out Gangubai's random earnings from concerts and recordings. Finally one fateful day, when an anxiety laden Gangubai was performing at a concert in distant Bombay, her husband succumbed to cancer back home in Hubli. Ironically perhaps, Gangubai's widowhood was more complete than her earlier relationship with her husband.

Financial worries, emotional traumas, untimely bereavements were all like the plucking on a musical instrument that was Gangubai Hangal. The deeper and harder the strikes, the more poignant the resulting music. At the core, she always remained the simple, small town girl, ready to confront any hardship for the sake of her duties towards her immediate world and her haven of music. Even when her horizons began to expand and her fame grew like the crescent moon, her feet were firmly grounded; she never dreamt of the luxuries and the trappings and the tantrums of a celebrity life. Hubli has remained her humble home for life. In her days of initial struggle, when moving over to Bombay or Pune would have opened up many more doors of income and opportunity, she did not have the heart to tear away from her relatives and dependents. And later, even when the outer world was at her feet, she could not walk away to a larger arena. It was the overwhelming love, respect and familiarity accorded by the art-loving people of Hubli that kept her anchored.

Gangubai, with her dedicated learning, her *sadhana* and her *guru-bhakti* has been a major torchbearer of the star-studded Kirana *gharana* throughout India. Her recitals have also been appreciated in America, Canada, Germany, France, and even Pakistan. Through her marathon struggle with life itself, and her triumphs in the world of music, she has compelled the world to believe that an artiste's ultimate identity is her art.

Gangubai has never cringed from life's flurry or fury. Yes, in her solitary moments of anguish, she has often plumbed her spiritual depths and emerged wiser. Rarely ecstatic in receiving, she has always found true bliss in the joy of giving. Even today she sometimes feels that her guru, Sawai Gandharva is singing through her voice. She is merely gifting her guru's music to the world. She has never thought of going elsewhere and learning from any other guru. She has never wished to sing any other music either! No recourse to popular light music, no artistic allowances to the lowest common denominator. Since the day she made her choice, pure classical music, *shuddh shastriya sangeet* has been her only *sadhana,* and her sublime *siddhi.* Like all her relationships in life, this ultimate one too has been based on genuine integrity.

She still remembers that wintry night long ago, when a couple of telegrams from Delhi had brought in the news of her being awarded the Padma Bhushan. Her uncle Ramanna, who had often accompanied her on the tabla, was beside her that night, sharing a deluge of haunting memories. The exaltation of the moment was all but drowned by the relentless waves of heart-wrenching nostalgia! Yes, the one person who should have lived to see this day was gone far too soon. The spirited Ambabai could neither see nor foresee this moment of recognition, which perhaps was no less hers than her daughter's. Perhaps the last link with a fading ancestry, she was much more than a mother to Gangubai. Ambabai had merged her own unspoken ambition with the promise and talent shown by her daughter. She had lovingly placed her dreams in the cradle and had rocked it gently for a while. In the wake of her premature demise, the cradle did not return to stillness, but expanded into a stage. An honourable and luminous stage on which, her little Gangu sat at the centre and sang pure Hindustani classical music in a compelling voice. Ambabai did not live to see it. Music loving audiences over the last few decades have had all the luck.

Living Memories...

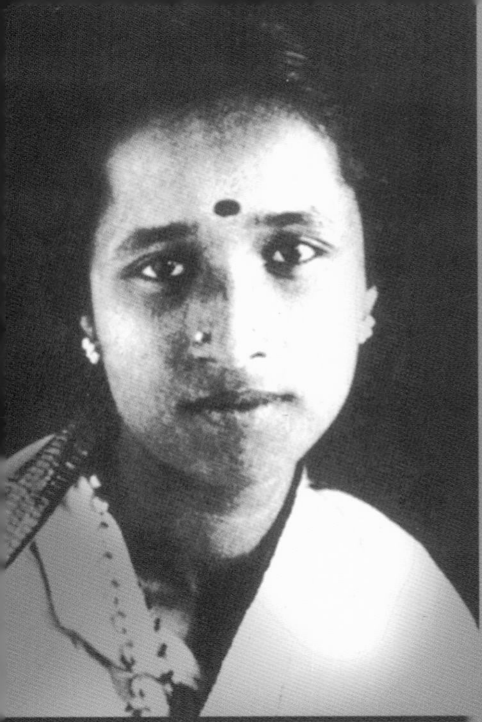

The age of innocence

Younger days

Vintage Gangubai

The traditional look

Younger days

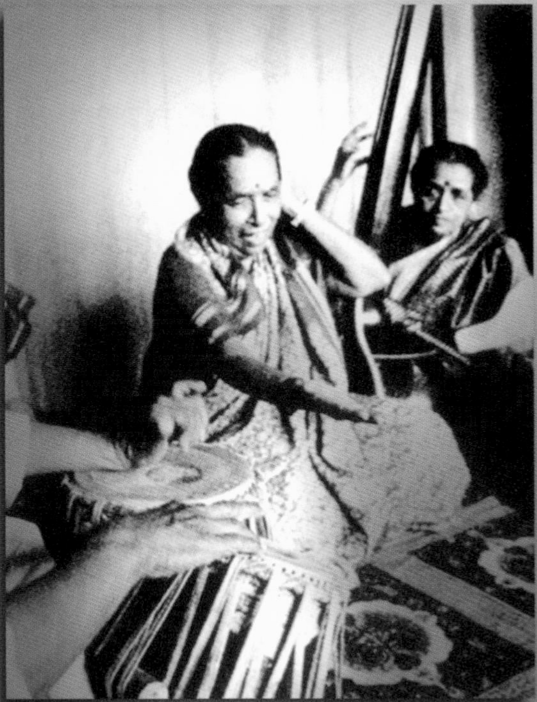

At concert with her talented daughter Krishna

Being honoured by Morarji Desai

With Pupul Jaykar

With Indira Gandhi

In tune with her tanpura

The typical gesture

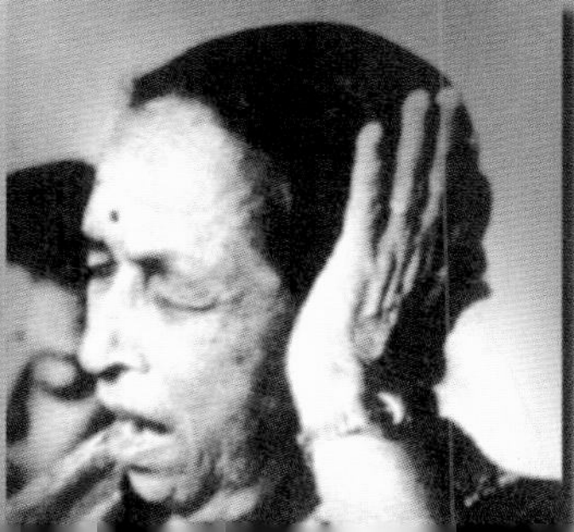

Q. The society's attitude to music must have been very different at the time when you began learning?

A. *Very much so. People's thinking was different. Learning music was confined to professional artists only. If others showed a desire to learn, they would often be discouraged, because there was no saying how the immediate society would view it.*

Q. Women performers faced the added problem of not finding established accompanists?

A. *I never experienced any such discrimination. Alla Rakha Khan played with me. Even Thirakuwa Saheb has accompanied me more than once.*

Q. You have had a difficult life. Did the pursuit of music help you forget some of your social and financial worries?

A. *Some people say that once you sit for your music riyaaz the whole world recedes into the background. But with me somehow things did not happen that way. When I sat down for riyaaz, I would begin to sob. All my sorrows, my financial worries, my family responsibilities would suffocate me...Except, when I would prepare for a performance, the concentration of wanting to do well would be powerful enough to push aside my mundane worries. But then again, there have been instances when I would be singing on stage, and floating strains of my little son crying backstage would put me in a quandary.*

Q. Who were the famous musicians you liked as you grew up?

A. *My mother sang very good javali and kirtana compositions. But I was attracted to Hindustani classical, and my favourite was Zohrabai. Then there would be small jalsas in our house. Stalwarts like Hirabai and Sunderibai would visit and sing. Film star Nargis's mother Jaddanbai would come. In fact, I got my first programme in Calcutta through the good offices of Jaddanbai.*

Q. Tell us something about how your guru-ji Sawai Gandharva taught you.

A. *He taught me a lot about how the presentation and elaboration of a raga should be approached. The swaras of the raga must be presented in varied combinations. The vistaar should be unhurried and serene. The listener should be kept eager to hear the next note; his interest should be maintained throughout. This is how the atmosphere of the concert, the mehfil is created. One must study the methodical use of the raga-swaras in presenting the badhat, or the elaboration of the raga. It would sometime seem boring to me then, but I soon realized that this approach would assist me in future in getting a quick grip of any new raga I might want to learn. Besides being taught, I also got to attend many of his programmes and learnt a lot by just listening.*

Q. But you did a great deal of riyaaz?

A. *I remember I used to practise for seven to eight hours a day. When I began my daily trip to guru-ji's house, it was three hours in the evening at his feet, and at least four to five hours every morning at my place. This was my practise for a number of years.*

Q. Do you still do regular riyaaz?

A. *Unfortunately, I gave it up long ago.*

Q. So you sing only in concerts these days?

A. *Yes. And that's also my riyaaz. (Laughs) And sometimes, while teaching my students, I sing.*

Q. How about your daughter Krishna?

A. *She had started singing along with me. She has heard a lot of music and has a natural flair to imbibe the good. And she has a light, sweet voice, unlike mine (Laughs).*

Q. Would you care to recount any of your memorable concerts?

A. *There are many. But let me tell you about the first time I sang before a really large audience. It was unscheduled and unexpected! HMV had organized a conference in a village called Goregaon near Bombay. After the scheduled programme got over, a lot of time had to be killed before people could catch the next train. So the people of Goregaon encouraged me to sing. And I gathered my courage and sang before that huge audience. And I was well rewarded. Many representatives of various art circles from all over Maharashtra were present there, and from then on I began to receive invitations to sing from far and wide.*

Q. You did a lot of radio concerts and HMV records. How were those experiences?

A. *Those days, going for a recording meant staying in Bombay for a fortnight. HMV would rent a house for the invited artistes, complete with caretakers and even a cook. Their sound engineer would come over from London. It would take about fifteen days for a couple of records. Wax records were prepared and dried. Once it so happened that we were called back again from the railway station for re-recording, because the records made the previous day were*

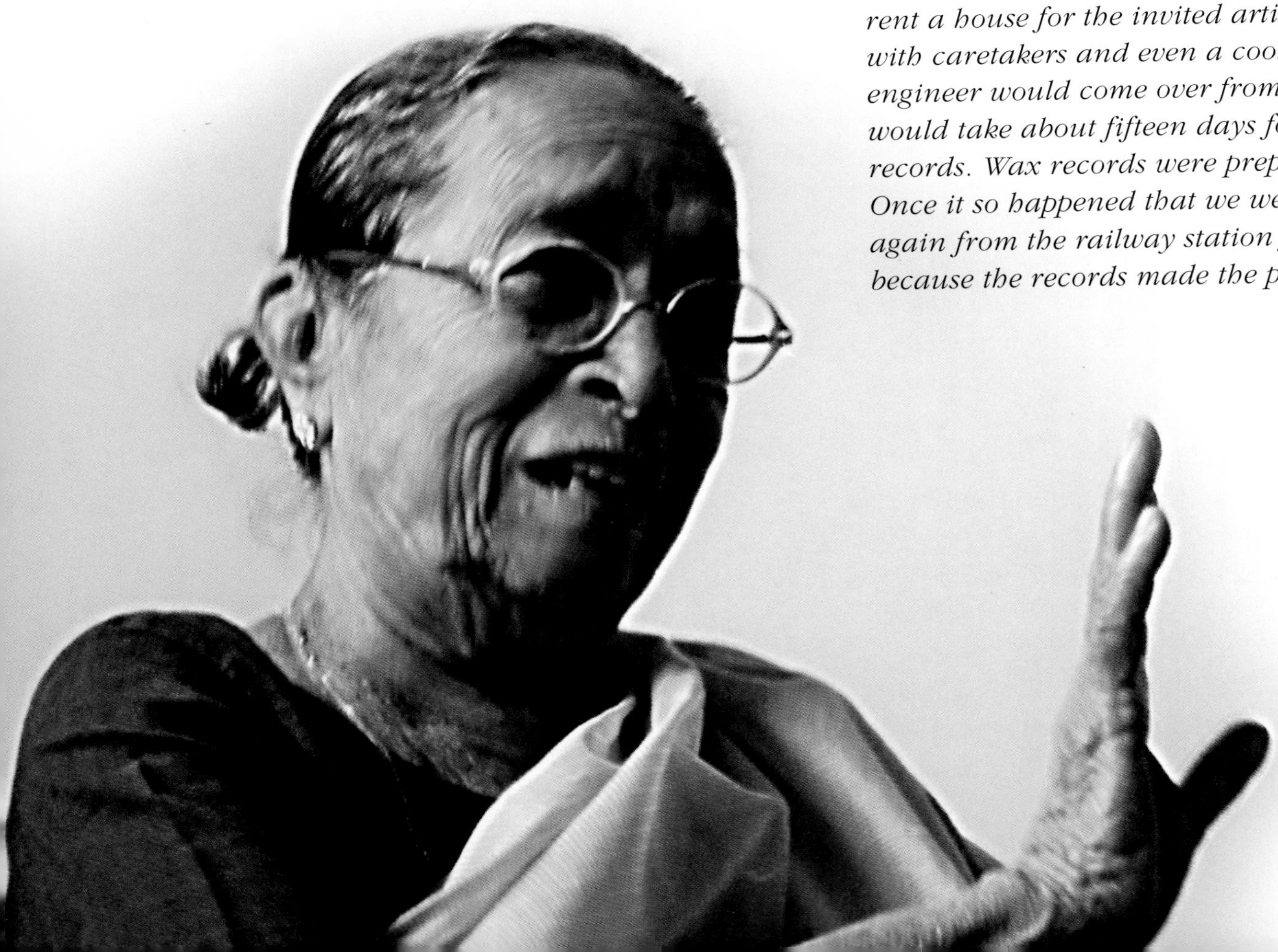

all broken!

Q. Once you had met your guru-ji's guru Abdul Karim Khan himself?

A. *Yes! He had come to our house to listen to some of his favourite Carnatic songs from my mother. Later on even I was asked to sing, and being too little I did not have much hesitation to sing whatever I knew. Khan saheb blessed me and said, "Dekho Beti, khoob gana aur khoob khana!" (Laughs)*

Q. Your mother's untimely death had left you shattered?

A. *Well, for months together I could not sing at all! Everyone was worried. Then my good friend Dattopant Desai would try to motivate me by reminding me that my mother had sacrificed her own music for my sake! I could not afford to let her down! Gradually, I fought my depression and got back to singing.*

Q. One finds a lot of projected glamour, and ego tantrums in star musicians today...?

A. *Ego and pride are detrimental to genuine greatness. In our earlier days, we have ignored the peripherals and concentrated solely on the music! When the occasion demanded, I have sat on layers of pillows to reach the mouthpiece of nonadjustable microphones!*

I have had to sing with single-stringed tanpuras, and even clarinets! There was a warm sense of accommodation those days. In music conferences, one could easily request other artistes to lend you their accompanists if the need arose. The greatest of artistes sat enthusiastically through the recitals of other artistes who performed after them. And there was open admiration and plenty of encouragement for upcoming musicians. Today, I notice, things are not quite the same...

Q. You are known for your firm principles of not compromising for the sake of earning easy applause. Don't you ever sing what the audience wants?

A. *I believe in the music I have spent my life to learn. And it is my endeavour to present it to the audiences of today and to that of future generations. See, it is not difficult to give what one thinks people want. But I would like to give them something higher, something more sublime. There may be some initial difficulty, but soon they will get to enjoy higher standards of classical music. That would make me really happy!*

Q. Which is more eloquent? Vocal music, or instrumental?

A. *Each has its place. Actually, music has its own language; it need not depend on words. When I returned from my American tour, some people asked me, "Bai, you did not know their language. How did you communicate?" I replied, "They knew my language: music. And that was enough."*

Q. Did you ever feel like learning to play any musical instrument?

A. *No. I had learnt dance for a while though. Kathak. Then they said, those fast movements would affect my singing voice. So I gave up.*

Q. Any advice for the young learners of music?

A. *Sing. And listen.*

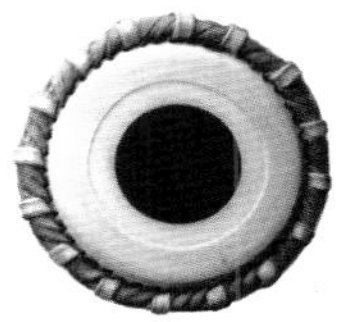

HARIPRASAD
CHAURASIA

Aeons ago, when Lord Krishna walked this earth in human form, he had given himself many a monumental task to accomplish. Most of them were acts of strife, violence and valour. Vanquishing demons, punishing evildoers, holding the reins at the Kurukshetra battle field, and even revealing his devastatingly spectacular *'Vishwaroop'* to Arjun.

The divine charmer, however, balanced it all out with his most endearing image. That of the flute-playing, stealer of hearts! Making music, that evokes in human souls, the most dramatic yearning for the divine! In fact, what Lord Krishna's gospel, the Bhagavad Gita has been preaching to the thinking minds, his flute has been singing gently to the listening hearts.

Such indeed is the power and significance of Lord's Krishna's flute. And it is only the specially blessed who are inspired to pick up the most pristine and natural instrument in their mortal hands and go on to make divine music with it. It is the power of this blessing that must have prompted the elders of the Chaurasia family of Allahabad in the monsoon of 1938, to name the family's latest newborn as *Hariprasad!* For, there was no immediate indication, that the large-eyed, bubbly baby would have anything to do with the flute, or even music. As Hariprasad grew up to be a tall, robust boy, his father, a renowned wrestler, was happy and proud to initiate him into the lion-hearted occupation of being engaged in physical contests of strength, skill and stamina!

From this rather down-to-earth pursuit, however, young Hariprasad's attention was soon claimed by the ethereal beacon of music. It was that 'blessing' at work, for sure. Hariprasad managed to persuade his father to allow him to learn vocal music from Pandit Rajaram. Lord Krishna, perhaps, wasn't willing to wait anymore. Within a year's time, Hariprasad attended the first flute recital of his life...and the divine melody from many past lives wafted across time and space and possessed him! It also gave him a fleeting vision of his life's mission. He didn't have to look around for a guru. His moist eyes couldn't see beyond the saintly man who was playing the flute in front of the rapt audience. Wiping his tears of joy, an adolescent

Hariprasad in concert. Flanked at the extremes by young talents Yogesh Samsi on the tabla and nephew Rakesh Chaurasia on the

Hariprasad approached the master, and touched his feet. With a sense of déjà vu, perhaps, Pandit Bholanath accepted the young boy as his disciple...

Hands that were taught to wield the bamboo staff for sporting combat, soon learnt to hold the bamboo flute in a gentle, reverential grip. Hariprasad could sense that his life had found its meaning, and his life-breath, its purpose. Pandit Bholanath was from Benaras, the eternal city, steeped in spiritual fervour. Young Hariprasad learnt from him for several years at a stretch without wavering. He followed up the difficult training with rigorous practice, and before long, he could convince everyone that he was not born to be a wrestler or anything else; his talents and energies were meant to be channelled through the flute. And he was ready and qualified to begin a career in music!

Hariprasad's proficiency with the flute was already of a high order, and he got a break at the All India Radio, Cuttack, as a performer and composer. But soon, his energy and enthusiasm at the new place spilled out of the confines of his routine job, and he began to circulate freely and famously as a bright young flautist in town! His office colleagues saw very little of him during work hours, and in due course, the seniors were obliged to take disciplinary action against the young man, by ordering a transfer. The transfer, deservingly, was chosen to be a long distance one, but it turned out to be a blessing in disguise for the humbled victim. Along with his immense talent, burning ambition, and his young, melodious wife, Anuradha, Hariprasad Chaurasia made his historic appearance in the metropolis of Bombay.

Taking up residence in a modest room at a suburban lodge, Hariprasad set out to explore the musical avenues of Bombay. On the one hand, were the duties and responsibilities of the All India Radio job, and on the other, were the untapped possibilities of recitals and concerts, and the unique opportunity that only Bombay could offer as the emerging capital of the film empire of India.

Just as the classical music scene had already experienced the bansuri of Pandit Pannalal Ghosh, so had the film music world. The *bansuri* had to be an important instrument in Indian film music, literally instrumental in lending mood and poignancy to the emotion-laden stories and sagas. Yet, the ropes had to be learnt fast, and sustained efforts had to be made

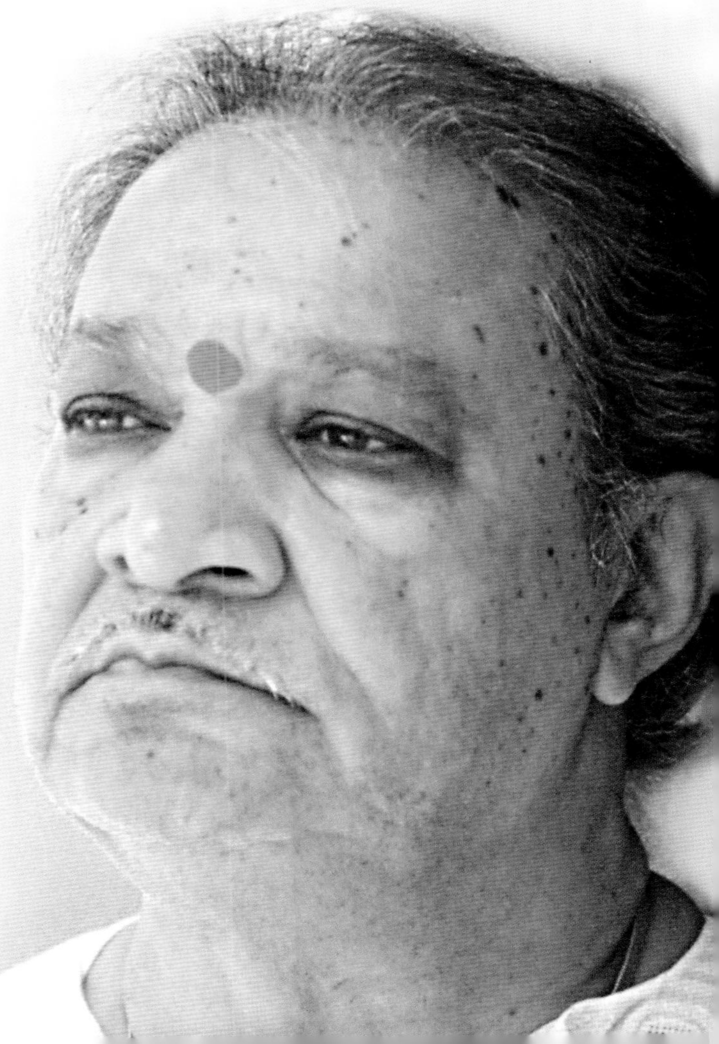

to unravel the circuitous paths around the many bastions of the film world. An artiste's ego had to be gently patted in place while seeking appointments and auditions in an industry that ticked at its own style and pace, and had its own methods and madness. Cradled between the swing of commerce and creativity, the Bombay film world, slowly but steadily, began to open its doors and arms to the new magician of melody. Talent, as always, recognized talent, and the legendary music directors were gradually warming up to the inspiring presence of Hariprasad Chaurasia in their recording studios.

The major task for Hariprasad, of course, was to keep investing in himself. Into the core of his musical mission. He had to repeatedly regain contact with the sensitive classical musician residing deep within. In the Indian classical music arena, his beloved bansuri had to measure up to the reigning stars—the sitar, the sarod, the shehnai...

Hariprasad knew that one of the most brilliant and rare gurus the classical music world had ever seen was right there in his city. But the reclusive Annapurna Devi wasn't easy to confront or convince. After much spirited effort, the 'princess' of *Maihar gharana* agreed to teach the eager and earnest young flautist. It was a major stride in the direction in which Hariprasad was ordained to proceed.

The 'musician's musician' Annapurna Devi had witnessed the genesis of Pannalal Ghosh's success, and now she recognized the destined relationship between young Hariprasad and the classical flute. She went on to bestow a deep musical maturity on Hariprasad, by enriching his vision and enhancing his repertoire of ragas and compositions. She also inspired him to focus on an unwavering performing career in classical music.

In the meanwhile, the other well-wisher who repeatedly advised Hariprasad to focus his energies on the cause of the bansuri, was the santoor maestro Shiv Kumar Sharma. Having met repeatedly in the recording studios of Bombay, and finding much in common as far as their age, their musical mission, and the stage of their struggle were concerned, the two fortune

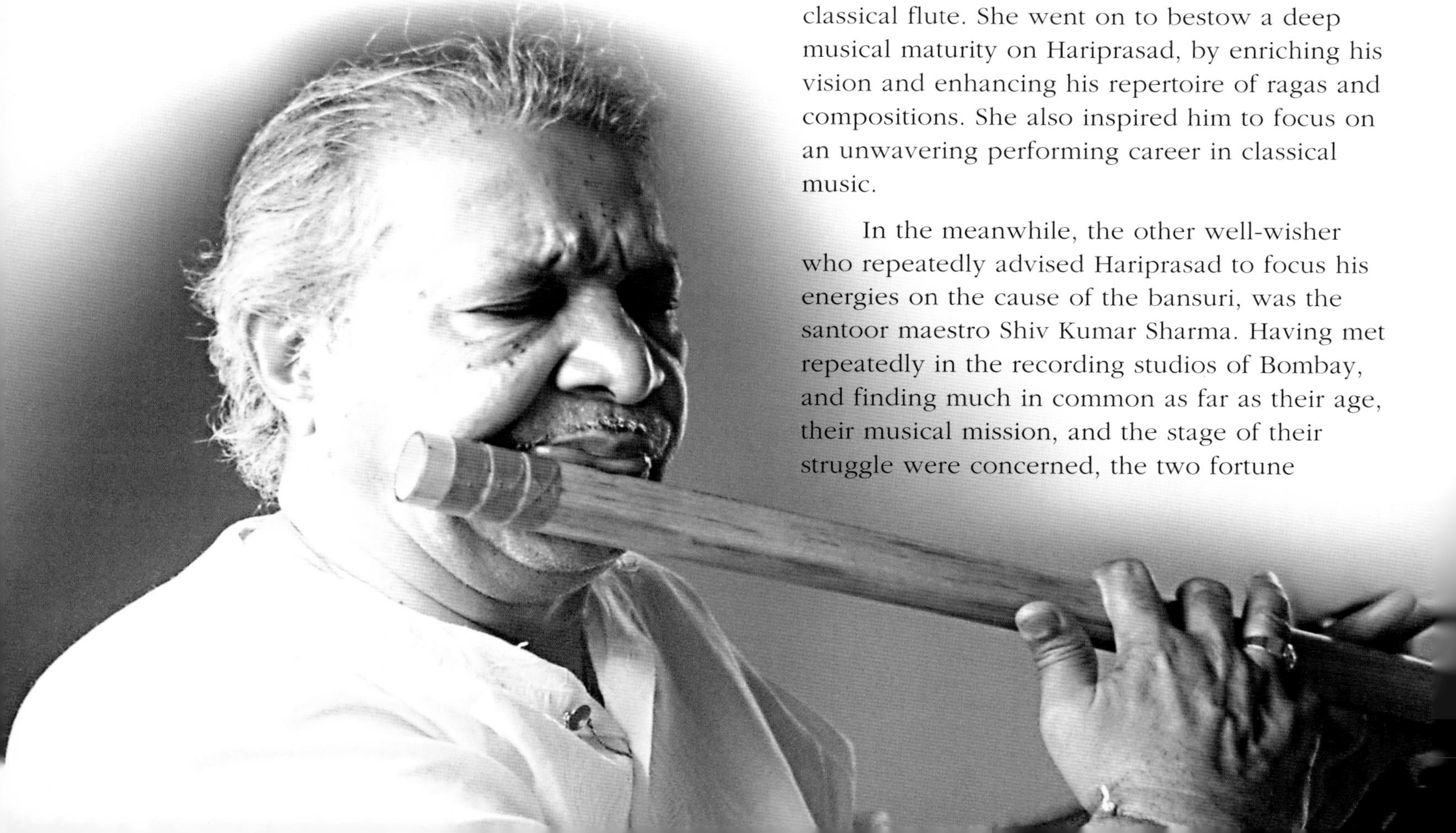

seekers in the hustle bustle of Bombay, had reached out to each other in a warm and reassuring friendship. A friendship, which was destined to blossom along many branches of alliance, both in their professional and personal lives. The two musicians spent a good part of their striving time together, grabbing a quick meal at cheap restaurants, exchanging professional notes, lightening loads of despair, enhancing joys of achievements, and inspiring each other to soldier on undaunted, through the barbed fences of professional progress. Like a responsible elder brother, Shiv Kumar urged Hariprasad to optimize his efforts, to stick to arduous *riyaaz,* and attend serious concerts and festivals. He helped his friend realize the futility of frittering away time and energy in distracting pursuits, when the Indian classical music arena was still dominated by the sitar and the sarod. They infused in each other the confidence and belief that it was time for the santoor and the bansuri to take their place in the elite league.

Touched with mutual respect and affection, this deep friendship had many spin-offs. Along with their wives, they made a joyous and effusive foursome, meeting frequently out of doors and at each other's residence for dinner and long chats late into the night, gradually feeling at home in the once alien metropolis. And in the professional sphere, the friendship led to very many creative alliances on landmark music albums, *jugalbandis,* and adventurous concert tours.

The film industry, however, wasn't going to easily surrender Hariprasad to the grasp of the classical music world. He continued to play some moody, poignant, scene-filling, heart-stealing bansuri for almost all the top-notch music directors in that golden era of film music! History

In humorous conversation with his audience

perhaps may never speak of how great a role was played by Hariprasad's bansuri in inspiring all those legendary music directors to live on a melodious high in order to make such memorable music, which today's generations can only envy. Hariprasad himself took on the role of providing music direction for many regional and a few Hindi films as well. Until, in a significant, inspired moment of shared dreams, Hariprasad and Shiv Kumar decided to forge a professional bond, and *Shiv-Hari* was born. The two maestros could harmoniously apply their classical, folk and personal dynamics of musicality in a string of challenging and eventually satisfying movies beginning with *Silsila* and *Chandni*.

The duo also collaborated in HMV's eternally popular music album 'Call of the Valley', a thematically interwoven string of eloquent ragas expressing the intrinsic relationship among music, man and nature. The tremendous success of the album widened their circle of listeners, as the santoor and the bansuri steadily gained acceptance and respect in the world of classical music.

Shiv Kumar, as a friend, echoed what Annapurna Devi as a guru had advised Hariprasad. It was time to give up his radio job and peripheral pursuits, in order to further sharpen the focus on his classical bansuri. Soon enough, Hariprasad's experiments with the flute technique were already meeting with eloquent success. A new tone, a new style, a fresh breath of life were being infused into the bamboo flute...and Hariprasad Chaurasia was steadily becoming an indispensable name in concert circuits and music festivals.

Considering the collective memory of Krishna's divine flute reverberating across eras and cycles of myriad lives, it wasn't difficult for Hariprasad to conquer the eager Indian hearts. It took just a single listening experience for audiences to realize that this was special. The bamboo flute, like the wooden baton in a relay race, had been passed on from one 'Hari' to

Teaching at the Vrindavan Gurukul

another, across many millennia. Except, there was no competition here; only audiences and spectators, too eager to surrender.

Soon it was time for Hariprasad to spread his wings further. Invitations began to reach him from concert circuits and festivals abroad. Sometimes alone, sometimes with congenial musician friends, including Shiv Kumar Sharma and Zakir Hussain. Hariprasad travelled extensively, performing in several countries in Asia, Australia, Europe and the Americas. Gaining audience adulation and critical acclaim from fellow musicians, such as Yehudi Menuhin and Jean-Pierre Rampal, Hariprasad made the Indian bamboo flute resonate with its magical melodies all over the emerging music world. Aspiring disciples flocked to him from countries as diverse as Mexico and Japan. Western greats John McLaughlin and Jan Garbarek collaborated with Hariprasad to record a major international album at Oslo, and as expected, it took the global market by storm. Back in India, Hariprasad's experiments with various sound and musical genres created landmark albums like 'Eternity', 'Soundscapes' and 'The Elements'...

Striking an aesthetic and melodious balance between traditional riches and innovative explorations, Hariprasad has been steadily expanding the expressive prowess of the classical flute! His unique and pioneering adaptation of the *alap* and the *jod* of *Khayal gayaki* into the realms of flute playing, has been energized by his masterly blowing style and technique.

With his warmth, charm and sparkling humour, his boundless energy and youthful enthusiasm, Hariprasad Chaurasia has been straddling the vast domain of music for decades. From his delightfully melodious lighter classical compositions rooted in the country soil at one extreme, to the boldly experimental multicultural fusion pushing the other, he has been the lord and master of all that he has touched with his musical genius.

Hariprasad has cast his spell on countless gatherings of music lovers. He has mesmerized alien and sophisticated audiences with his simple bamboo flute! With his own unique technique, he has made his instrument whisper, hum, weep, speak and sing!

He began life with the blessings of Lord Krishna's name. Since then, he has reverentially concentrated all his talents, inspirations and energies to channel them into that short piece of hollowed bamboo. And through its outlets, his personal spirit has reached out and merged with the universal consciousness. His very life-breath has sublimated into divine music.

Lord *'Hari'* himself must have been happy with his *'prasad'*. He too must have enjoyed the worldly strains of his inspiration, his cosmic flute. He has blessed Hariprasad yet again, with another life-spanning dream! With a most ambitious mission of making the melodies of the divine flute spread to all landscapes of the modern world, Pandit Hariprasad Chaurasia's *Vrindavan Gurukul* is fast taking shape...

Living Memories...

As a young boy in Allahabad

At home with wife Anuradha

Exchanging notes with John McLaughim

With the great Lata and Usha Mangeshkar at Tirupathi

As a young conductor at All India Radio

With collaborating maestros Brij Bhushan Kabra & Shiv Kumar Sharma

'Shiv-Hari' discussing music of 'Silsila' with Amitabh Bachchan & Yash Chopra

With tabla maestro Allarakha

With the legendary Ustad Amir Khan & the magnetic singer Begum Akhtar

In a lighter moment with actor Peter Sellers

Receiving a national honour from President R Venkatraman

A spiritual recital at the Osho ashram

Happy grandparents

Q. Besides the three gurus you have had, was there ever anyone from whom you had felt like learning, but could not?

A. *Yes. Kesarbai Kerkar.*

Q. How many disciples do you have?

A. *Countless. My disciples are from a diverse range of races and regions. American, European, Pakistani, Japanese, Negro...*

Q. Any special reason for this wide spectrum?

A. *More diverse people seem to be drawn to the flute because as a basic instrument it is not alien to anyone. Unlike the other Indian instruments like the sitar, the sarod or the sarangi...*

Q. Is it necessary to be a good human being to become a good musician?

A. *Hmm...yes. You have got to be a good person to handle music.*

Q. Does one have to be deeply spiritual, to delve deep into Indian classical music?

A. *Some may not start off to be spiritual but may still have a good musical temperament. But when you acquire the two most crucial qualities for music, which are concentration and devotion, you begin to literally feel the presence of the divine. Spirituality, ultimately is an integral part of music, and if one has embraced music, one cannot be too far from spirituality. I was never so spiritual. But my music has changed me. Today, music is my only religion.*

Q. Do you follow rituals?

A. *I do not have a set routine, I comply with my family's wishes if there are special occasions. But yes, whenever I go to my hometown Allahabad, I do take a dip in the holy Ganges. That's special.*

Q. A musician's temperament is so finely tuned. How do you cope with frustrations?

A. *God has been backing me in most of my endeavours. That's why, when something seemingly goes against my wishes, I pause to realize that it must be God's wish, and ultimately, it must be for the best. And I believe in learning from my failures. It is only in the face of failure that one appreciates the value and sweetness of success.*

Q. Would you care to name five of your favourite ragas?

A. *All the ragas I have learnt are my favourites. That's why I have learnt them (smiles). And they are many more than five...*

Q. The ragas you created?

A. *Shivanjali...Manohari...well, they too are many.*

Q. Name three of your most memorable concerts?

A. *All my concerts are memorable to me. Because when I sit for any concert, I think of it as my first...and also probably my last (smiles)!*

Q. That's an attitude. But in terms of memory, there must be some concerts, which were special.

A. *Every recital is special. You see, when I commit for a concert, the moment I know the date, I begin thinking about it in my mind...I get ready. And when I am on stage, I do not think of it as a performance. I think of it as a prayer!*

Q. ...Your offering to God?

A. *Yes, my offering to God. Who is present there between my audience and me...listening to my music...*

Q. What do you think of the lighter forms of classical music—Thumri, Dadra, Chaiti...

A. *All forms of music in India are wonderful.*

Q. What about film music?

A. *I admired all the old time music directors! They were wonderful...*

Q. Name some?

A. *All! All of them were great! There isn't a single name I can ignore. They had their distinct identity. Their gharana of music! I loved them, I played for them; those were wonderful days...*

Q. What's your impression of Western classical music?

A. *Wonderful! Such great composers! I love listening to all of them...*

Q. It's so difficult to get you to name anyone...!

A. *(Laughs) See, if you have five children, how do you label anyone as your favourite?*

Coming back to Indian films, I have worked with Husnlal Bhagatram, Naushad, SD Burman, Shanker Jaikishan, Kalyanji Anandji, C Ramchand...I have worked with them, I have learnt from them...Different sounds, different styles,different sources, different gharanas...

Q. What do you think of the current generation of young musicians ?

A. *They are brilliant! They are doing a wonderful job. They may not have much time to practise, yet they are able to perform well...*

Q. What might be the reason?

A. *I think God has given the new generation more talent! When we used to study and get about thirty-five per cent marks, we would be happy. Today they weep even when they get ninety per cent marks!*

Look at the junk food they eat, yet they have such good brains! (Smiles).

Q. Any unfulfilled dreams?

A. *I am contented.*

Q. Any ragas you haven't learnt?

A. *There are so many from the south and the north combined! They are like stars in the sky...many lives are needed to learn them all...*

Q. During your film music creation, did you ever have any problems with the lyricists?

A. *Hmm...at times I felt that the words were not good enough. Just as they may have felt that my music was not good enough (Laughs)! But this was healthy, otherwise how does one improve?*

Q. Who is your favourite poet?

A. *All saint poets of olden times.*

Q. Who is your favourite writer?

A. *Mahadevi Verma...Harivanshrai Bachchan...*

Q. Finally, I got you to name names!

Tell us something about the relevance of the gurukul institute you are planning? Are you facing hurdles?

A. *It is not easy. You see, the awareness about gurukul is incredibly low among modern people! Is the guru 'cool' or something, people ask! (Laughs)*

In reality, it is a wonderful tradition. And it is as relevant today as it ever was. The shishya has to surrender himself, and the guru has to adopt him. Then they are closer to each other more than even a family!

Q. Any spiritual experience you'd like to recount?

A. *Many times when I play my flute, I feel this special power surging in me. I forget myself. I get transported to a different planet...*

Q. This happens more recently?

A. *Off and on for the last forty years! That's how my music has become my love, my religion, my language, my life!*

Q. If you believe in reincarnation, what would you like to be in your next life?

A. *I would like to be in the same music field.*

Q.A vocalist, perhaps?

A. *No, a flautist.*

Q. What were you in your previous birth?

A. *I think I played the flute.*

Q. What, according to you, is so profoundly unique about the flute?

A. *Man can tune almost every other instrument. But the bamboo flute is one instrument where you have to tune yourself to it! And when you are thus tuned, you are already in meditation! Every pore of your body breathes music.*

I consider it a yogic instrument! Some people play music in the background when they practise yoga. But when you are playing the flute, you are making music and at the same time you are doing yoga! This is truly unique!

God is love.
JASRAJ

If you can imagine an unbridled emotional odyssey of the human voice through the ever-expanding galaxy of music, you may be able to conjure the charismatic image of Pandit Jasraj in concert. As his mellifluous voice travels to heights and depths hitherto unexplored, his persona reigns majestically over the transient musical kingdom he creates.

Flowing along a mysterious spring of intuition, his *alaap* ripples all around your being, as if you are yourself the source of these pristine *swaras*. The music seems to be all pervading, embracing in its fluency the passage of time. You are barely allowed a faint feeling that you have heard or known this music before, perhaps in some previous life, while your current attention is held taut and rapt by the dancing glides of his unfolding raga.

Teasingly and sensuously, his notes lead and lure one another into a fluent pageantry of sequence. His chosen raga takes form, shape and *sringaar,* and begins to dance in front of your eyes. Unable to contain yourself, you begin to sway with the lilting notes gathering momentum in harmony with the quickening beats of the tabla. But then, the maestro soon invades your very breath! You suddenly realize that you are breathing *only* when he is sending his voice dancing into the ether! He takes a pause, and you hold your breath! His next note takes a swaying glide into an incredibly low *khadj,* and you experience a free fall through outer space! If you ever thought his music would help you meditate, you stand corrected. In fact, you are swept off your feet like a storm-tossed wind surfer who had wanted to straddle the crest of his voice. But do you regret the failure? Far from it! Enthralled beyond dreams, you actually relish losing your self, as you feel one with the dynamics of the universe.

Foremost among the legendary maestros of contemporary Indian music, Pandit Jasraj has travelled the world as a cultural ambassador of India. And in preparation, he has travelled the dust roads and the boulevards of musical experiences that make a musician reach out and touch the divine.

Blessed with rare sensitivity and emotional energy, Pandit-ji has refined his musical voice to the extreme, through lifelong *sadhana* and enduring enchantment towards his art. As his voice has travelled the octaves with mercurial fluency, he has himself enjoyed his musical journey and has taken audiences in its wake, through experiences beyond recall.

It is indeed a challenging task to confront his multifaceted personality from a single perspective. Human endeavour and spiritual fervour have combined beautifully to make his life's journey no less enthralling than any of his electrifying music recitals.

Pandit-ji's first memories are from historic Hyderabad, where his father Pandit Motiram, the stalwart of the famed *Mewati Gharana*, had migrated from their ancestral land of Rajasthan, to flourish under aristocratic patronage of music. But when Jasraj was barely three and a half, his father departed to the realms of a higher patronage, leaving his youngest son just the seven notes of music as legacy. The sudden demise of the breadwinner landed the family into an old dilapidated dwelling place, where the devoted riyaaz of music was among the very few sources of joy and pride.

Pandit-ji on stage, with disciples Tripti Mukherji and Pritam Bhattacharya, accompanied by Abhijeet Banerjee on the tabla

His elder brother Pandit Maniram managed to send him to school but Jasraj seemed to prefer the open outdoors to the walled classrooms, and even at that early age, it was music, which seemed to lure him away from pursuits of the prosaic kind. There used to be a typical tea-stall on the way to his school, which, quite typically, played a Begum Akhtar song over and over, on its gramophone, *"Deewana banana hai, to deewana bana de..."* A five-year old Jasraj, forgetting school and home, would hover around the stall for hours, mesmerized by that magic of music! Indeed, one had to be a *deewana* himself, to make the world fall madly in love with one's art...

Soon enough, Jasraj's path began to move further away from that oft-forgotten school, towards the compelling, full-time university of life. His immediate elder brother, Pandit Pratapnarayan taught him to play the tabla. A quick learner, Jasraj began to accompany his brothers in concerts, and on occasion, he would even be invited to play solo on the Indian percussion. Incidentally, an open insult to his

tabalchi status pushed him to take up vocal music with a rock solid emotional resolve. But that's a story Pandit-ji doesn't always relish telling, probably because of his own regard for today's tabla maestros.

Time then changed its beat, and Hyderabad got engulfed in communal conflicts. So much so, that one fateful day, their patron, Babu Nawab saheb, had to advise the Pandits to renounce the city for good.

With a heavy heart, loaded with bittersweet memories, the family had to uproot itself and move on...towards the walled city of Ahmedabad.

It was at the royal state of Saanand that a fourteen-year old Jasraj was accepted as state musician along with his elder brother and guru, Pandit Maniram. It was here that he encountered the first miraculous incident of his eventful life. At Ahmedabad, Pandit Maniram suddenly lost his singing voice. A traumatic experience for a dedicated musician whose life and livelihood depended solely on it. When every medical treatment proved futile, a friend referred them to Maharaja Jaywant Singh-ji Waghela of Saanand, who then invited the brothers, Maniram and Jasraj, to the sanctum of the temple of his deity, the Divine Mother. There, despite the inability, the Maharaja asked Pandit Maniram to try and sing for the goddess, while he himself sat in prayer to his Divine Mother. Accompanying his elder brother on tabla, young Jasraj witnessed the incredible! As Pandit Maniram tried to sing, his voice actually began to revive and ring true! And very soon, he regained the crystal clarity that he had lost! The significance of that incident sunk deep, as young Jasraj gratefully embraced the first ripples of spirituality in his musical consciousness.

Life at Saanand then began to enrich him in many wonderful ways. Maharaja Jaywant Singh was himself a gifted and scholarly musician and he began to lend a hand in tilling the soil of Jasraj's musical mind, preparing it for a lifelong harvest of sublime music.

Time and events too played their roles well, chiselling and shaping the young musician with the tests and turmoil of life...

The next dramatic twist came as Saanand lost its statehood with one historic stroke of the political pen. The family of the state musicians, Pandit Maniram and Pandit Jasraj, with tear-soaked blessings of their beloved patron, had to move on once again, far into the eastern wing of India. It was like following the strains of their own immortal musical composition for Mother Kalika...the resident deity of the bustling city of Calcutta.

Far removed from royal patronage, yet textured richly with the emotional energy of the common folk and music lovers, the city of Calcutta inspired Jasraj to live a life of passionate struggle during those crucial formative years as a vocalist.

Even in the face of big city distractions for the young blood, Jasraj managed to remain focused, and pursue his musical maturity with a hermit-like sincerity and dedication. Sometimes he starved for days, but did not let it affect his long hours of arduous practice of music, his breath of life, his real sustenance.

Soon after, even before she could hear the news of her son's first big singing break on national radio, Jasraj's mother passed away, leaving him immersed, yet again, in grief and dejection.

With the passage of time came marriage and fatherhood, as happy, synchronous events, bringing in that semblance of worldly order and family bliss to his fluid and demanding life-style.

His romantic conquest of wife Madhura, the talented daughter of legendary film doyen V Shantaram, complemented Jasraj's first love, his music, in a manner that inspired him to strive even harder and recognize the importance of achievements... Horizons expanded, and destiny, with its own hands, began to open up the avenues of fame and fortune.

While national and international accolades, honours, titles and trophies were being showered upon him, Pandit-ji was engrossed in ascending the heights of spirituality by exploring the depths of his music. Riding the waves of success and adulation, he, the true artist, never paused in his evolution as a creative explorer and innovator.

A privileged audience saw him bring down unseasonable rains while singing the monsoon Raga *Dhulia Malhar*...On another occasion, in the city of Varanasi, his fervent rendition of *Ragini Todi,* inspired a deer to come bounding inside the cordon of a bewildered human audience! But then, miracles have had a life-long tryst with Pandit Jasraj...

A deep inquiry into his own man-woman relationships and duality, leading up to that ideal sense of completeness in the male-female principles of nature, inspired him to present an exciting new dimension to the musical *jugalbandi,* which was spontaneously christened *Jasrangi* by an enthralled live audience in Pune. *Jasrangi* is essentially a magical interface between two singers, male and female, when they complement each other and their music, by singing two different ragas entwining into one another through the performance.

From the most insignificant ones, to the most compelling engagements, Pandit-ji honours his commitments despite a jet-set life-style. The annual music festival in Hyderabad, a tribute to his musical ancestry, is a function he presides over with unfailing, pilgrim-like devotion...just as the treasures of his own hard-earned realizations and sublime intuitions get showered generously upon his students and disciples from far and wide...

In this era of speed and impatience, his personality as a teacher and guru, reflects the ancient tradition of India. Secure in a delicate balance between strict discipline and affectionate care, his students have always received knowledge free, emanating like sunshine, from the *Sangeet Martand*...

Energized and propelled into the grand orbit of Indian music, the galaxy of Pandit-ji's students has begun to shine in its own light. A record number of his students command a good audience at live concerts, and adorn audio albums that continuously expand the domain of Indian music...

As a revered guru, and a high priest of Indian classical music, Pandit-ji's presence in person, name and spirit has enriched universities and institutions of music and culture in far-flung places like Prague, Vancouver, Toronto, Oklahoma, Harvard, Tampa, New Jersey, New York... Deeply felt insights, and inspired research into the philosophy of music and its universality, have run parallel to Pandit-ji's trailblazing path of a much-celebrated performing artiste.

From the blissful state of being immersed in music, Pandit Jasraj does surface, as often as he can, to partake of the simple joys of life, like watching the Indian team play cricket, and to celebrate that warm sense of belonging with his near and dear ones.

His family, his disciples, and the distant shores of his human interest, peopled with friends and fans, do vie with one another to bind him in an embrace, but soaring on the wings of his music, he escapes all efforts of definition and ownership, as if smiling mysteriously upon enchanted audiences.

From the inner circle of his family, to the expanding sphere of his chosen field of activity, Pandit-ji today lives a varied and rewarding life. His music not only caresses the soul, but is also known to heal the mind and body of listeners. Indeed, through his pilgrimage of music, he has been a true cultural and spiritual ambassador from the East to the distant lands of the Western world.

Textured richly with life's significant thoughts, issues and events, his utterances are well known as a music historian's treasure, and a journalist's delight. In the face of widespread pessimism, he remains an ardent propagator of the grand cultural resurgence, and a staunch believer in the impending golden era of Indian music and spirituality. And the fact, that even after such diverse and sustained personal achievements, he still continues to evolve as a supreme creative artiste, makes his prophesy for India ring true.

After creating a vibrant musical trance even among the most secular audiences with his *bhajan, 'Govindam Gokulanandam',* Pandit Jasraj can suddenly be lost in himself within the very epicenter of that spiritual storm. Insiders have come to know it as a moment from a higher realm. A moment when, like the fading echo of many of his standing ovations, the everyday world recedes into oblivion, leaving him alone with his music...and his Maker. When that audience of one, the Supreme One, inspires him to even further musical ascendance... whispering to his soul what to sing next.

Living Memories...

Young Jasraj as a talented tabla player

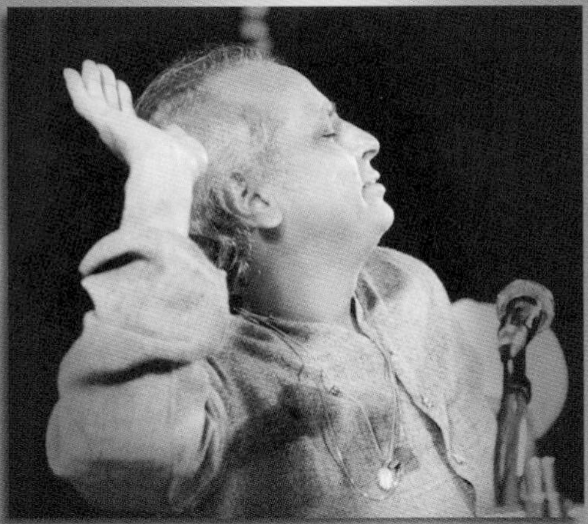

The maestro in full flow

In concert with his swaramandal

Maharaja of Saanand, Jaywant Singh Waghela

With wife Madhura

Elder brother & guru Pandit Maniram

With father-in-law, the movie legend V. Shantaram (flanked by his two wives), Madhura, nephew and disciple Rattan, daughter Durga and son Shaarang Dev.

With Prime Minister Atal Behari Vajpayee

Lost in music

Family ties. With nephew Rattan, daughter Durga, son Shaarang, wife Madhura, daughter-in-law Sarita, and grand daughter Avani

With Hariprasad Chaurasia and dance legend, guru Kelucharan Mahapatra.

In the circle of disciples

The long-haired sangeet saadhak

With daughter Durga, music director and tabla player Kedar Pandit (top right) and a galaxy of eminent disciples

Q. Pray tell us something about the Mewati Gharana. How important is your lineage to your personal exploration as an innovative musician?

A. *The significance of the gharana can never be forgotten. I'd like to mention here that in my younger days, Ustad Bade Ghulam Ali had once asked me to be his disciple, but despite all due respect to him, I had to decline, by telling him that I would like to carry forward my own gharana. And he appreciated that decision.*

The Mewati gharana began with Ustad Ghagge Nazir Khan, from whom my grandfather Pandit Natthulal-ji and Pandit Chimanlal-ji learnt the music...to then pass it on to their nephew Pandit Motiram-ji, my father. Pandit Motiram-ji taught this music to his brother Pandit Jyotiram-ji and his sons Pandit Maniram-ji and Pandit Pratapnarayan-ji. Thus, my singing guru has been Pandit Maniram and my guru of tabla, Pandit Pratapnarayan. Every gharana has its own special character...some go along the swar, others go along the laya. Some emphasize the vilambit, and others, the Madhya-laya. Every artiste will agree that swar is the mother, and laya, the father. We too go by this realization. The salient feature in our gharana today is the elaborate knowledge of all the four quarters of a composition. Namely, Sthayee...Antara...Abhog... Sanchari. These four aspects extend the raga to its fullest potential.

Q. How did you arrive at this concept of 'Jasrangi Jugalbandi'?

A. *Often when one listens to male-female jugalbandi, one wonders as to why the recital appears somewhat incomplete? Whereas in the case of Wind-Water...Earth-Sky... Radha-Krishna...Shiv-Shakti, two aspects unite to become one, and together achieve completeness. Then why can't this jugalbandi achieve that kind of completeness? The answer came from within. Our ancient sages, who founded the norms of our Indian music, gave prime importance to the principles of harmonics, upon which is based this jugalbandi, dual interface. So, I thought, if the man performs at his own pitch and accompaniment, and the woman, at her own higher pitch and accompaniment, each element is separate, yet they unite into a wholesome jugalbandi. Two different ragas interact, and achieve completeness! It was an audience in Pune, who heard this for the first time and gave it the name 'Jasrangi Jugalbandi.'*

Q. How do you see the future of Indian classical music?

A. *(Excitedly) Extremely bright. In fact, I consider the present time as the Golden Age... moving towards the Platinum Age. And mark my words, India will soon occupy the top place in the world in many ways...*

Q. How do you see the difference between vocal and instrumental music?

A. *Indeed, there are many great instrumentalists today. But our shastras used to indicate the difference by saying, "Uttam Gana, aur Madhyam Bajana". Interestingly, (smiles) even the best of instrumentalist gurus, while teaching, prefer to use their vocal chords...and many of them nurture a secret desire to sing...*

Q. The West was exposed to Indian classical vocal music much later than instrumental music. What's the status there today?

A. *I myself have four to five teaching institutes in America where Indian vocal classical music is taught. And each has about sixty to ninety dedicated students. And as far as the listeners go, their number is steadily rising, because the spiritual element in Indian classical music manifests very well in vocal music.*

Q. For quite some time, you've been voicing some constructive suggestions to motivate the government policy makers in our country to encourage classical music...?

A. *Although I am personally happy with the respect and recognition I always receive from the government, I feel that the powers that be can do a lot to promote the most precious legacies of our culture. Why can't they, for instance, start at least one separate TV channel for classical music?*

Q. Any special advice for the aspiring musicians?

A. *First of all, fill your hearts with respect and gratitude for your parents. Remember, they have nurtured your human form so that you can strive to reach for the divine. And then comes your guru. Do everything you can to learn from him, but most importantly, earn his heartfelt blessings. This can multiply your talent and learning ten times over!*

Q. Any special incident you'd like to share with us?

A. *(Reflects) There was a strange dream, which used to blow my mind every time I saw it. It was the 'darbaar' of Lord Krishna, where, on his left sat kings and emperors, and on his right, were poets and musicians. I was in the middle, and Lord Krishna was telling me, "Jasraj, prayers and rituals are meant for the others. Whereas, what you sing reaches me directly! Sing on..."*

KISHAN MAHARAJ

An invited audience had gathered at a prominent industrialist's palace in Bombay to enjoy an evening of classical music. The elite gathering was getting a little restive in its cushioned chairs and velvety sofas. The rustle of silks and chiffons was creating a buzz, as if in polite enquiry as to why the announced artistes had still not taken their positions upon the majestic Persian carpet spread on the marbled floor in front! Their simmering wonderment changed to stunned silence, when the host walked in hurriedly to announce with folded hands, that all the sofas and chairs would have to be removed and the audience would have to sit on the floor at the same level as the performing musicians. The tabla player Kishan Maharaj had refused to sit at a level lower than his audience. It would be an insult to Indian classical music, he had said, if Ustad Ali Akbar Khan with his sarod, and he, Kishan Maharaj, with his tabla, had to sit at a level where the audience would rest its feet! It took but a few moments for the enlightened audience to agree with the apologetic host, that the elevated seating be banished, and everyone take his appropriate place on the floor as privileged recipients of some divine musical bliss that was to flow from the two gifted performers.

The incident just recalled may have taken place about half a century ago, in 1953, and may have even been tinted with some narrative license, but the light it throws on the persona of Pandit Kishan Maharaj is incisive as a laser beam. It brings into gleaming focus his supreme confidence as a performer, his high self-esteem, his deep reverence for his music, his superior personal equation with the artistes he accompanied, and above all, his courage of conviction. The conviction which, backed by relentless efforts, has been a major driving force in elevating the status of the classical tabla player and his art, to the level where it belongs.

As if to accomplish this historic task with the greatest of legitimacy and moral right, Krishna Prasad was born in Benaras in 1923 in an illustrious family of tabla players, strung into an unbroken tradition of almost two centuries. As soon as he was born, two potent mantras of *swara* and *laya* were whispered deep into his two ears by his grandfather, prompted by family custom. Since mothers do not take the birth names of their sons in their family, Krishna Prasad's mother began to hail him as 'Kishan', and with time, this endearing name endured, and took on the 'Maharaj' suffix in due course.

Although born exactly after midnight on Krishna *Janmashtami,* and named Krishna Prasad, young Kishan chose Goddess Sharda and Lord Ganesh in quest for his personal *ishtadev.* With due respect and recognition to the entire pantheon of deities present in the family temple, including *kul devi* Durga, Kishan must have realized soon enough that his life's mission of service to the performing arts required the continued blessings of Saraswati and Ganesh.

The *gharana* into which Kishan Maharaj was born was well known as *Benaras Baaj,* and had already emerged as the premier tabla playing tradition of north Indian music. His father, Shri Hari Maharaj, a brilliant tabla player, was so obsessed with attaining the ultimate success, or *siddhi* in tabla that one of his extreme esoteric efforts left him mentally imbalanced. Uncle Kanthe Maharaj, perhaps the greatest tabla genius and guru of his time, was without a son, and he took little Kishan under his wings, both as adopted son and formal disciple. When Kishan became six years old, his *dadaji* brought the ritualistic flowers and sweets and a *dakshina* of rupees five, and asked his son Kanthe Maharaj to formally accept Kishan as his disciple. Little Kishan was more than ready for the solemn occasion. As the great Kanthe Maharaj tied a bonding string around Kishan's tiny wrist, and instead of the customary *'Dha, Dha Te The',* recited a *paran,* a complete verse, little Kishan reproduced it admirably on the tabla! His grand, historic journey through *laya* and *tala* was set in motion with the blessings of his guru, and Lord Ganesh.

Along with the techniques and the mathematics of the tabla, Kanthe Maharaj began to teach his 'son' the ideal temperament and approach to other music related arts as well. He initiated Kishan into learning Hindi from the *pujari* Brahmin who manned their family temple. There too, instead of the first alphabets, Kishan began with a poetic invocation to Lord Ganesh, as he began to read up the *Ram Charit Manas* three times over! The study of Hindi whetted his appetite and Kishan began to learn English from Ashu Babu, one of his guru's learned tabla disciples. His sense of challenge and application took things further, as he got into the habit of deciphering all the English signboards he encountered along the road to the *Sankatmochan* temple, which he visited frequently on his bicycle. Life has always been a fluent stream of wonderment for his rich and observant mind.

Guru Kanthe Maharaj kept close company, and pampered Kishan in good measure throughout his growing years. From a rather weak and sickly child, Kishan was gradually transformed into a robust and handsome youth...but only after his uncle broke Brahminic norms of the family and encouraged Kishan to eat meat and practise wrestling, as prescribed by an Ayurvedic expert. Then, only when Kishan was all of fifteen years of age, was he asked to begin nightlong rigorous *riyaaz* of the tabla.

Riyaaz under Kanthe Maharaj was very scientific. It had a well-planned structure devised to help Kishan soak in all the varied facets of tabla playing which distinguished the Benaras gharana from its lesser rivals. Unlike most other *gharanas,* where the tabla maestros excelled in just one or two major roles, the Benaras Baaj ensured an all-round aptitude and a versatile temperament. Soon, Kishan became a true representative of this lineage through a year-long training each, of all intricate *talas* or beats, accompaniment with classical dance forms, accompaniment with instrumental music like that of the sitar and the sarod, accompaniment with vocal music, and finally the most demanding art of solo performance, accompanying no one but the unbridled dictates of one's inner rhythm.

The blessings of Devi Saraswati and Lord Ganesh often come in a generous sweep. Although the tabla was always the voice of his soul, Kishan's irrepressible artistic spirit courted other art forms in youthful exuberance. As his father Hari Maharaj passed away when he was sixteen, Kishan rediscovered his father's modest collection of literary classics and through voracious reading he developed a desire to write, and soon he began to fill pages with impassioned poetry. Similarly, watching folk artists at work during festive adornments, his dormant desire to become a painter found instant expression on floors and walls. Observing idol makers at work at a friend's showroom, young Kishan discovered a sculptor waiting in him to be chiselled out; he sculpted idols of Ganesh to set him free.

When Kishan became a handsome young man of twenty, his guru granted him the latitude to go and play his tabla wherever he pleased. With this freedom, however, came an inner awakening of a far greater freedom for his beloved instrument. His mission of taking the tabla to its well-deserved status of respect began to pick up an inspiring rhythm. He challenged the prevailing practice

followed by all the top-notch tabla maestros in Benaras, and told his guru, that he did not wish to play the tabla for the courtesans. He found it demeaning to the worshipful regard he had for his art. And since it was difficult to make a career in tabla playing in Benaras those days, without collaborating with the courtesans, Kishan sought his guru's permission and blessing to go to Bombay and try to establish himself.

The 'city of opportunities', however, did not present him anything on a platter. Careful not to tarnish his family reputation, Kishan took on his other name, KP Malik, and began his professional struggle from a dark, stuffy room, which just about served him as an address. Unable to bear the cockroach infested musty room, he took his pillow onto the pavements to sleep, after the tramcars went off the roads at midnight. His diet too was limited to the bare minimum on most occasions, comprising thick *rotis,* salt and onion. Once in a while, when some money was earned, he and his friends would enjoy some meat and rice. Memories of a pampered lifestyle in Benaras made things a little more poignant, but at the same time strengthened his resolve to soldier on.

Kishan's first break came in the form of a challenging assignment for a Hindi film. No one was able to play a difficult piece of composition for dancer Sitara Devi, and the director sought out Shri KP Malik from his obscure address and took him to the studios. The 'challenging' piece proved to be just up his street. Very few tabla players could rival Kishan Maharaj when it came to accompanying dance. The money earned from this effort was enough to buy a decent cot and pesticides to drive off the pests, and Kishan Maharaj, alias KP Malik, could finally sleep in his own castle at night!

More assignments began to flow in as newcomer Malik's name was being recognized in the film and music circles of Bombay. And soon the inevitable happened, as destiny unfolded its hardbound script. Sitar maestro Ravi Shankar's conquest of Bombay had just begun, but his search for a suitable tabla player of his class was being met with frustration. Someone introduced him to one KP Malik at a private concert, and within minutes of their playing together, Ravi Shankar—himself a master of *taala* and *laya*—stopped playing and began to stare quizzically at his accompanist. Suddenly he embraced Malik confidently and said, "You must be Kishan, the able disciple of Kanthe Maharaj, whom I have already heard a lot about!" It was a dramatic moment in a historic evening, when two momentous things happened. Kishan Maharaj and his tabla had stepped under the spotlight of recognition, the light that would gradually become the halo of fame around him as his long and illustrious career would unfold. And Pandit Ravi Shankar had found his match. He was particularly impressed with the observation that Kishan Maharaj did not merely

follow his sitar, but he approached his role in a spirit of complement, adding a semblance of conversation and surprise to conventional norms of percussive accompaniment. This suited Ravi Shankar fine, as he was already pioneering a trend in Hindustani classical concerts, whereby, the accompanist was given enough opportunities by the main artist to assert his identity and raise the status of his craft. In fact, the familiar echo of repeated audience applause extracted by tabla maestros of recent times had its seeds sown in that historic evening, when two charismatic musicians from Benaras matched their talents and merged their spirits at a venue in distant Bombay!

The newfound chemistry between Ravi Shankar's sitar and Kishan Maharaj's tabla took the music world by storm and the prolonged applause went on to take a decade in its stride. Ironically, as his struggle in Bombay was easing out, Kishan was called back to Benaras by an anxious Kanthe Maharaj, who had heard rumblings from 'well wishers' that young Kishan was getting too engrossed in the film world and was revelling in the constant company of film heroines. Marriage seemed the ideal antidote, and the ever-obedient Kishan gave his consenting nod to the alliance engineered by the elders of the family. However, when he realized that his newly wed wife was just an adolescent, a twenty-four-year old Kishan decided to stay away from home for a while. He went and took refuge at the famous Sankatmochan shrine of Lord Hanuman, and spent endless hours in austerity and *riyaaz.* When the legendary *ustad,* Baba Allauddin Khan arrived in Benaras for a concert, he was accompanied on the tabla by a quaint young *sadhu* adorned with long hair, a flowing beard, a huge sign of the trident on his crimson stained forehead, and *rudraksh* beads around his young neck and arms! At the end of their performance, Baba Allauddin was as impressed with Kishan's appearance as with his artistry with the tabla. He embraced the young man and blessed him profusely.

After a long enough stay at the temple complex, Kishan settled down in his ancestral home as a family man. His marathon productive period seemed to have begun in right earnest. Invitations to concerts and music festivals kept pouring in from all corners of the country. He played as a preferred accompanist to the biggest names in the world of music and dance. His feel for aesthetics and sculpture, his inherent sense of *laya,* his dexterity with intricate and innovative *talas,* showed the world how classical dance and its percussive counterpart can inspire and energize each other. He gave electrifying performances with the all-time greats of classical dance: Achchhan Maharaj, Shambhu Maharaj, Birju Maharaj, Mohanlal, Gopi Krishna, Sanjukta Panigrahi, Roshan Kumari and Sitara Devi...

In the field of classical music, his range of accompaniment was like a horizon-spanning rainbow! He has had the honour of accompanying almost all the music greats of India who have been active during his lifetime. He played with most of the living legends from the earlier generation, and received their hearty appreciation and blessings. He has played with his contemporary greats on an equal footing, and with a rare sense of understanding and mutual enhancement. And the momentum and enthusiasm have been unabated when he has played graciously and affectionately with the rising stars of the succeeding generations as well. Even today, at eighty, one can expect him to suddenly switch his posture to 'Vajrasan' and like the *vajra,* or lightening, explode into an utterly electrifying performance!

Although Kishan Maharaj has participated in highly successful concert tours abroad, his identification of pride and priority have always been with his motherland. While Prime Minister Nehru had once sent a special chartered plane to transport Kishan Maharaj from Afghanistan to Russia to catch up with the rest of an Indian cultural delegation, on another occasion, just being homesick was reason enough for him to turn away from an American tour. But then, whenever he has represented Indian music and culture on foreign soil, he has done it with a sense of pride and patriotism. It was Pandit Kishan Maharaj who had insisted that the Indian tricolour must flutter along with the host country's flag on the concert stage.

His continued zest for life and art has helped him ripen into a delightful source of knowledge and experience. He can speak to any gathering of men with great charm and authority. Even some of his occasional excesses in speech and candour are endearing, and quite in character with someone so obviously brimming over with blessings from all quarters.

Kishan Maharaj's sense of belonging must have had its roots in his illustrious family lineage, but it grew and blossomed in his passionate personal chemistry with the unique city of Benaras. He has breathed the very essence of this enchanting land all his life, and it has energized his large-hearted spirit with its famous *masti* or *joie de vivre!*

He has flown kites in its winds...he has ridden horseback along its dust roads...he has swam and bathed in its guardian river...practised penance at its burning *ghats*...he has rubbed the brown earth of its wrestling rings on his body...he has worn the *sindoor* of its lofty temples on his high forehead...yes, the city of Benaras has blessed him with all its elements, and has almost personified itself through the life and times of Kishan Maharaj! He, in turn, has been at the forefront of the revival of its many fading traditions and customs, keeping alive and celebrating its unique and vibrant character. He has been one of the premier citizens of this eternal city and has brought it immense honour and glory.

Indeed, a music lover's pilgrimage to Benaras is incomplete without a visit to the abode of the *Laya Samrat,* where Pandit Kishan 'Maharaj' holds court under the shadow of an imposing idol of Ganapati, which he has sculpted with his own worshipful hands. And it is no surprise that Lord Ganesh looks happy playing the *mridang*, celebrating the cosmic ecstasy of *laya* and *taala.*

Living Memories...

In solitary 'sadhana'

With the great vocalist Amir Khan

With Ravi Shankar and Ali Akbar Khan

With the gifted vocalist Parween Sultana

Accompanying Ravi Shankar

Exchanging thoughts with Zakir Hussain

Receiving the Enayat Khan Award from the sitar maestro Vilayat Khan and Viren Shah, the Governor of West Bengal

Man and wife

Instructing the talented tabla player, Kumar Bose

Two tabla greats. With Ustad Allarakha

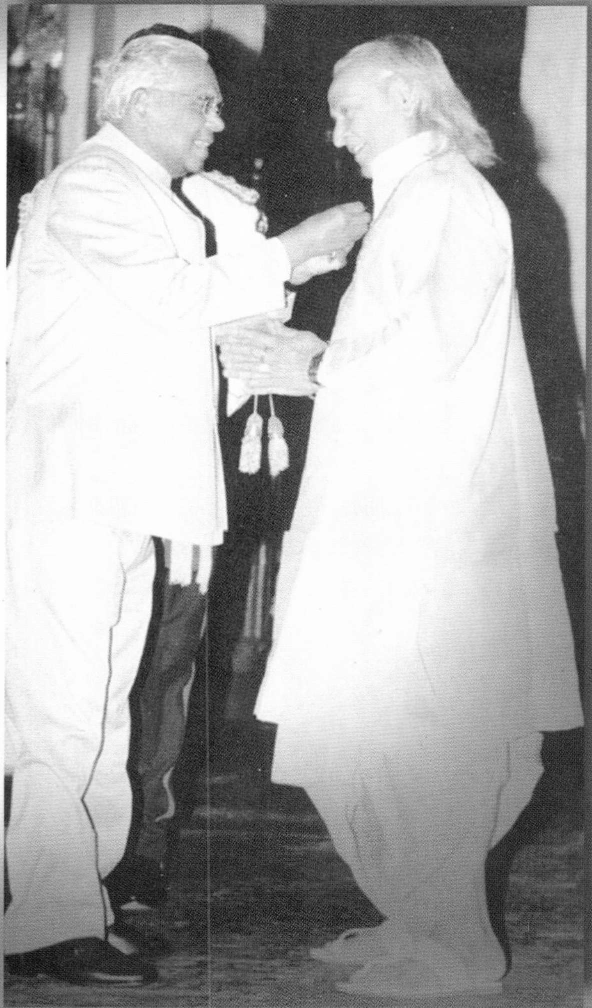

With Indian president K R Narayanan

Q. When you had announced that you will not play the tabla for the courtesans, what was your guru-ji's reaction?

A. *Since he had himself accompanied courtesans, like the other top tabla players of his time, he might have felt a little slighted at my decision, I don't know for sure. But he supported my stance. Although by the time I had turned my stance into a resolve, I had already played for Siddheshwari Devi.*

Q. How did that happen?

A. *She was to perform at the Kashi Naresh's mehfil, and my guru was to accompany her. But somehow, Kanthe Maharaj-ji was called away at the king of Durbhanga's concert. So he asked me to substitute for him at Siddheshwari Devi's performance. I could not refuse.*

Q. Were you able to play well?

A. *Oh yes! The king Hari Singh-ji was so pleased that he asked me what inaam I would like. In my youthful exuberance I asked for a motorbike, and he gave it to me.*

Q. Your father Hari Maharaj-ji had lost his mental balance in pursuit of some Durga Siddhi. Did you ever think of trying anything tantrik?

A. *While in Bombay, someone told me that there was a secret mantra for tabla siddhi, which had to be practised and realized at the smashan, the cremation ground. So I used to go to the Shivaji Park and Borivali smashans and chant some malas of that mantra. One night, two shadowy figures confronted me and they told each other that I should not be allowed there henceforth. I wasn't unduly worried, because I was to finish my mission that night itself! Soon, the two figures went near the pyres and vanished!*

Q. Didn't you feel scared?

A. *Not much. I did such things at the Benaras smashans as well!*

Q. Would you name some of the legendary musicians you accompanied as a young man?

A. *I played a memorable concert with Ustad Faiyaz Khan in Taal Dhamar.*

Pandit Omkarnath Thakur used to make sure I was available to play for his concerts at Benaras. Among the legendary instrumentalists I had the good fortune of playing with Ustad Haafiz Ali Khan, and Ustad Allauddin Khan...

Q. Have you found any difference between the audiences of today and those of fifty years ago?

A. *Earlier audiences used to be intensely attentive. Today, in the era of loud speakers, some people conduct private conversations during a recital (smiles).*

Q. What about this practice of clapping in the middle? While it is supposed to encourage, it also seems to distract some artistes.

A. *I welcome it as a spontaneous, natural and positive response. Those who don't get enough, they complain (laughs).*

Q. How do you react to Carnatic music?

A. *What we do not know well enough, we should not comment on...*

Q. Don't you enjoy listening to it?

A. *Of course, I do! And I have played with many great Carnatic vidwans! In fact, I have done something that no other tabla player may have done! I have played a two-and-a half hour duet with Shri Palghat Mani Iyer in Calcutta! I have played many times with Shri Palghat Raghu, and Shri Sivaraman. I have even played with their senior vidwan Ramnadeshwar! This much I am qualified to say, that the way most north Indians think that Carnatic music is alien and difficult, it surely is not so! Both these systems of Indian classical music are very similar in essence.*

Q. You are a pioneer in demonstrating how to accompany dance correctly and confidently. Is it very difficult, really, to play the tabla with classical dance forms?

A. *I have found a parallel between the process of folk painting and that of accompanying classical dance on the tabla, directly without rehearsal! When the dancer introduces a tukda, or a piece, you create a framework in your mind, just like the painter sketches an outline of his design. Then, as the dancer begins to dance that tukda, you follow the painting procedure of filling the colours and the shades within that outline. Then, when the last tehai is danced, treat it as the dark outline the painter puts around his forms for emphasis and the final delineation. Once you remember these three steps, it is no problem playing with the best of dancers. You need to be smart and sensitive.*

Q. If you were to choose from among vocal music, instrumental music, and dance...which one would you prefer to accompany?

A. *I would choose the artist, not the art. There are wonderful artistes here, in each art form, who can make accompanying them a source of joy and pride.*

Q. Do you believe in reincarnation?

A. *Oh yes!*

Q. What were you before this birth? Would you make a guess?

A. *Definitely, a musician. But this field of music is so vast, that you might spend one lifetime in just observing and listening. Then you will be born with a deep yearning for music, and spend that lifetime in learning. Then be born yet again and practice profusely, fill the world with your music and make a name...*

Q. Would you like to take a rebirth?

A. *(Smiles) I have already covered all these three births in pursuit of music. I am sure I won't be born again! Besides, our shastras say that those who receive 'sawa lakh' blessings, attain moksh! I must have received that many blessings from millions...*

KISHORI
AMONKAR

The great sages from antiquity conjure a certain image for us. Tall, wiry figures with glowing eyes and flowing beard suggest themselves as the likes and likenesses of Vashistha, Viswamitra, Agasthya...But the images of the *sadhvis* and the *vidushis* like Gargi and Maitreyee are somewhat difficult today for us to visualize. A mental picture of present-day Kishori Amonkar might be of some assistance in this endeavour. She is the female embodiment of brilliant, inborn talent taken to dramatic fruition through an intensely introspective quest for musical wisdom. She is perhaps the closest example of the quintessential *sadhvi* as described in India's ancient cultural treatise. Lit early in life by the able hands of her guru, she is today the self-fuelled flame, burning with passion and purity to illuminate unexplored paths of Indian classical music.

Much before Kishori's own sense of purpose and destiny crystallized in her meditative and adventurous mind, providence had lovingly placed her in the ideal environment. She was in intimate touch with her guru even before she was born...because her guru was none other than her own mother

Memories of younger days: Learning from her mother Mogubai Kurdikar

Gaan-Tapaswini Mogubai Kurdikar, one of the most revered vocalists from the Jaipur *gharana*.

Mogubai was taking lessons from her preceptor *Gaan Samraat* Alladiya Khan saheb while Kishori was in her womb, and thus, perhaps, the most subtle and unusual bond was forged between the mature music of the Jaipur *gharana* and its unborn protege. And when the very first notes from Kishori's voice resonated in the world they were greeted by the affectionate gaze of her guru. The future relationships of mother-daughter and *guru-sishyaa* swirled into a joyous embrace of boundless promise.

As she was sheltered in a temple-like abode of music, Kishori saw the world around her from an intellectual distance. Having lost her husband early in life, the spirited Mogubai was left alone to bring up three young children in a taxing yet dignified struggle against poverty. All banal distractions were banished from the Kurdikar home, which was forever fragrant with musical and spiritual pursuits. Apart from their schoolbooks, the only other books the youngsters could lay hands upon were spiritual books, and each one was taught to respect the arts, the *shastras* and a disciplined way of living.

Driven by her inborn talent and intelligence and her rare capacity to observe and assimilate, Kishori was quite playfully able to reproduce the melodious intricacies that emanated from the music room of her mother. As she was flowering into a fine young woman, she discovered that apart from being a brilliant student in school, she was remarkably proficient in sporty activities like field games and table tennis, and artistic expressions like intricate knitting, embroidery or exquisite *rangoli*...and as it became increasingly apparent that it was impossible to live in that musical haven without being immersed in music, she began to learn formally from her illustrious mother. If one last bastion remained to be bypassed, providence took care of that as well. There was this desire to become a doctor, and Kishori had duly chosen the appropriate science subjects to pursue the medical course. But a sudden bout of sore eyes prevented her from appearing for some examinations, which led to an academic default, thus aborting her attempts at joining the medical college. The world may have lost a potential physical healer, but soon it was to find instead, a magical musician with the power to heal the soul.

Mogubai had already inculcated the right values and *samskaras* in her children; she began teaching her promising daughter by first placing music in the right perspective. Music was not to be mistaken as a means to just earn money or make a career, not even to merely

please oneself or impress large audiences to earn popularity or fame. 'Music is *tapasya*. It should take you towards inner fulfillment, towards completion.' This did not seem like sermonizing to her teenage daughter, because Kishori, through her own introspective and meditative quest, had herself arrived at a similar mindset. She was ripe and ready to channellize all her multifaceted talents and qualities into one, all encompassing mission: classical music.

Mogubai had imbibed all the greatness and characteristic qualities of the Jaipur *gharana,* including the correctness and purity of structure and grammar, and also the ideal balance between the ever-rivaling *swara* and *laya*. While teaching her disciples, she added the fruits of her own quest as well. In Kishori, she instilled one more factor: austerity.

Introducing Kishori to *swaras* and *alankaras* before delving into the actual raga, Mogubai taught her to recognize the notes and their movements, for 'that is the real language of music.' And the raga, when taken up, was not introduced by its name, but by its character and movement. Having acknowledged her daughter's razor sharp mind and remarkable power of concentration, the doting mother let the strict mentor take total charge of her progress. Even a difficult new raga was taught only a couple of times; it was up to the disciple to grasp it with exemplary concentration and end up owning it completely with dedicated *riyaaz*. There was a tacit duel raging between escalating expectation and responsive fulfillment.

Kishori, however, wasn't satisfied being just the bright student. She was born to explore other horizons. While as a young attractive girl she had enough wisdom to refuse offers to act in films, the appeal of good lyrics and enchanting music in films could not leave her aloof. The sheer emotional appeal in film music and light classical music of that era inspired her to explore those spheres. With her mother's permission, she lent her voice for a major film, *Geet Gaya Pattharon Ne*. It made waves in the film music world and also created ripples of jealousy and insecurity among established playback singers. Thousands of her records reportedly vanished overnight from the stores! Embittered by this very first experience, Kishori never did an encore to playback singing.

Plunging deeper into her real world of classical music, Kishori allowed shades of heartfelt emotions to embellish and energize her style of singing. With time, it extended to the soul of her music and began to underline her performances and characterize her emergent identity in the widening music world. She had imbibed all the rules well enough to dare to break them. She had confronted convention squarely to bedazzle it by the brilliance of her own hard earned conviction. Kishori was trained in the highest tradition of *classicism* in music, yet she explored the appeal of *romanticism* with an open mind, to return ultimately to add colour and vibrancy to that classicist approach.

Destined to be repeatedly controversial, Kishori faced warm accolades in overwhelming measure. But she had to bring into play all her natural courage of conviction to deal with the frosty fumes of disapproval from many quarters. It still inspires debate in music circles as to whether it was a genuine sense of outrage at heresy, or an expression of envious resentment, which prompted most of the senior stalwarts and even music critics to deny Kishori the natural encouragement due to a flowering new talent who was making fast inroads into the hearts of audiences...

Absorbing all hurt and pain, Kishori did what she did by the dictates of her inner self. She was gifted with a naturally sweet voice, a sharp analytical mind, and an honest meditative soul. The real Kishori, if one got to know her, is like a dynamic confluence of wind, fire and fragrance. She took pains to enrich herself from every natural source around her. On occasion, she took brief training under various gurus from even other *gharanas*. Anwar Hussein Khan saheb of Agra *gharana* taught her a single *cheez* in *Bahadur Todi* for nearly three months...Anjanibai Malpekar helped perfect Kishori's delightful *meend* (glide)...Pandit Husnalal gave Kishori instructions in lighter music like ghazals...But her best teacher was always her own introspective mind. Once, in the middle of her musical journey, she had suddenly lost her voice! A heavy curtain of gloom and anxiety threatened to descend upon life around her. Oscillating between hope and desperation, mother Mogubai tried everything within human reach to get her daughter to sing again. But months stretched to years...with no real hope in sight. Until finally, complementing her own private faith and confidence with some potent spiritual and medical help from Sardeshmukh Maharaj of Pune, Kishori was able to defeat that mysterious affliction. She must have read destiny's cryptic message in that rare experience, because she converted it into a rare opportunity. That entire period of vocal silence was not wasted in idle acrimony or self-pity, but in harvesting some deep spiritual insight by meditating deeply on music...and singing within her soul.

Passing through different eventful stages of her long musical pursuit, Kishori has often emerged triumphant in the deepest sense of artistic fulfillment. Guided by her fierce sense of commitment to her profound realizations, she has scarcely done anything just for the sake of effect or novelty. Nor has she allowed the rumblings of opposition to distract her from her chosen path. She has never accepted anything at mere face value or out of passive convention. Deviating from the established, even revered dictates of the Jaipur *gharana,* she explored and reveled in *alapchari*. If the picture of a raga, as she saw it, demanded additions, deletions or alterations in structure, she went ahead and rendered it her way, swaying audiences and stirring up critics in the process. If the mood of a raga was in conflict with the meaning of the accompanying *cheez,* the poetess in her picked up the pen and composed a new bandish. In total integrity with the way a raga has unveiled itself to her mind and soul, she has presented it to her audiences without dilution or compromise. The effort has always been to gradually eliminate herself from the production of the raga, so that what remained was just the soul. If a raga delving in *Karun Rasa* appeared incompatible with fast and robust *taans,* she has shown the courage of presenting it only through the *alaapi*. Similarly, if a piece in furious *Veer Rasa* did not have to follow the meandering approach, she has broken convention to omit the *vilambit* part. She may have often shocked the myopic critics, but those with a broader vision have eventually come to appreciate her role in the right scale and perspective. This, after all, is how genres and *gharanas* draw their sap of rejuvenation. This is, perhaps, how music celebrates its essential vitality and dynamism.

On that antiquated meditative image of a *sadhvi* or *vidushi* like Gargi or Maitreyee,

Kishori has unconsciously wrapped the devotional and emotional garb of a modern-day Meera. Life and family have showered their bittersweet experiences on the loving, giving and dutiful Kishori through the umbrella of an exemplary mother, the companionship of a sensitive and supportive husband, and the joy of worthy, loving children, extending the cycle of a blissful wholesome life. All this, however, may be considered a steady drizzle compared to the stormy winds that spiral around Kishori the music maker. Like Meera, all aflame and entranced by her vision of Giridhari Gopal, Kishori's tryst with her life's music too has been all pervasive, all consuming. All her life's crescendos so far, almost all the conflicts and concerns, criticisms and controversies, aches and ecstasies have been centered around her *musical persona,* lending colour and character to her quest for the ultimate.

In that entranced pilgrimage to the *sangam* of god and music, she has chosen her own gait and path, her own *swara* and *laya*. While detractors have been left gasping along the wayside, her audiences have happily followed her spirited, enchanting voice into the promised realm of divine music.

Living Memories...

The glow of talent

Father, Shri Madhav Bhatia

Mother, the venerated Mogubai Kurdikar

Newlyweds

Three great vocalists.With Giraja Devi & Parween Sultana

Emotional relationship with the audience

Flanked by children and grandchildren

Honouring the harmonium wizard Appa Jalgaonkar

Being honoured by president Gyani Zail Singh

With two other masters of their art. Zakir Hussain and kathak legend Birju Maharaj

League of extraordinary women. With four great vocalists, Manik Varma, Prabha Atre, Saraswati Rane, Gangubai Hangal. Flanked by two great dancers, Sitara Devi and Kanak Rele

With Prime Minister Atal Behari Vajpayee

Mutual respect. With Balamuralikrishna

In musical nirvana

Q. Early in life, when your mother began to formally teach you, there must have been many other disciples learning from her. Do you remember feeling any pressure of rivalry or a desire for special treatment?

A. *Not at all. Since I was by far the youngest, all the other students treated me with great love and affection. Many of those relationships have continued into adult life and beyond. Today, when my mother is no more, I miss all those wonderful fellow students. Yes, I miss them very much.*

Q. Your mother never taught you separately, away from the rest?

A. *Not in a routine manner. But yes, since we were living together, there were random instances of one to one interaction. She was rather strict with me because, perhaps, she expected a lot from me. Without praising me or pampering me, she always put me gently, yet firmly, on the right path to the highest form of music. I am eternally grateful to my mother for whatever I have achieved in life so far.*

Q. How about your husband? Did he admire your music?

A. *He was a great admirer of my mother's music. (Smiles) He wanted me to be as great a singer as Mogubai Kurdikar. Ravi himself was a great soul in many ways. Extremely supportive of my musical dreams, he instinctively and sensitively offered a lot of constructive criticism during my long hours of riyaaz. As far as people around me go, I must say I have been very fortunate all my life.*

Q. Beside your mother, who were the other great artistes you heard in your formative years?

A. *Hirabai Badodekar...Saraswati Rane...Bade Ghulam Ali Khan...Kesarbai Kerkar...*

Q. Gangubai Hangal?

A. *Of course! I call her 'Aai'. All these artistes had the great desire to seek and pursue at any cost the real musical bliss! (Sigh!) They were much closer to the real art; we in comparison seem to have drifted away, giving priority to making money, cutting records and planning foreign tours...*

Q. You look so meditative, lost in yourself even when you are performing on stage. In that scenario, does the audience mean anything to you? Are you even aware of their presence?

A. *My god! The audience is the soul of the mehfil! A performer strives to touch that collective soul...*

Q. But suppose, hypothetically, you did not ever sing in public. You could have still learnt music and got immersed in it...

A. *Hundred per cent! Because, I actually studied music as a subject. I did not study music to perform. Performance is a negligible part of the great ocean of music. My mother taught me the difference between rendering a raga and singing a raga.*

Q. What's that difference?

A. *Rendering is presenting it to an audience. While, singing involves doing sadhana of that raga, knowing the raga as intimately as possible...*

Q. ...That's when you are complete in yourself? You do not need anyone else around...

A. *I only need to be in the bosom of the raga, that's all. That's where I experience that music is the language of the notes. Not words, nor beats. It is the ultimate in sound. On the other hand, when I am singing for my audience, I try to sing in such a way that they are able to forget themselves, their pain, their problems. They love me because I always try to take them along with me and gift them that feeling of exaltation.*

Q. Does it always happen the way you want?

A. *Not always. But often enough, to keep me going. Suppose four thousand people are sitting in front of you. How many souls can you communicate with? How many atmaas can you please? It used to worry me...until I found the solution. Sing for God.*

If the Parmatma is happy, ordinary souls will also feel that happiness! That's why I usually sing with my eyes closed. I am even referred to as the 'blind artiste'! (Laughs)

Q. There's a lot of pain and pathos in much of your singing. Does it spring from real life?

A. *Pain is a very real part of life. Samsar mein sukh kise milta hai? That's why in singing, the ultimate rasa is Karun rasa. It contains pain, pathos and many other shades. When its notes are extended sensitively, the real colours of the mind come to the fore. And when universalized with inspired singing, it can lead to 'ananda',*

On stage with her disciples, accompanied by young Balkrishna Iyer on the tabla

the sublime joy...and the state of bliss...

Q. How true! Joy, in fact, can bring tears to the eyes more readily than sorrow! I remember, years ago I had heard your Bhoop...

A. *Bhoop presents a wonderful relationship between Shadaj and Gandhar...it is almost mystical. Yes, it does bring tears to the eyes! A strange chemistry of sentiments...*

You know, I had to read Sanskrit in order to do a complete study of the shastra of sentiments - the Rasa Shastra. The music treatise did not have it. So I had to study and acquire this from literature.

Q. The classics?

A. *Yes, the classics...like Kavya Prakash...where I could find an echo of my own intuitive exploration of emotional elements. I have been trying to apply this knowledge, this complete theory, onto my music. To accord 'feelings' the pride of place in the scheme of a raga. I do not know whether I shall be able to reach the destination I have visualized, but I know that my path is right. I just need to proceed along that path...with the blessings and good wishes of all of you maybe I shall reach the ultimate.*

Q. Have you ever had any spiritual experiences, like visitations, while in a musical trance? Something that you might not have spoken about as yet?

A. *If I say yes, people are going to say I am insane...*

Q. No, they won't. I assure you...

A. *Well, what if I tell you that Shadaj is Purush and Gandhar is Prakriti...? The male and the female principle...*

Q. Have you seen it that way? It has been said that through proper sadhana, a raga can actually manifest in front of you...

A. *That is not possible in this world, now. Yes, a raga may have a form. If you consider it an entity, it has its emotional elements as well. But how much sadhana will it require from us, just imagine! You might need to sing just one raga all your life! Even then, who knows whether it will actually manifest or no...That's why I follow a simple rule. No matter how many different ragas I may present in concerts, for my riyaz, I stick to just one raga.*

Q. How do you relate to Carnatic Music?

A. *The main distinction is in the prominence of notes. Our raga, as elaborated through the alapi and vistaar, blooms by the movement of notes. Whereas in Carnatic music, since it is the music of compositions and kritis, the accent is on words and beats. There's virtually no extension or expansion of the swara, the notes. Still, while these are two different systems, the music is essentially the same. Our shrutis are the same, our ragas are almost the same. The very religion of musicians is the same. You can reach God through words, you can reach Him through taal, you can reach Him through notes...*

Q. Also, through silence, perhaps?

A. *Actually, musicality should lead to silence! A stage comes when sur begins to move and speak within one's mind. That's the realm of silence. After the pronounced 'sa' we must reach to the un-uttered 'sa'. After 'aahat', our yearning should be to feel the 'anaahat'. I must also see what is even beyond. This is not idle philosophy, mind you, this is the domain of practical reality. Practise, and you will achieve! Coming back to* *the difference between Carnatic and Hindustani classical music, I feel that the so-called difference should gradually vanish. It should become just one: Indian classical music.*

Q.That would really be good!

A. *Isn't it? Nothing could be more desirable!*

Q. And what about Western classical? Do you enjoy, analyze, or compare it with our kind of music?

A. *I see the atmosphere of Western classical music as very powerful. They believe in chords. We believe in melody. We basically pursue the manifestation of a single note at a time, without taking the help of other notes. So our music leads to depth and subtlety. Theirs leads to effect and grandeur. Harmony, co-ordination and discipline are factors that make their music great. There may be other analytical differences, but the meeting point is the inherent simplicity. Listen to Beethoven's Moonlight Sonata...much of it seems uncannily familiar to our kind of music. It is that simplicity, again. Simplicity is the hallmark of all great art. One must realize that.*

Q. What is your opinion of our light classical music?

A. *A wonderful world in itself! I have sung bhajans, Marathi abhang, I have my popular compositions in devotional music. And most people do not know that I have delved deeply into ghazals. After learning from Husnalal-ji, I have myself studied the aesthetics and the nuances of Urdu alfaaz, and how it should be applied to music in the classical ghazal form.*

Q. That's a revelation. Who's your favourite ghazal singer?

A. *My all time favourite is Noor Jehan. And then, Begum Akhtar, Mubarak Begum...*

I do not appreciate those who try to show off their pure classical acrobatics in ghazal gayaki and thereby impede the flow of the lyrical impact, the poetic richness.

Q. You surely like Jagjit Singh then?

A. *Oh yes. I just love his ghazals. So much so, that I even watch him on TV sometimes. I also like the Sufi exponents. Abida Parween is exceptional...The point is, there are various musical paths to the ultimate. To me, it is the Khayal. The raga is the supreme form.*

Q. There are studio recordings for music album productions, and there are stage performances...how do you reconcile the two?

A. *I am utterly uncomfortable with the clinical and clock-bound atmosphere of the recording studio. That's why I do not readily submit to album projects, unless it is of some exceptional worth. In fact, I even charge a lot of money just to discourage producers. Live concerts are much closer to my heart...*

Q. How do you see the basic difference between a vocalist and an instrumentalist in the context of classical music? There's this perpetual rivalry between the two...

A. *Well, like the instrument 'veena', our body is an instrument too. While the outer 'veena' can produce only notes, the 'Shareer-Veena' also pronounces words. Yes, being the direct outlet of the inner light, the human voice does have an advantage. But I must also say that, when an instrumentalist plays with total involvement with the raga, his heart sings from his fingertips!*

Q. Your image on stage is that of a performer totally oblivious of her surroundings. Do you remember actual instances when you have been lost in a trance?

A. *Oh, that happens quite often. While internally I am lost in the 'kavya' of the raga, I strive to remain aware that my platform is that of the 'natya' of the raga. I am presenting the raga to a large audience. Yet, sometimes I am so lost to the outer world that I can just about manage to hold on to my swarmandal out of sheer habit! In fact, I sometimes wish that it should be while singing in a trance that I pass away to the other world...my stilled hands clutching on to the loyal swarmandal.*

Q. Do you like any other musical instrument?

A. *Veena is my favourite. It expresses meend (glide) very well. The interface between notes in veena playing is something wonderful. I am also a devotee of Shri Raghavendra Swami—the veena playing saint from the south. I must tell you, sometime ago, an orphaned and broken veena reached my hands in the most unexpected manner. Although I do not play the veena, I was very excited about it. From an almost unrecognizable condition, I got it restored to its shapely and tuneful state. Then I noticed, it is the same kind of ancient Saraswati Veena, which Shri Raghavendra Swami holds in his hands, in the picture I have of him. This is uncanny. And since nothing ever happens without a purpose, I am waiting for this mystery to unravel someday...*

Q. Amazing! Tell me, do you believe in reincarnation?

A. *Of course I do. Definitely.*

Q. Then what do you think you might have been in your last birth?

A. *Well...in my previous birth, or in the one even before that, I must have had an intimate relation with music. And this might explain how so many things in music come to me unbidden...seemingly through intuition! It cannot be a matter of just one life...*

Q. If you take rebirth, what would you wish to be?

A. *Actually, to be frank, I do not wish to die with any wish within my heart. That's because I do not want to take birth again...*

Q. But, like you said, it may not be possible to learn everything in music in just one life... so, what if some destination remains unattained...?

A. *That's why I am evermore at the feet of my gurus...with the soulful request to be taken to completion...I...I have a wish. When I die, God should take me at his feet, and let me lie there. After all, music is only a path, not the destination...It is a means to reach ultimate peace...*

LALGUDI
JAYARAMAN

The shop owner near the marketplace was a benign, elderly man, and he revelled in an abiding sense of satisfaction that he was doing much more than those lesser mortals who strove along to manage just one good deed a day. The pride of place at his shop was justifiably occupied by a huge radio set with speakers that distributed loud music, with the lofty air of a lighthouse sending off beams of light into the darkness of human mire. His self-satisfied eyes that panned the vicinity would, however, trip over a discordant sight from time to time. His round spectacled vision could never get used to the suspicious presence of a small, lean boy with scruffy short hair, who would hover around his shop without ever buying anything. Repeated observation had revealed that the boy's presence had an uncanny synchronicity with the schedule of the radio programmes. Whenever the best of classical music would be aired, he would be there, drifting close to the shop, almost like a sleepwalker. But then, the plot would thicken every time a great piece of music would end, because, the boy would then suddenly hasten away with big strides. As if he had just lifted an irresistible piece of music and escaped!

The old shop owner at Lalgudi might have never got to know just how close to truth his incredible suspicion had come. Because, it was only much later in life that a famous Lalgudi Jayaraman revealed that he actually used to run away with pieces of music that appealed to him from the shop with the loud radio! Radio programmes were rich in content those days, and since he did not have a radio at home, he would go hunting. And the moment a piece appeared inspiring enough, he would trap it with all its vivid details in his mind, and rush home to recreate it perfectly on his violin! Given his musical intuition and 'phonographic' memory, listening to a composition just once, would often be enough for him to claim possession and make it his own...

Lalgudi G Jayaraman was born in the state of Madras in a famous village, whose name he was to make even more famous along with his own. Lalgudi was a scenic place, which aroused Jayaraman's sense of harmony with nature, and his passion for music, quite early in life. Destiny's favoured child, Jayaraman was blessed with everything a budding musician could dream of. A brilliant brain and a sensitive heart, lovingly nurtured by exemplary parents, along the natural flow of a glorious lineage! Lalgudi Rama Iyer, a famous disciple of Saint Thyagaraja himself, was a direct ancestor of Jayaraman, and their blessings must have had a role to play in taking their descendant to great ascents of Carnatic music.

Jayaraman's father, Lalgudi Gopala Iyer, was a spiritually inclined versatile musician, and he had kept his great musical lineage alive and thriving. This provided young Jayaraman with an ideal atmosphere at home, resplendent with the best of Carnatic music. The violin was like a household deity, an idol to be held close to the heart and worshipped with the music of the soul...

Reluctant to wait till he grew up, Jayaraman began to learn Carnatic music under the family tutelage of his father, and also his paternal uncle Kandaswami Bhagavatar. Six busy years of vocal music, overlapped with four years of rigorous and meticulous training on the violin, ensured that before Jayaraman could reach his teens, he ascended the concert platform with his gurus' blessings!

Quite apart from invoking awe, affection and admiration in audiences, Lalgudi's violin accompaniments began to open up grand vistas of golden opportunities for the gifted young musician. He played with a wide spectrum of seasoned musicians, some of whom were frontline stalwarts of contemporary Carnatic music. This helped him complement and nurture his inborn music sense and sensitivity with practical musical wisdom blossoming through intimate interaction with great performers.

Even as a young man, Lalgudi distinguished himself as a thinking musician. With great sagacity, he also achieved a rare chemistry between his vocal experiences and instrumental explorations. That's how, with time, even the finest vocal *gamakas* would find an enhanced expression on his singing violin! He explored the instrument like an inspired scientist and devised a method and style that was to change the entire face of violin playing in Carnatic music. The perfect Carnatic training he received early in life provided him with a strong and enduring foundation on which he could craft lofty musical towers of rare beauty. Precise,

liquid glides of his bow, coupled perfectly with dexterous fingering technique, where all four fingers assume equal importance, have gone to create that distinct style known as *Lalgudi Bani*. A style that has ushered in a new era of violin playing in the traditional world of Carnatic music. Lyrical contents and emotions, with all their nuances are central to the *Lalgudi Bani*.

Unlike meteoric prodigies who burn out without a trace, Jayaraman's composed genius was recognized intuitively by his father. As his music guru, he fuelled it gently and protected it like a temple flame, lending it stability and sanctity. As a growing boy, Jayaraman was kept away from rough sports on the field, and sharp instruments at home, including kitchen knives, and even fire crackers during festive revelry. The concert 'stage' was 'all the world' for the focussed young Jayaraman. Even much later, it took a persuasive Palghat Mani Iyer to secure the senior Lalgudi's consent to get Jayaraman on the plane to Europe. The veteran mridangam magician and the young violin virtuoso had been invited to perform at the prestigious Edinburgh Music Festival.

The Western world was intrigued and agreeably surprised to see their favourite and familiar instrument produce some soul-stirring other-worldly music. Yehudi Menuhin, perhaps the most celebrated name ever associated with the violin, invited Lalgudi to get to know him better. As the host in his London home, Menuhin urged Lalgudi to play for him. Since Lalgudi had not taken his instrument along, Menuhin brought out a violin for him! The Italian beauty that held memories of the harmony of Beethoven, Schubert, Chopin and Mozart, was ready to change its tuning to produce some exotic Carnatic melodies. That violin remains a present from Menuhin to Lalgudi. A memento of musical amity between the West and the East. It was a historic moment, and Lalgudi's heart must have danced with joy; he presented Menuhin with an ivory *Dancing Nataraj* when Menuhin visited India.

In 1965 itself, Lalgudi travelled with sitar maestro Ravi Shankar, and later he embarked on other concert tours as the West began to wake up to the fact that Indian classical music was not just Hindustani from the north; there was an equally wondrous and tradition-rich world of Carnatic music to be experienced. As the witty Raja Gopalachari, the then chief minister of Madras, had commented during the send off ceremony of Palghat Mani Iyer and Lalgudi, "For a change, some unadulterated stuff is going out from India...!"

Lalgudi himself has had the greatest respect for Hindustani classical music too. Just as his violin successfully captured the characteristic glide of the Carnatic nadaswaram, he was once inspired by Bismillah Khan's shehnai, and as a ten-year old, wanted to capture the maestro's magical continuity of notes on his own violin. He also enjoyed listening to other Hindustani legends like Amir Khan and Bade Ghulam Ali Khan. After he became famous, Lalgudi's very first *jugalbandi* with a north Indian musician was with the great maestro Vilayat Khan.

Although India was always his first priority, once the doors of the West opened up, Lalgudi responded selectively to invitations from across the oceans. An extensive tour of America and Canada compressed as many as twenty-four concerts on a string, followed by lectures and demonstrations under the East-West Exchange programme. One resounding success led to another, and soon again, he was travelling across

East European countries, followed by a cultural delegation tour of Russia. Other nations and cities like Singapore, Malaysia, Manila, Cologne, Belgium and France also got a taste of the Lalgudi magic on the violin! The Government of India chose him to represent the country at the Festival of India in London. He gave some memorable solo and duet concerts in London, followed by music centers in Germany and Italy. In 1984, it was the Middle East venues like Oman, UAE, Qatar and Bahrain that revelled in Lalgudi's exotic music, and the following year it was the Festival of India in the US that was graced by his participation. More recently, the Bharatiya Vidya Bhavan conferred the title 'Bharatha Jyothi' on him after his memorable recital for the millennium concert in New York...

While on one hand, Lalgudi's solo concerts were gaining for his violin an unprecedented prestige on the concert platform, rivalled only by vocal music, the master accompanist in him was in no mood to take a backseat. With his dynamic thoughts, and insightful approach to music, he was constantly raising the standards of classical accompaniment to greater heights. In contrast to the amiable Hindustani style of accompaniment, the Carnatic accompanist has to be like a gladiator in the music arena.

Rhythmic puzzles, melodic challenges are thrown at him without warning, and he has to have an aesthetic answer, if not a fitting reply to it all. The audiences have been thrilled like never before to find that Lalgudi, with his rare grasp and genius, has always been more than equal to the challenge, giving back more than everyone's expectations!

His solo odyssey takes a unique path altogether. Being his own master and guardian

In front of a portrait of Saint Tyagaraja

angel, he takes his concerts to the realms of a spiritual experience. With his essentially vocalistic leanings, Lalgudi's music flows like a continuous fountainhead kept alive by the finest and subtlest of grace notes, and the most sweeping flight of glides. The music is never bereft of the beauty of inherited Carnatic idioms, yet it simmers with the promise and energy of intuition and innovation. Threatening to burst the bounds of tradition but eventually just pushing the horizon a little.

The logical and poetic consequence of his resounding success in solo performances was his surging interest in composing. The mountain stream which was blocked by boulders for too long began to gush forth. The Lalgudi touch brought alive the obscure *Dhanasri Thillana* in vivid colour and form. His gliding bow gave shape to the contemporary favourite *Nadaloludai Krithi* in the newly embellished raga *Kalyana Vasantham*. Numerous *Varnams* and *Thillanas* began to glide out of his creative, meditative violin in a victory parade. Some of these compositions are often presented by other contemporary musicians as a tribute to Lalgudi's contribution. A time came when his emerging identity as a composer of rare originality began to complement his luminous image of a premier performer on the Carnatic stage. Bedazzled prima donnas of classical dance began to embrace Lalgudi's moving compositions to energize their performances.

The temple flame of genius that was sheltered and fuelled by a father's foresight and teaching, had gradually proliferated and begun to burn bright as the *panchadeep*, the multi-flamed lamp, illuminating the Carnatic music world. With the passage of time, Lalgudi found himself surrounded by eager and devoted disciples who wanted to seek guidance from the master. The Indian spirit of traditional continuity has an impel that no musician can ignore. Whoever acknowledges his guru's contribution in his life, feels morally bound to accept his own disciples and pass on the knowledge. Like a flame finding its fulfillment in igniting many more.

Lalgudi's spirit of teaching, however, soars much higher than moral or professional compulsions. His ever-widening circle of disciples is a joyous family, which includes his own son Krishnan, and daughter Vijayalakshmi, among many other talents that are poised to light up the future. As a strict, sincere and impartial preceptor, Lalgudi gives of his best to each individual disciple. Each teaching session invariably transcends the structured routine, and becomes an inspired exercise in creativity. Lalgudi enjoys it as much as his concert performance.

Lalgudi, the lover of elephants

Lalgudi Jayaraman has had an enchanted life. The force above, the 'fiddler on the roof' has not only blessed Lalgudi's violin, but he himself seems to have played harmonious tunes for him all along. Not too many geniuses get to live a life of poise and serenity, not too many philosophers get to practise what they preach. When Lalgudi makes music, he is totally lost in himself. His violin becomes an extension of his body and his music, a voice for his beautiful mind. An obedient son to his loving parents, a protective elder brother to his three talented musician sisters, a responsible and generous father and guru to his children, Lalgudi has lived an exemplary family life despite demanding concert and travel schedules over the last few decades. His love for nature and man, his compassion, his luminous sense of humour, his simple *satvik* habits and ascetic demeanour, are indeed rare qualities in this era of eroding values. One could even find it quite incredible, until, of course, one listened to the music he makes.

Lalgudi's father, Sri Gopala Iyer, had lived a mendicant's life for several years in his youth, before providence brought him back from his *sanyas,* into the householder's life. Many beautiful compositions then came to him unbidden. As if his spirituality was sublimated into music, before Jayaraman, his eldest son, was born. As his guru, Jayaraman's father used to tell him, "Don't think of name and fame, concentrate on the music of the moment. Go deep into it; the rest will follow." And it did.

Sometime in 1979, a panel of judges at the International Music Council, Baghdad, was evaluating seventy-seven competitive entries received from various countries of the world. And although there was no Indian on the jury panel to explain things, an ordinary recording of a solo violin composition, sent in by All India Radio, Delhi, was being played again and again to the rapt and roused group of listeners... In the early hours of the following morning, a telegram reached the doorsteps of the Lalgudi residence in Madras. It was a one-line message of congratulations for being adjudged the very best! Yes, it was a grand moment of recognition for the genius of Lalgudi Jayaraman. But above all, it was a precise statement of what the contemporary world thought of a rich, vibrant heritage known as Carnatic music.

Living Memories...

Young and famous

Contemplating on music

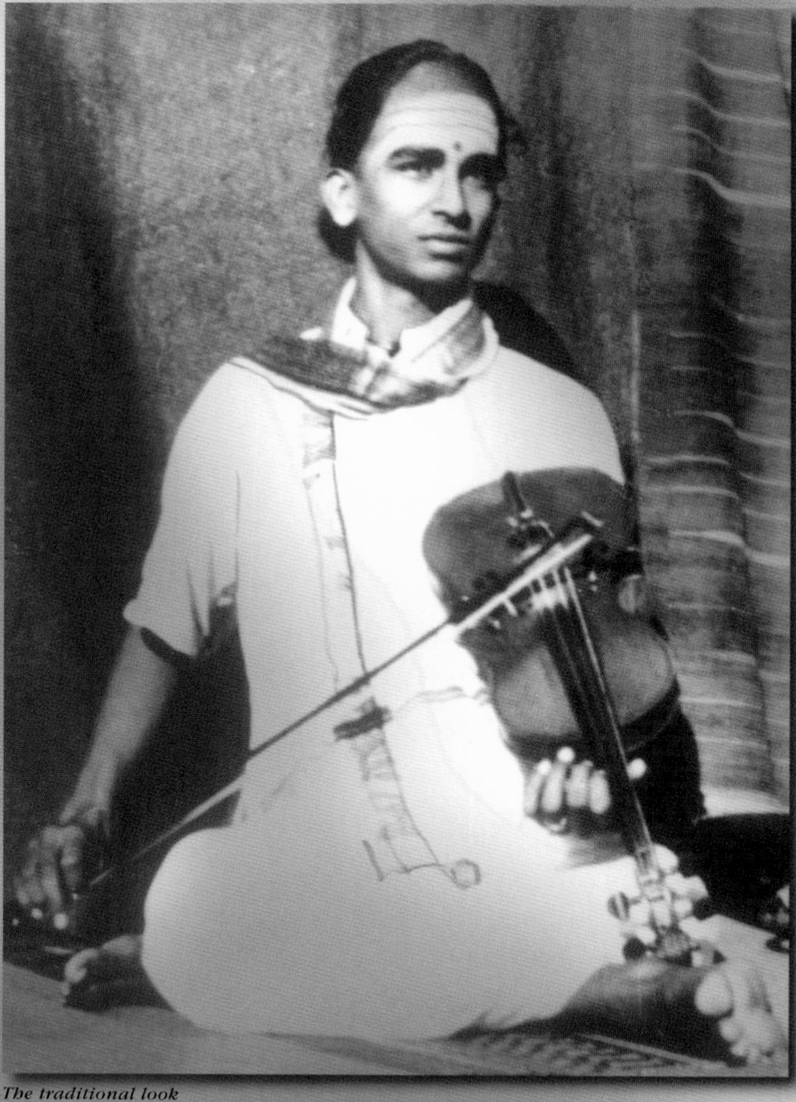

The traditional look

With sitar maestro Vilayat Khan

With celebrated violinist Yehudi Menuhin and reputed musicologist Raghava R Menon

Wielding the magical bow

On stage with veteran vocalist G N Balasubramaniam and mrudangam maestro Palghat Mani Iyer

Q. What prompted you to take up the violin as your chosen instrument?

A. *In a way, I inherited it. My great-grandfather had lived in Mysore as the 'State Vidwan' at the Mysore palace. Many musicians congregated there from far and wide. That's when he was exposed to the Western violin. He took it up as his chosen instrument for making Carnatic music, and it flowed into the family. My grandfather Shri Valadi Radhakrishna Iyer accompanied topmost musicians of his time, and was the 'Asthana Vidwan' of the Samasthana of Ramnad. My father too was a very good violinist.*

Q. Who were the Carnatic stalwarts you accompanied as a budding musician?

A. *Ariyakudi Ramanuja Iyengar...Musiri Subramania Iyer... Maharajapuram Viswanatha Iyer...Chembai Vaidhyanatha Bagavathar...Semmangudi Srinivasa Iyer... Madurai Mani Iyer...M M Dandapani Desikar... G N Balasubramaniam...Alathur Brothers... Dr S Balachander...it's a long list of great music makers.*

Q. Apart from your violin, you have given so many vocal concerts also. Which do you enjoy more?

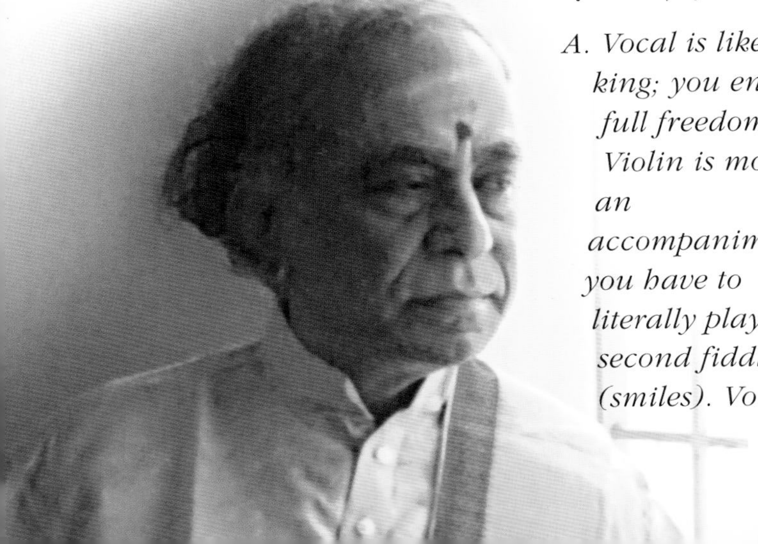

A. Vocal is like the king; you enjoy full freedom. Violin is mostly an accompaniment; you have to literally play second fiddle (smiles). Vocal Carnatic music attracts more people, because it has the advantage of words. In instrumental solo, you have to imagine the words.

Q. But to you, violin is special, isn't it?

A. *As a violinist I enjoyed the rare good fortune of associating with great musicians at an early age and learnt a great deal from them. The veena, the flute, the nadaswaram... no other instrument in Carnatic music gets so close to vocalists as the violin does. My first love, my first child is the violin. Even if I take rebirth, I would like to become a violinist again and again...And mind you, violin is 'sarvavyapi'...it is in solo, in accompaniment, it is in cinema, in dance, in flute concert, in veena concert...it is virtually everywhere.*

Q. Your dexterity on the violin, and the other refinements like the minutest of the gamakas, can rival the best of vocal music. In fact, if a vocalist ever tries to accompany you, he will have a tough time!

A. *(Laughs) People say my style is vocalistic. I have tried to imbibe the best of both.*

Q. How did you conceive the dance ballet 'Jaya Jaya Devi' ? It was premiered outside India?

A. *It was an inspired musical composition portraying 'Devi Shakti' in six different incarnations. It was first presented at the Ohio University in Cleveland. It was then well received at other parts of the world as well, including our very own Chennai!*

Q. This inspired the observance of the date 2nd April as 'Lalgudi Day' in Ohio?

A. *(Looks embarrassed) That's their generous*

style of appreciation.

Q. And what about the other great dance drama 'Pancheshwaram'?

A. *That too was premiered outside India, in London. It was based on the theme of temples built long ago in Sri Lanka by Indian kings like the Pallavas and the Cholas. Current generation Sri Lankans found it particularly fascinating.*

Q. How do you select your students from the many that aspire to learn from you?

A. *Depending on the students' aptitude, I teach violin, veena or vocal music. But I prefer students who show not just talent but a serious sense of purpose. I take them along in a spirit of interaction, and I myself learn while I teach. In fact, I often tell them, "I am a senior student; you all are junior students..." (Smiles).*

Q. You do not accept personal remuneration, but you divert all collections towards your Trust. What's the basic objective of the Lalgudi Trust?

A. *The Trust has been offering scholarships to young and deserving students. It also seeks to sponsor concerts of young and upcoming artistes through various organizations.*

Q. You have also helped raise funds in order to renovate the dilapidated birth houses of the great trinity of Carnatic Music: Thyagaraja, Dikshitar and Shyamashastri...And have also raised lakhs of rupees to help expand and modernize the Government Boys High School at Lalgudi?

A. *The first was my solemn duty as a Carnatic musician. And about the boys school, the idea appealed to me because it was an opportunity to give back something to my birthplace, Lalgudi, whose auspicious vibrations have been enriching my name all my life.*

Q. You have always been a favourite with saints and god-men...

A. *I feel blessed that they have liked my music. Once when the Parmacharya of the Kanchi mutt was observing 'kashtha maunam', and was not meeting or speaking with anyone, a hoard of devotees who had gathered there, felt very dejected. I had my violin with me, and I began to play some devotional tunes. First his windows opened up, and after a while the saint himself emerged to bless everyone present with his darshan! I, of course, received the blessings of the lucky devotees too, as a bonus! (Smiles).*

Q. Your music compositions have often had your poetic and lyrical support. Is that a natural talent?

A. *I believe all art is interconnected. If you have a poetic vision, you can see the simile in painting and music, for example. When a painter paints, he uses seven colours, his brush, and his imagination, to bring out the strokes. In music, the seven colours are the seven notes, the brush strokes are the phrases that come out of his voice or instrument.*

And yes, just as the painter needs a clean, white canvas, the musician needs the attentive silence of the audience...

Q. Beautiful! Before I fall silent, can I request you for a message for the young, aspiring musicians?

A. *Well...just remember that music is a great boon to humanity. From childhood to old age, it makes you human; nothing can bring as much satisfaction. Surrender your ego; make room for music to come to you. Stay focussed, and give yourself completely to music. Surrender your body, mind and heart...and they will all come back to you much enhanced.*

M.
BALAMURALI~
KRISHNA

In this *kaliyug,* the ultimate era of karmic chaos and confusion, when it is difficult to hear even your own inner voice, the divine music of Creation could well have become elusive to mortal ears. The *Kinnaras* and the *Gandharvas* may have drifted away to a different time and place, the singing sage Narada too may not roam the earth any more to sing the praises of the Supreme Lord. Yet, all is not quite lost.

While with his conceited intellect, man struggles to make sense of his life and fate, the language of communication with his Maker is still in his grasp. As long as there is music, as long as man is able to communicate musically with the Divine...there is hope.

God continues to send in the prodigies and the geniuses in his own time, as per his own *laya.* They are the chosen souls. Human *instruments,* tuned by the Maker himself, set alive with a single stroke of the Divine finger...to resonate for a lifetime on earth.

A child prodigy, M Balamuralikrishna was born on 6 July 1930, at Sankaraguptam, a tiny village in the east of river Godavari in Andhra Pradesh. It is utterly credible that the very first cry of his arrival into this world must have been distinctly melodious. Such was the aura of music that enveloped him as he began to grow into a sweet, endearing boy.

Since his father, Shri Pattabiramayya, was a noted musician who played the flute, the violin and the veena, and his mother Suryakantamma was a gifted veena exponent, it was only natural that Balamurali's unbridled melodic energy and talent made intimate playmates out of the musical instruments strewn around the premises. By the time most children begin to outgrow their toys, Balamurali's interest in musical instruments like the veena, the violin, the khanjira and the mridangam was on the rise. But young Balamurali's greatest asset was his rare talent for singing. It was undoubtedly a gift from God, a *prasad,* which he freely distributed on request, with a smile and a glint in the eye.

Friends and well-wishers advised Balamurali's father that formal education could not be ignored and it was high time his son was put in a school. As an eight-year-old when Balamurali walked into the local municipal high school with his father, he was heartily welcomed by the principal. Balamurali was readily admitted into the 6th standard, but not before the principal had asked him to sing a song! It was only a prelude to the routine that was to follow, because from the very next day, as everyone gathered at the prayer hall in the morning, before the classes began, Balamurali was asked to sing the prayer! And the hitherto short ritual would turn into a concert as one song would lead to another!

This went on for a few months and soon it was time for the quarterly examinations. Young Balamurali duly received his white sheets, his pencil, and his question paper. But he respectfully returned every answer paper without a scratch, because he simply could not read the questions! While most teachers did not mind it much, the mathematics teacher wasn't amused. He inscribed a huge and perfect zero and asked Balamurali to get his father's signature on the paper. But his calculations went wrong, as Balamurali's father too had a similar experience in his childhood and he signed the paper without much ado. And so when Balamurali returned happily with the requisite endorsement, all that the mathematics teacher could ask him was whether he was ashamed to get a zero or not. The innocent answer was, "No, Sir. In fact I was trying my best to draw a circle as perfect as you had drawn, but could not! You are a great artist, Sir!" The mathematics teacher, sadly, was not flattered. Finally, the head master advised Balamurali's father that his son was a genuine artist and he should not be forced to waste his time in the school. If and when he would feel the need for mundane education, he could easily get it! That was the end of Balamurali's formal schooling; it lasted just six months. A rather curious point of reference for the five

honorary doctorates he was to receive from major universities, later in life.

A born musician, Balamurali's music training from his guru Parupalli Ramakrishna Pantulu too, did not extend beyond a six-month span. Before he was even nine years old, it was time for his first radio broadcast from Radio Madras. And after that successful debut, every three months Balamurali would be required to come to Madras from Vijayawada, and return after the radio performance.

There used to be a spiritual guru at Vijayawada who would often come with his entourage of disciples and live in the mutt opposite Balamurali's old residence. One fine day, as Balamurali was singing a song for him, the holy man took him aside and engaged him in an in-depth conversation. At the end of it, Balamurali's mind was suffused with glowing inspiration backed by some compelling logic. There surely was devotional and other music even before Thyagaraja, but the legendary saint did not spend his life singing just that. He composed new music, created a body of original lyrical work. His kritis went on to encompass all aspects of life! Today, everyone, including the best of singers, is immersed in Thyagaraja's legacy. Young Balamurali should also decide now, whether he wants to be just a singer, or an original composer! Should he seek to contribute to the treasure trove of Carnatic music...or simply take from it! It was a rhetoric question, and the answer kept echoing within his tender heart! Windows opened up in his virtually unschooled mind, to allow cross ventilation between long-forgotten talents and wisdom, and his ordained calling in life.

Glimpses of rare and precious musical *melakartas* began to flash within...poetic phrases in unknown Sanskrit began to well up in his mind...and a fourteen-year-old child prodigy began to create astounding lyrical compositions using all the seventy-two *melakartas*...and even sing them to wide-eyed audiences.

Inspiration courts miracles. One late night, just before daybreak, a saintly Sanskrit scholar barged in to wake up Balamurali's father

An assembly of diverse stalwarts! Balamurali being honoured by artists and chief ministers in Mumbai

Pattabiramayya. He introduced himself as a devotee, a *Devi upaasak,* and demanded that young Balamurali should wake up, take a bath and come away with him within fifteen minutes! Like young Rama following Rishi Vishwamitra, Balamurali went with the old man to his residence. He was taken straight to the sacred *puja* room..."I have heard your Sanskrit compositions," said the old scholar, "they are coming from above; they are not yours." Then, pointing to the deity he said, " Devi has asked me to teach you some fundamentals of poetry. And you must bear those in mind when you sit down to compose..."

Young Balamurali entered an intellectual trance...and it kept him charged with creative inspiration for a span of two years, until he composed some exquisite lyrical poetry in Sanskrit using all the seventy-two magical *melakarta* ragas. These were later put together in a book. Unknown, unheard words and melodies kept flowing out of his voice, which was tuned to some unfathomable mystical source. As if Lord Krishna was playing some divine music having chosen young Balamurali as his instrument...

Someone else in this situation would perhaps have been overwhelmed and lost his balance, but his worldly engagements kept Balamurali grounded in reality and sanity. He was in tremendous demand for his recitals and concerts—both private and public. Sometimes he had to accommodate as many as three performances in a day...like three consecutive shows in the local cinema hall!

Without any major setback, Balamurali's life progressed like a musical river broadened and strengthened by many diverse streams of talent flowing into it. He sang for movies, even acted

in them. He played the violin and introduced the viola into the Carnatic concert scene. He achieved the rare distinction of being appointed the state musician for two states—Andhra Pradesh and Tamil Nadu, and the *Asthana Vidwan* to a number of famous religious conglomerates. His very presence became a source of excitement and inspiration to every *sabha,* institution and forum of contemporary Carnatic music.

Describing Balmaurali's craft in words is not easy. He packs tremendous power in his voice yet he controls it like fluid lightning. The magnetism of his voice rivals the magnetic charm he exudes through his smiling demeanour, as he sings without the slightest hint of strain or effort. The voice is wonderfully vibrant and in full command as it glides through the three octaves like one celestial river flowing through the three worlds. Now it frolics like a butterfly; the next moment it swoops like the desert eagle. It is indeed a roller-coaster ride for the listening ears, an odyssey marked by surprises at every turn.

It must be with consummate ease, and fluency of the wind, that he has created ripples and waves on the placid surface of the deep reservoir of traditional Carnatic music. Many new ragas got conjured as if by magic. They all sparkle today with befitting ornamental names like *Trisakthi, Omkari, Vallavi, Lavangi, Mahati, Sumukham, Manorama, Rohini, Pratimadhyamavati, Janasammodini...*

Some of these newborn ragas have danced to the rhythm of his new, innovative tala patterns. Percussive artistes on the *mridangam* and the *ghatam* have been led playfully beyond their known limits while accompanying Balamurali on the concert platform. Like an invisible puppeteer, Balamurali has tugged at many heartstrings at once, and has actually created music, which had existed earlier only in the realms of possibility.

Aware of the power of the broadcasting medium in this vast geographical arena, Balamurali has always given the radio its due importance. The radio stations in turn, have given him the power and position to accord his ideas and talents the maximum reach and expression. He was one of the two very first 'Producers of Music' while serving the All India Radio for over a decade. Later again, a special position of 'Music Supervisor' was created for the first time in order to capitalize on the creative contributions of Balamurali on radio.

An accomplished devotee of art and culture in their panoramic entirety, Balamurali founded the Balamuralikrishna Trust with the view to let his legacy take root while his image flowers. The Trust is doing some extensive and inspired research on music therapy, which might be revealed to the world in the fullness of time. The Trust is taking rapid strides in the education and propagation of Indian music and dance.

An unassuming and humble man, Dr Balamuralikrishna has never flaunted his genius in any facet of his versatile persona. Presidents and ministers have paid their obeisance to his talents in public, and have confessed to having been soothed and inspired by his music in their private moments. High profile holy places have honoured themselves by conferring on him titles like *Aasthana Vidwan*. Quite apart from his expanding list of honorary doctorates, which make him nostalgic about his brief tryst with formal schooling, Balamurali has had the rare distinction of serving a central university as its pro-chancellor! Even in his family life he has conducted himself with the quiet dignity of an exemplary householder. Since music came to him naturally, he has never felt the urge or need to force it on his descendants. He has brought up his children to become professionals like doctors and surgeons, and have encouraged them to pursue their own paths with freedom and pride.

With Hindustani music greats, Ram Narayan, Dhondutai Kulkarni and Kishori Amonkar

Balamurali's music has been the light of his vision, revealing to him the wonders of the manifest world. He can feel the inner vibrations of the places he visits...he sees God in every soul around him...and in his profound simplicity he perhaps wonders as to why good souls are in such slumber, why can't every human mind open up to its inner music! In the wake of that unuttered emotion, another new raga takes shape and shines through his twinkling eyes before his crystal voice releases it into existence! If a disciple happens to be around, he captures it in attentive memory. Or else, it vanishes, floating into the atmosphere, like a misty cluster of joy.

There have been many child prodigies in the long and vibrant heritage of art and music. But in rare instances like that of Balamurali, where the prodigious elements span across decades, evoking the same sense of awe and wonder all around, one feels the need to coin a term like 'adult prodigy'!

The world has seen maestros who have emerged as 'instruments' of God. We know how their highest music was created by the deepest strokes of pain and strife, and how they had to keep re-tuning themselves at every turn of their tumultuous journey through life. In utter contrast, all along his charmed ride through life, M Balamuralikrishna never had to labour over his enormous body of creations. He never ever needed the daily riyaaz to keep in shape! Evidently, he has been the one 'instrument' sent to earth tuned perfectly by the Master's own hands!

And since we all know the God who played the *murali,* it is not difficult to visualize the existence of a God who loves playing the 'Balamurali'...

Living Memories...

Balamurali, the child prodigy

Playing a part

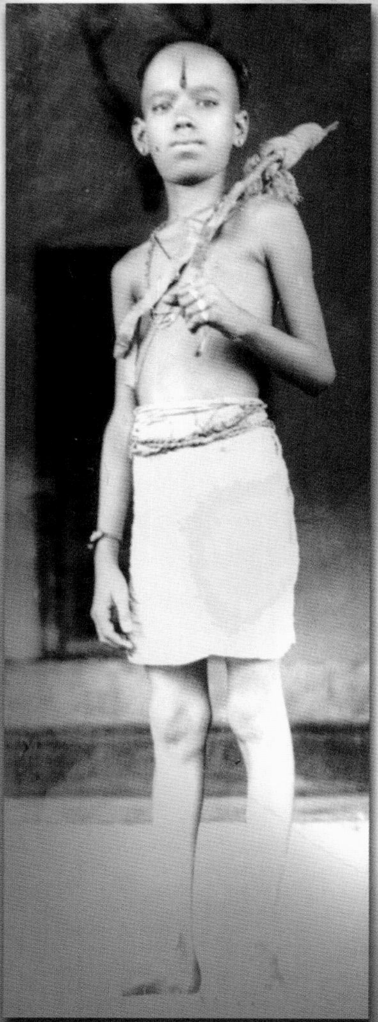

Seated in his father's lap

Playing a musical role

Boyhood medals

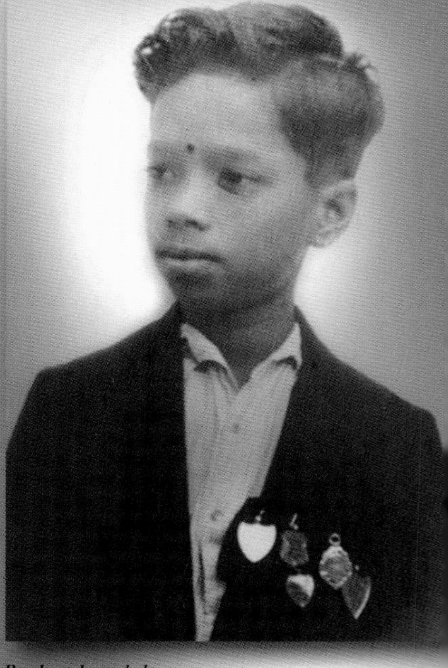

Boyhood medals

The historic town of Madurai. Circa 1920.

The main streets around the imposing Meenakshi temple complex were resonating with austere chants and frenzied music. The temple deity had been taken out in one of its spectacular, ritualistic processions, which was making steady but slow progress, like a huge serpent that was swallowing up the wide arterial road. Approaching the vicinity of a particular house, the procession seemed to slow down further. If one did not notice that, there was at least one thing, which was very obvious. The temple musicians who led the procession, were suddenly charged with some added enthusiasm. The *nadaswaram* players appeared to have saved their crescendo for this stretch of the journey. And as they glanced collectively at the well-recognized house, they finally got the nod of approval they sought. Their musical efforts were duly acknowledged by the pleasant smile on the dignified face of the lady of the house, who stood poised within the premises.

Standing in her shadow, quite literally, was a little girl with pigtails, whom no one perhaps noticed. She hardly moved. Transfixed, she scrutinized all the passing musicians with their various instruments, and soaked in every nuance of their *swara* and *tala*. She loved the music. And she loved the context to devotion. No one knew then, that music and devotion were destined to be inseparably woven like a jasmine garland around her persona. As if to celebrate her eventual deification by the music loving multitudes of her country.

The beautiful house the procession had paused at, was itself a temple of music, adorned by the presence of Shanmukhavadivu, heir to a

traditional lineage of talented women, who dedicated their lives to the service of god through dance and music. Her mother was a reputed violin player, and her father, a music lover who zealously patronized many fine arts. Shanmukhavadivu herself was a celebrated veena player, who had earned the respect of the art and music lovers of the great city of Madurai. In the fitness of things, Madurai has stood for the 'M', and Shanmukhavadivu, for the 'S' in M S Subbulakshmi, the future goddess of Carnatic music, who stood beside her mother that afternoon watching the august temple procession pass by. It would later be apparent that perhaps after many lives of musical pursuit, destiny had placed her perfectly in time and place, to touch the pinnacle of artistic achievements in this life. And, as if the abiding devotion of the *Devadasis* was rewarded by the emergence of a goddess at the end of their lineage.

One might say, that M S Subbulakshmi's entire life so far has been like her own flawless rendition of one of her favourite ragas. Born in a town which preserved and represented the very best of India's religious and cultural heritage...placed in a home that resonated with music...ensconced in the midst of a loving family where everyone, from parents to siblings, was either a musician or a music lover...taught by the best of gurus who seemed to come along at the right moments...loved and supported by a spirited husband who orchestrated her life and career like a virtuoso conductor...befriended and felicitated by the greatest celebrities from every field...blessed by an entire pantheon of saints and god-men who lived in our time...and above all, she has basked in the abiding belief and satisfaction of having taken her art to a higher plane of spirituality, and brought immense joy, bliss and elation to millions of lesser mortals through her divine music and angelic generosity! She surely has been God's favoured child.

Like her favourite Krishna, Subbulakshmi too began life by lighting up the surroundings where she grew up. Mother Shanmukhavadivu had longed to be a vocalist herself, but since she did not have the requisite voice quality, she had opted for the veena, and with her great talent, had made it sing. When she would sit and practise for concentrated long spells, daughter 'Kunjamma', the little MS, would lovingly accompany her by learning the ragas just by listening and humming along the with the veena. And when other *sangeeta vidwans* would visit the hospitable household, to sing or discuss the nuances of Carnatic music, Kunjamma would quietly absorb every word and note. Later, there would be a musical threesome revelling in family bliss! MS would sing, her sister Vadivambal would play the violin, and her brother Shaktivel would play the mridangam. Although MS also learned to play the veena and even the mridangam out of genuine appreciation and youthful enthusiasm, what filled her mother's heart with great joy and rekindled expectations, was the fact that her daughter's voice was being recognized by everyone around as a god gifted asset!

It must have been a universally auspicious day when Kunjamma was formally initiated into vocal music by the well-known Carnatic musician, Srinivasa Iyengar of Madurai. The lessons guided her emerging talent, and before long, MS had absorbed the basic tenets of Carnatic music, the *alankaram,* the *kirtana,* the *varnam*...After the guru had exhausted his repertoire, Shanmukhavadivu herself took on the task of enhancing her daughter's musical

MS, in front of the portrait of her mother, Shanmukhavadivu

maturity. Soon, MS began to accompany her mother in her concerts. At these *'kacheris',* the audiences were surprised to see a tiny little girl with a clear, sweet and fluent voice, complementing the masterly notes of her mother who played the veena!

When Kunjamma was barely ten, her mother had taken her along to Madras for her own recording of some veena compositions. There, almost on an impulse, she asked the record company to try out her daughter's voice. This resulted in a twin record, featuring mother and daughter, which was an instant sellout! Back in Madurai, Kunjamma continued to sing with her mother in her veena concerts. The consistent, loud audience applause left no doubt in anyone's mind that it was time for little Kunjamma to graduate to M S Subbulakshmi, and take her deserved *aasana* on the solo concert platform.

Her first public solo recital was arranged in Madurai, where the fifteen-year-old demure and confident MS was hailed, both by the audiences and the critics, as the new rising star on the horizon of Carnatic music. Soon, she began to cut records and travel on concert tours to all the major centre of Carnatic music. Despite the heady success, she, like a true music student, sought out reputed *vidwans* like Ariyakudi Ramanuja Ayyangar, Musiri Subramania Iyer, and Semmangudi Srinivasa Iyer, to learn some special *kirtanams* from them. Like ascending an easy, even paced flight of stairs, MS began to scale the heights of popularity through concert after major concert in the south. To keep pace with her meteoric rise, the entire family shifted residence to the metropolis of Madras.

Bombay's Matunga Sangeet Sabha had heard of MS, and decided to invite the new star of Carnatic music to perform in the city. It was also an invitation for her destiny to expedite the preordained by getting the act together.

Thiagarajan Sadasivam was a tall, lean young man who had devoted his mind, body and spirit to the cause of India's freedom struggle. Freshly converted from a firebrand to the path of *ahimsa* by Mahtma Gandhi's blessings, Sadasivam had energetically propagated the use of khadi and had efficiently marketed the concept in the state of Madras. This experience had helped him in his current job as the young business manager of the premier Tamil publication, *Ananda Vikatan*. Destiny brought him close to MS and her family as he undertook the responsibility of escorting the shy and innocent MS in her first trip to Bombay. Sadasivam witnessed from close range the magic of MS in concert, and was deeply moved by the divine music that enveloped her entire persona. Later he began to attend all her electrifying concerts and was charged with the inspiration of joining forces with her, in life and mission. Shanmukhavadivu too had intuitively realized that MS and Sadasivam were destined to be a happy and auspicious couple. So, despite the fact that Sadasivam was married and a father of two daughters, and was also much older than MS, she responded to Sadasivam's request for her daughter's hand with a mother's blessings.

So, after a simple marriage ceremony in the monsoon of 1940, at Tiruneermalai, a temple town near Madras, MS began her conjugal journey with the man she had come to deeply admire. It was the beginning of a lifelong alliance, whereby Sadasivam took upon himself the responsibility of grooming MS, shielding her from life's mundane distractions and problems, and easing her gently and lovingly into the orbit of her astronomical potential in the universe of music.

Perhaps more than MS herself, Sadasivam was convinced that although she already shone with noticeable brilliance in her musical accomplishments, her inner luster was still waiting to shine through! And it was the *bhakti,* the devotional appeal in her voice that needed further refinement, so that it would ultimately make her realize her true potential. After all, her kind of music transcended the confines of performing art, and was a language for the soul, a medium to reach God. So, while on one hand,

Sadasivam wanted MS to play a role in the nationalistic movement and had already introduced her to leaders like Mahatma Gandhi, Pandit Nehru and Raja Gopalachari, on the other hand, he wanted her music to be a potent force to unite diverse people with their spirituality. He stressed the clarity of MS' diction, so that the meaning of her songs came out loud and clear and touched the hearts of even the simplest of listeners. Under Sadasivam's watchful guidance, MS continued her music lessons from Semmangudi Iyer, and expanding her performance repertoire with instructions from diverse composers like Papanasam Sivan, T L Venkatrama Iyer, Dwijendralal Roy, and Pandit Narayanrao Vyas. Siddheshwari Devi of Benaras lovingly taught her the basics of Hindustani classical music, while she learnt *bhajans* from Srinivasa Rao. The famous Carnatic singer Brinda instructed MS on the art of rendering *padams* and *javali.* At Sadasivam's behest, MS applied herself and learnt to speak languages like Kannada, Telugu, Hindi and even Sanskrit. Without stifling her creative freedom, Sadasivam charted and propelled MS' entire musical career with rare insight and understanding of her temperament and potential.

The beauty and appeal of MS' singing had painted a luster of divinity on her charming, good looks. This held out a strong lure for film-makers of that era, when artistes like K L Saigal, Kanan Bala, Suraiya and Noor Jehan used their singing prowess to set the silver screen aglow. MS was persuaded to do just four film roles in her life. The first was that of an idealistic heroine in a movie based on a Munshi Premchand novel. The second was from the immortal love story of Shakuntala, followed by a male portrayal of Narada Muni in the mythological film *Savitri*. All these films met with great commercial success, with their songs becoming extremely popular. The film *Savitri* was accepted by MS so that she could hand over her remuneration to Sadasivam, who, with his writer friend R Krishnamurthy, was planning to launch a new Tamil weekly named Kalki. MS was to do just one more film later in life. But before that historic event, she scaled further heights in the Carnatic music world, to become the most popular and the highest paid concert artiste. Music stalwart Musiri Subramania Iyer once commented that organizers who needed to raise funds vied with one another to hold MS concerts!

Nationalistic at heart, it must have rankled MS and Sadasivam that the north-south dividing line in Indian classical music, had remained like a dark, long stain. While some rare north Indian singers like Paluskar and Saigal were able to make a place in the hearts of the south Indians as well, no south Indian musician could successfully return the favour. So MS saw it as a golden opportunity when she began to receive invitations for concerts up north. With meticulous prior preparation with Sadasivam, MS went on to conquer the first bastion of north Indian classical music—the Vikramaditya Music Festival in Bombay. She poured her heart out in presenting amidst an august gathering her favourite raga *Sankarabharanam!* Major stalwarts of Hindustani classical music joined in the thunderous applause that followed! MS was personally congratulated by the likes of Bade Ghulam Ali Khan, Omkarnath Thakur, Amir Khan, Pannalal Ghosh, Roshanara Begum and Ravi Shankar. The music-loving audience too got a taste of what they didn't even know they were missing! Once this barrier crumbled, MS' popularity began to spread freely and fluently to many more parts of the country. Her repertoire now included some well-chosen *bhajans* of Meerabai, Tulsidas, Kabir, and Guru Nanak, which sent her steadily expanding Hindi-speaking audiences into devotional ecstasy. Jawaharlal Nehru became an admirer of her music, and Mahatma Gandhi invited her to sing his favourite *bhajans* at his prayer meetings...

When Kasturba Gandhi passed away, Sadasivam, prompted by the great Raja Gopalachari, decided to raise funds in the south for her memorials. MS performed in five concerts in a string to help raise adequate money. Gandhi-ji conveyed his gratitude and blessings in a touching hand-written note inscribing his name in Tamil. Like the holy waters of the Cauveri, the stream of pure devotion began to flow unhindered in Subbulakshmi's music. Gradually it flooded her entire being, her very existence! She began to see God everywhere, and in everything. The devotion in her heart for the Almighty also manifested as affection and compassion towards humanity. MS and Sadasivam quietly made a pledge. Henceforth, MS would sing only for charitable causes. For projects that were dedicated to social, religious and humanitarian missions. Not everyone knows, that perpetual royalties from the treasures of Subbulakshmi's recorded music, bestsellers, sung in many languages, and the huge collections from her thousands of concerts have been the lifelines of many worthy projects all over the country. The entire amount of the Ramon Magsaysay award, which she received later in life, was also respectfully donated to charity.

Subbulakshmi's conquest of the north, and thereby the hearts of all Indians, was completed with the most dramatic impact conceivable! It came in the form of her fourth and last feature film, Meera! It bridged many points at many levels. North India with south India...history with the present...art with life...and above all, the human spirit with the divine! Mounted lovingly and lavishly by director Ellis Dungan and produced by Sadasivam, Meera marked the culmination of Subbulakshmi's charisma and creativity. Released at a difficult period for the just liberated India, Meera went on to unite hearts all across the country and create new hallmarks of artistic and musical success! Poetess Sarojini Naidu, the 'Nightingale of India', made a special appearance in the beginning of the movie to introduce MS to the world audience! And after witnessing the inaugural screening in the presence of Lord and Lady Mountbatten, and the entire Cabinet of India's ministers, including Pandit Nehru, Sarojini Naidu announced that MS was more deserving of the title, 'Nightingale of India'! Those who did not believe it, should only listen to the divine songs of Meera. It is quite possible that with Subbulakshmi's angelic, ethereal screen presence merging with the image of the Rajasthani saint poet, and her devotion laden voice singing the immortal bhajans, the celluloid wonder Meera must have converted countless non-believers into devotees!

Mahatma Gandhi, another MS admirer, who was depressed and away from all this revelry due to the raging Hindu Muslim friction, was not forgotten either. MS recorded a special Meera *bhajan* "Hari Tum Haro" and presented it to the Mahatma on his birthday. This favourite *bhajan* of the heart-broken 'Saint of the Freedom Struggle' was broadcast immediately after the radio announcement of his assassination just four months later! Gandhiji had once commented, "Subbulakshmi, while singing, comes closer to God, and the same happens to those who listen to her." The void left in Subbulakshmi's life after the death of Gandhiji was somewhat filled by the affection she received from Pandit Nehru, who attended every MS concert in Delhi, and was heard exclaiming, "What am I, a mere Prime Minister, before the Queen of Music!" Similar adulation was showered upon MS by the future prime minister Indira Gandhi as well. Quite expectedly, when the National Awards were first instituted in 1954, MS was honoured with a Padma Bhushan. And by the end of the century it was the nation, which honoured itself by conferring the ultimate, Bharat Ratna on M S Subbulakshmi.

Once MS became a national celebrity, the powers-that-be always endorsed the view that she could be an ideal cultural ambassador for India to the world. The various festivals of India abroad had MS gracing the inaugural concerts. Her overseas tours began in 1963 with a special invitation to sing for two days at the world famous Edinburgh Cultural Festival which showcases the best of world talent. What pioneers like Ravi Shankar were doing in the outer world for north Indian classical music, MS set out to achieve for her Carnatic music.

The resounding success at Edinburgh was followed by many other programmes in Europe. The United Nation's secretary general invited MS to perform at its General Assembly in New York, where, in the midst of a host of international celebrities, MS presented her devotional gems, followed by an English song dedicated to world peace, which was written specially for the occasion by Raja Gopalachari. This rare melodious glimpse of the quintessential India was received with thunderous applause. The UN concert opened the gates for a seven-week tour of America with dazzling performances at fifteen centres. MS returned to New York later in 1977, when her performance at the Carnegie Hall made the music critic of the New York Times exclaim, " Subbulakshmi's vocal contribution transcends words...a revelation to the Western ears..." The Far East wasn't far either. Along her journey to receive the Magsaysay Award in Manila, MS touched the hearts of Tokyo, Osaka, Hong Kong, and Bangkok with a string of barrier-shattering recitals.

It is not just her Hindi *bhajans* that made the north notice and admire MS. Her contribution to India's national integration included an unprecedented achievement of opening up the 'Hindustani ear' to the exotic appeal of her Carnatic music. Her God-gifted voice, and her personal style, embellished with the best of Carnatic musical idioms, spoke eloquently even to those music lovers who did not know a word of Tamil. Indeed, Sangeet Kalanidhi M S Subbulakshmi's pure Carnatic roots, like her favourite jasmine, produced flowers whose fragrance transcended all cultural and religious confines! In entranced pursuit of this fragrance, countless music loving souls have repeatedly reached nirvana!

It must be this very essence of her music that transforms into an ethereal glow around her when she prays silently to her God, or even smiles at a simple human soul. Something that even the contemporary saints and god-men have recognized in MS. Mahesh Yogi had said to MS, "You have already reached where we are trying to reach". Saints like the Sage of Kanchi, Sankaracharya of Kamakoti Peetam, Swami Ranganathan of the Ramakrishna Math, Anandamayi Maa, and Satya Saibaba, have all showered their personal admiration and blessings on MS. Through her life and living, MS has also been the epitome of traditional Hindu womanhood.

Subbulakshmi's genius may have begun as a gift of God, but discerning listeners also know that her music was refined and crafted with great *sadhana*. It can be explained as a unique chemistry of *rasa,* where the purity and devotion of her heart, her appropriate choice of *raga* and *sahitya,* her balance of mood and technique, her timing and voice modulation, and the poetic harmony between the singer and the listener, the conscious and the unconscious—everything combined like magic during a performance! As her lifelong secretary, K R Atmanathan mentions, "She may have learnt from any vidwan, but when she sang, it became her own piece. The world might possibly see more talented singers, but there will never be another MS."

The title Bharat Ratna, the *jewel* of India, conferred on MS in 1998, must have lost some of its luster, because her husband, who had helped polish a rough diamond into that ultimate *jewel* through lifelong love and dedication, was conspicuous by his absence!

A ninety-five-year old Sadasivam had just lost the race of life against a galloping pneumonia by the margin of a single calendar year! Today, at eighty-seven, M S Subbulakshmi does not sing to any audience anymore. But people from far and wide flock to her Chennai bungalow hoping for a *darshan* of the living legend. They return quietly with a subtle radiance on their faces. Like pilgrims, who have just had a glimpse of a goddess.

Living Memories...

At the age of divine innocence

With Mother Teresa

Just married

With a legend of Hindustani music, the great Alladiya Khan

With her favourite vocalist Bade Ghulam Ali Khan

Ethereal look, sublime music

Playing Narada Muni in a film

In a scene from the legendary 'Meera'

With Mahatma Gandhi

With the Queen of England

With Sarojini Naidu and Padit Jawaharlal Nehru

With India's first president,
Dr. Rajendra Prasad

The epitome of beauty and talent

Taking centre stage

In the words of MS...

About her mother:

"My mother (Shanmukhavadivu of Madurai) was also my music guru. What little knowledge of music I possess today, I owe, in the first instance, to my mother."

About her husband:

"I owe everything I have achieved to my Pati Dev. By his loving care, he is my parent; by his unerring guidance, he is my preceptor. He gave artistic shape and definition to my ideas on music, which were almost running wild."

About raga rendition:

"The 'ragaswarupa' must be established at once. Don't keep the listener in suspense whether it is Purvikalyani or Panthuvarali. This difference must come through in the way you dwell on the notes common to both the ragas, even before the introduction of dissimilar notes..."

About Bade Ghulam Ali Khan:

"What a moving, melting voice Khan Saheb had! He used to put his entire heart and soul into his singing. I wish I could have heard him oftener..."

About Raja Gopalachari:

"Raja-ji...that 'Purushottama' is the personification of virtue...It is his blessing and the force of his personality that have watched over our welfare at all times..."

About Mahatma Gandhi's assassination:

"When I heard the terrible news, I fainted with sorrow!"

About music and divinity:

"Indian music is oriented solely to the end of divine communication. If I have done something in this respect, it is entirely due to the grace of the Almighty who has chosen my humble self as a tool..."

About herself:

"I am only a singer who just sings where I am asked to sing..."

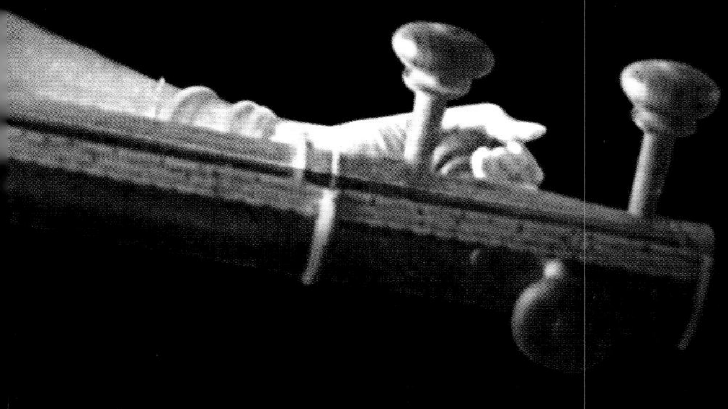

N. RAJAM

Rajam, in front of the portrait of her guru, Omkarnath Thakur

Along the march of civilization, the bow that shot arrows must have been followed by the bow that made music. Otherwise, our claim to have made progress would have a hollow ring to it. In fact, today, if the modern civilized world looks for just one living symbol of human refinement in mind and soul, in art, craft and music, that symbol would be the ever elegant and eloquent violin—the bowed musical instrument that strikes a common chord across cultural divides.

It was amidst the lingering refrain of this violin that a musical prodigy was born in Kerala, in a family that was already making music for six generations. She was a girl child, with dark eyes and an angelic smile. But her soft features were complemented with shoulders and arms that looked eager to wield the bow over the classical violin and make it sing! In spirited defiance to a violent civilization, at a time when the Second World War was about to explode!

By the time she was three, N Rajam was actually holding the violin with open arms. Her father, A Narayana Iyer, was a renowned Carnatic *Vidwan,* an excellent violinist who performed and taught classical music to students with great artistry and devotion. He was also a man of vision who had distilled the essence of his rich ancestral music legacy and through his own relentless research had created a unique violin technique of *Gayaki Ang,* based on qualities of the human voice and the veena. He was a man who worshipped music and followed a simple lifestyle bound by strict discipline. Qualities that were imbibed by his many students and his gifted children quite naturally. His son, T N Krishnan grew up to become a renowned violinist in the Carnatic style. For daughter Rajam, it was to be a slightly different story with a unique historic twist.

Given the perfect environment and an ideal guru, the journey that began with holding the first violin in a delicate grip at the tender age of three, took a somewhat predictable path. With the natural facility of a child prodigy, little Rajam learnt the finer points of classical Carnatic music and mastered the *Gayaki Ang* researched by her father. Soon, the tone of her violin became an extension of her musical voice...the flow as natural as humming a tune under one's breath. Before she was ten-years old, Rajam had already become a radio artiste, and her first historic radio broadcast was in the national programme, where she accompanied the legendary M S Subbulakshmi!

As she entered her teens, however, Rajam's musical journey took a deviation, which was as deep as it was dramatic. That was when she took a decision, which was going to break convention, shatter mindsets and bridge chasms in its wake! It may well have stemmed from a hidden desire nurtured by her father even before Rajam was born... Immersed as he was in Carnatic music, A Narayana Iyer had an open-minded liking for Hindustani classical music, which was further intensified by his personal exposure to stalwarts such as V D Paluskar, while he stayed in Bombay. Understandably, young Rajam was encouraged to roam free in a musical orchard where north Indian music was not a forbidden fruit. With some whispered prompting by providence, perhaps, she had already developed a liking and taste for the *khayals* and the *thumris,* via the radio and the gramophone. The likes of Bade Ghulam Ali Khan, Nissar Hussain Khan, Thirakuva *sahib* and Kanthe Maharaj-*ji* held great fascination for her eclectic ears.

Then came the momentous decision that would change the entire course of her beautifully budding career, and in the process, add some new shades to the complexion and character of the versatile violin itself! Out of the blue, as it were, a unique male voice had spiralled out of a 78-RPM record and had taken possession of her musical sensibility! The voice belonged to Pandit Omkarnath Thakur at his prime. If the *bhava,* the emotion in the voice was riveting, the passion and the appeal were utterly infectious. Omkarnath's *Malkauns* and *Nilambari,* laden with magic and mystery, beckoned her northwards. A thirteen-year-old Rajam declared that she would switch to Hindustani classical music, and learn from Pandit Omkarnath Thakur and no one else! His father and guru, who had guided her career in Carnatic music to such a promising start, however, was neither shocked nor hurt. He must have quietly smiled at the thought that his heartfelt desire of having at least one of his children pursue Hindustani classical music was destined to be fulfilled after all.

Rajam's facility with the violin by then was already remarkable! The versatile instrument that came in from the harmonic West was already

producing in her hands the most complex passages of the rhythm-driven music of southern India. A young and ambitious Rajam visualized another giant stride for the violin, where its prime quality of continuity of tone, the *swara,* could be employed in playing the north Indian ragas in full elaborate glory. Her newfound passion for Hindustani music merged with her success in pioneering the *Gayaki Ang,* and a new door in classical music was flung open! At age fifteen, she stirred the music world with a historic recital that demonstrated the undeniable possibility that with her novel *Gayaki Ang* technique, the violin could now sing *khayals* and *thumris!*

Having secured a double promotion earlier in school, Rajam found herself 'underage' for the local colleges. The Benaras Hindu University offered her a private course, and Rajam enrolled herself there, further aiding her destined gravitation towards the north. In the meanwhile, her chosen guru had reciprocated her musical feelings and Rajam's introduction into the Gwalior *Gharana* was solemnized amidst the echoes of Omkarnath's impassioned singing!

The majestic and mercurial ascents and descents of her celebrated guru's voice were at once the greatest musical inspiration to Rajam, and the toughest challenge for the innovative *gayaki* style of her violin. A magical alchemy combining diverse forces was at work within her. Strong Carnatic roots, grounded in a time-honoured family ancestry, reaching out to embrace an alien cultural ethos of the north,

On stage with her talented daughter Sangeeta Shankar

needed more than just youthful passion. It needed sustained research and application of her musical discipline for it to go beyond the initial blossoming and begin to bear permanent fruit. Within a short time, under the affectionate tutelage of Pandit Omkarnath Thakur, Rajam could emulate on her violin, not just the vocal intricacies of Pandit-ji's singing but also the *bhava* that characterized his music. By the time she was eighteen, she had already crossed a major landmark by accompanying Omkarnath Thakur on stage and receiving resounding applause and a shower of blessings from her guru.

Rajam's participation in music festivals invariably created a buzz around her as more and more listeners were exposed to this new voice and diction of the age-old violin. The impact on conventional violinists was even more significant: many adept exponents of the *gat-kari* style of playing began to switch over to the *Gayaki* ang pioneered by Rajam. With time, it was quite apparent that this *Gayaki Ang* was ideally suited to almost every form of Hindustani music—from the majestic *dhrupad* to the playful *tappa*.

While Rajam marched on as a rare and exciting performing violinist at concerts and music festivals, a parallel pursuit made her contribute to the service of music in a quiet and sustained manner. Her brilliant academic achievements, including university gold medals, an M.A. in Sanskrit, and a Ph.D. in music, led her to foster a scholarly career. The famous Benaras Hindu University, which had once graciously accepted an underage fresher from the south, was finally served by the same brilliant child of destiny for over four decades in music education, including a long and enriching tenure of deanship.

Over those four decades of disciplined life, her reputation as a performing musician and a pioneering violinist has systematically swelled and has reached the far corners of the music world. Concert halls of the West have echoed with thunderous applause, as incredulous expressions on the faces of musicians and musicologists have melted into joyous enchantment! Listening to the quintessential Indian music of pristine classical purity being coaxed out of a popular Western instrument by an unassuming apostle of charm and serenity, has often been a living testimony to the universality of music. The East and the West have rarely embraced each other with such palpable yet symbolic significance. Her concert conquests of Canada, America, New Zealand, Australia and the European countries have not only fanned audience interest in Indian classical music, but have also encouraged students and even professional violinists of the world to study her technique and seek her guidance in enhancing their craft.

Acclaimed scholars and dedicated academicians, historically, do not shine for long under the concert spotlights. Dr N Rajam's long and illustrious track record as a major solo violinist continues to dismiss such precedents with disdain. Aside from her very many memorable solo recitals, music lovers over the last decades remember with a great surge of nostalgic refrain her sublime *jugalbandis* with many other legendary instrumentalists like Pandit Ram Narayan, Pandit Hariprasad Chaurasia, Dr N Ramani and Pandit VG Jog. And of course, some privileged audiences will never forget her string of landmark *jugalbandis* with the large-hearted Ustad Bismillah Khan. Despite the age difference, their temperament was well-matched and so was their unique *gayaki* style, elevating their chosen instruments into extensions of their musical persona. It took time for the hypnotized audience to realize when the violin paused and the shehnai took over, and who complemented whom in that magical interface of sublime virtuosity.

Both in life and music, Rajam has remained a purist. For someone residing so high in the music lovers' esteem, her feet have been firmly on the ground. In charmed harmony with her supportive, music-loving husband, she lives a simple and worshipful life, and continues to excel in her art and serve the cause of pure classical music through concerts, tours, international workshops, and her easy and warm human interactions. In respectful memory of her guru Pandit Omkarnath Thakur, she organizes annual music festivals, which regularly bring stalwarts and emerging talents on the same platform. As 'professor emeritus' of the BHU, she is still very alive to the cause and status of music education.

And while her own brilliant daughter and disciple, Sangeeta Shankar, is already an established violinist, and her grandchildren too are happily initiated into classical music, Dr Rajam feels passionately for the growing number of flowering talents that are in danger of withering away for want of opportunities to perform.

In this era of unabashed self-projection and stage-managed career paths, Rajam quietly follows the dictates of her family tradition of self-effacing reticence and genuine humility in the face of achievements and adulation. But even in a state of inner poise her unfathomable contributions to the magic of classical violin surfaces with stunning eloquence within just a few glides of her majestic bow. And a lifetime's contentment shines through a single flash of her angelic smile.

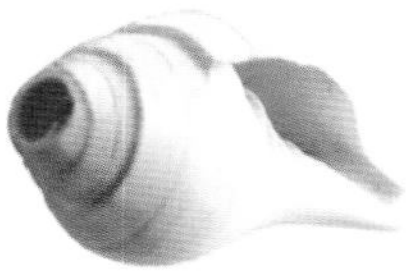

Living Memories...

Ready for the violin at age three

Making magic with Zakir Hussain

Under her father's supervision

The stealer of hearts

In perfect bonding with her violin

In charge of Music education at the Benaras Hindu University

With fellow violinist from the Western world, Yehudi Menuhin

Flanked by her husband and Prime Minister Indira Gandhi

Teaching them young

Jugalbandi with shehnai-nawaz Bismillah Khan

Violin & shehnai. Jugalbandi with Bismillah Khan

In company of film starAmitabh Bachchan, classical dancer Raja Reddy, and her music loving husband

Q. Why did you choose a Western instrument like the violin to play Indian classical music?

A. *The violin has always been played in our family. Besides, when you call it Western, do you know that the violin is very similar to an ancient bowed instrument mentioned in Sangeet Ratnakara? It was called Ravan Hatha. I believe it was taken out of our country long ago and has returned in the shape and complexion of today's violin.*

Q. Which instrument would you choose if you were not a violinist?

A. *I just love the violin; nothing comes close to it. Even if I am born again, I would like to be a violinist!*

Q. What were you in your previous birth? Can you guess?

A. *I do not know. Must have been a musician. Otherwise such early and deep involvement with music is inexplicable.*

Q. You began learning music at a tender age, did you ever feel that you have missed out on the fun of a normal, carefree kind of childhood?

A. *I was very scared of my father's strictness in terms of discipline. I had virtually no other childhood activities except hours and hours of concentrated music. I may have felt bad for fleeting moments, but looking back, I have no regrets. I am happy I gave my all to music and eventually achieved something worthwhile.*

Q. What is your attitude towards light classical music?

A. *I like it very much. I have taken training in light classical music from Pandit Mahadev Prasad Mishra. He used to sing Benarasi thumri very well. In fact, in my view, singing a thumri well is much more difficult than singing Khayal.*

Q. Have you ever desired to take up vocal music? Perhaps when you were younger?

A. *Well, what I play is essentially vocal. Even when I learnt Carnatic music, there was only the*

vocal style in all Carnatic instrumental music.

Q. What are your favourite ragas? And have you created any new ragas?

A. *Darbari...Bageshri...Bhairavi...Jhinjhoti...are some of my favourites. And about creating new ragas, well, I do not believe in it. So much has been handed down by our forefathers...even if one dives into that oceanic depth there's no end. And although I have nothing against those who try their hand at creating new ragas, I myself find it futile. Besides, it is no big thing to combine notes and create new ragas.*

Q. Any response to Western music? And say, fusion?

A. *I know nothing about Western music; never had the opportunity, since I was mostly in Benaras. And I am not enamoured by fusion. I am a confirmed purist.*

Q. Some people say Indian classical music is dying. They are worried.

A. *Not at all true. If it had to die it would have died long ago. It has survived many eclipses over the years. It has shone again, and is in front of us in all its glory! It has an inherent strength; it can take care of itself. Nobody needs to worry about its survival or continuance. Modern trends that might appear to pose a threat, are like gusts of wind. They'll come and go. Classical music is eternal.*

Q. One last question: Does one have to be deeply spiritual to become a great Indian classical musician?

A. *I would put it this way: going deep into Indian classical music will definitely make you spiritual.*

N. RAMANI

When Lord Krishna had walked the earth, he may not have spent much time south of the Vindhyas, but the strains of his flute must have wafted across, and lingered over the southern landscapes for centuries. Indeed, Krishna's human avatar may have been guided by cosmic promise and purpose, but his music was fluent and free. It energized the elements, enriched the flora and fauna, and awakened the human soul, reminding us of our true potential and our forgotten divinity.

He showed us the simple instrument of his music, the bamboo flute in his hands...and as he put it to his lips, he left behind an enduring image, an eternal message for mankind.

With all its sensuous qualities, the human body is an instrument, and the fulfillment of residing in it, is in making music with it. The bamboo flute is both a symbol, and a device, which nature has placed in our grasp, inviting us to make music with our thought and action, our heart and soul, with the force and warmth of our very breath. In repose, it is an expression of human potential; in full play it is a celebration of human accomplishment.

When Natesan Ramani had first picked up the bamboo flute in playful intrigue, perhaps he wasn't aware how blessed he was, and what

In front of a portrait of his guru, T R Mahalingam

power and magic had drifted within his tender grasp. As a child of four or five, he was oblivious of the fact that he had taken birth on the same sacred soil where the great 'trinity' of Carnatic music had been born. Nor was he actively conscious of the fact that his own uncle was perhaps the greatest living exponent of the Carnatic flute.

Ramani's maternal grandfather had no male child, so Ramani was a pampered boy invited to live with him, lighting up the premises with his energetic presence. But very soon, it was little Ramani who had more to gain from the arrangement, because Aazhiyur Narayanaswami Iyer, his grandfather, was a great flautist and a renowned music guru. Under his loving care, almost as a swan takes to swimming, little Ramani was inducted into music and the flute, in an atmosphere where many other students learnt a variety of musical instruments. Thanks to the energized ambience and his guru's blessings, Ramani's progress with the flute was so rapid that he soon began to guide even older students through the intricacies of flute craft. His *arangetram,* the first public performance, was held at the holy shrine of Chikkil Singara Velan temple, and the eight-year-old Ramani was applauded heartily by the enchanted audience.

However, an event, more significant than his *arangetram,* happened the following year in 1943. At a concert in the nearby town of Nagapattam, young Ramani heard his uncle, the celebrated genius T R Mahalingam for the very first time! He was as proud as he was thrilled with the magic of his flute. In his exuberance, Ramani went and replayed before the great 'Mali' some of the intricate pieces he had absorbed at the recital. Mahalingam was impressed by the youngster's understanding of *shruti* and *laya,* and had blessed his talented nephew. He was even willing to take Ramani under his wings immediately, if he came to the city of Madras.

The meeting opened up a whole new world of fervent pursuit, as Ramani began to commute to Madras to mature further as a flautist under Mali's guidance, and at the same time, he attended to his formal education at the local school. Within two years, Ramani accompanied Mali on an important concert on stage, and a discerning audience of rasikas was delighted to see that Ramani held enough promise to become a worthy successor to the eccentric genius T R Mahalingam. In 1945 itself, the All India Radio of Thiruvananthapuram invited an eleven-year-old Ramani to air his first radio recital!

Like the continuity of mellifluous notes, one music milestone led to another. While Ramani began to regularly accompany Uncle Mali on stage, the other contemporary stalwarts

In the family puja room, with his mother

of Carnatic music were eager to experience him as an accompanist. Playing with an entire spectrum of music legends like Tiruppampuram Swaminatha Pillai, Palladam Sanjiva Rao, Ariyakudi Ramanuja Iyengar, Chembai Vaidyanatha Bhagavathar, Madurai Mani Iyer and Alathoor Brothers widened his repertoire and enriched his musical vision. *Sangeet sabhas* and music centres in Madras began to vie with each other to get the young genius to grace their concert stage. Similar enthusiasm got replicated in other culture capitals like Bombay, Delhi and Bangalore.

Those were the days when rivalries were healthy and practitioners of the same art were like a band of brothers. Everyone inspired everyone to become better and blossom together. Money was never a priority; music was a reward unto itself.

As Ramani began to realize that the Carnatic flute was not just his source of joy but also his responsibility, he began to inspect various types of flute and research the bamboo flute deeply. Although he never got to meet Pannalal Ghosh who had brought classical status and concert glory to the north Indian flute, Ramani studied his recordings and the characteristic differences between them. He also took a close look at some western flutes. Since the transition from the mike-less era of concert performances to the advent of loud speakers, there was a growing preference for lower pitch instruments. Guru Mahalingam had already ventured into the eighth hole of the bamboo flute in his exploits of the lower octave. Ramani began to explore the tonal qualities of different types of flute. He ushered in the long bass flute for a longer reach on the lower octave. This invested his devotional compositions with an unprecedented mellow and sublime emotion. Even the size and placement of the holes on the flute are closely related to the facility with which his fingering and blowing techniques create magic on the steadily evolving bamboo flute. Apart from his expansive music knowledge, the benefits of such technical research too are shared with music lovers, students and musicologists in lecture demonstrations all over the world.

Ramani's open mind about the universality of music has had a rich reciprocal effect. Ravi Shankar heard him over the radio at an airport transit lounge and was so intrigued that he sought him out the very next day, and got to know him better. This prepared the grounds for a perpetual string of *jugalbandis* between Ramani and music maestros from the north.

Posing sportingly for the camera with a showpiece glass flute

Ramani's very first *jugalbandi* with a Hindustani musician was with Hariprasad Chaurasia at the Balasubramania Sangeetha Sabha in 1970. It impressed everyone in the audience, including Ravi Shankar, and a fragrant new romance between the music streams of the north and the south was in the air! Once the horizon expanded, it beckoned Ramani's musical mind even further. As he began to travel to some of the Western centre of music on concert tours, there was free and fervent exchange of ideas with Western virtuosos, leading into unprecedented collaborative experiments. The East and the West indeed found a thousand meeting points on the musical spectrum of seven basic notes. The family of metallic Western flutes with its engineered precision found a melodious counterpoint in the simple Indian bamboo flute tuned lovingly by Nature.

Enriched and energized by his cross culture adventures, Ramani's musical exploits found some new excitement on his home terrain as well. He explored the spirit of *jugalbandi* within the Carnatic musical milieu itself. In Coimbatore, Ramani presented a *jugalbandi* accompanied by duet mridangams. His guru Mahalingam was present at the concert and was inspired to take the experiment further. Soon the celebrated guru-shishya duo was seen together on stage in a historic concert with double mridangams. This ensemble of melody and rhythm encouraged a new era of experimentations in the tradition bound Carnatic concerts. All major centres of music, including the most circumspect, Madras, sat up and bestowed appreciative acknowledgement. This was also the time when Lalgudi Jayaraman had introduced his novel

Ramani, with his wife

violin-venu-veena concept in collaborative performance, and Ramani participated in it with his characteristic spirit of camaraderie.

All the collaborative accomplishments of Ramani are richly coloured by his individualistic style of handling the bamboo flute. Even in the most intense spirit of merger, Ramani's individuality shines through as an enriching factor. His subtle yet compelling sense of aesthetics guides the overall performance towards a listeners' delight. Critics the world over have been almost unanimous in appreciating Ramani's panoramic range of power and beauty, residing within the scope of his simple, unassuming piece of bamboo. Ramani's continued conquest of the Western world of music spans decades. It began in 1962, with his gracious response to the invitation of the Asia Society, New York. It was probably the very first time that the Carnatic flute cast its magic on the international stage. The same year, Ramani toured America with S Balachander, the veena maestro. This triggered off a series of concert tours of the US, Europe, Canada, Singapore, Australia and the Middle East. The Munich Olympics arena heard Ramani's inspiring flute in the spirit of 'stronger, faster and higher' in 1972. He has been wielding his magic wand over diverse music audiences spread over thirty

international concert tours. Much of his melodic magic is captured in music albums with prestigious music labels of the world.

Many original compositions in the form of *pallavis, varnams* and *tillanas* have danced out of Ramani's prolific flute. His generous nature, like the breath put into his flute, has found many laudable outlets. Several charity concerts by Ramani have been lovingly dedicated to the benefit of the socially underprivileged. His lecture demonstrations, all over the world, has had no other motivation beyond the proliferation of classical Carnatic music. Despite the demands of a hectic jet-set lifestyle, Dr Ramani has enthusiastically served worthy organizations like the Music Academy, Chennai, for over fifteen years.

Of course, the greatest *dana,* or gift, for Ramani has been *vidya dana,* the generous gift of knowledge. Domestic sessions of tuition and training have, over the years, expanded into a dream like vision. The rich, multi flavoured harvest of his musical investments unto himself, through years of exploration, interface and concert experience, is placed on a platter, as an offering to the divine spirit of music, to the cause of Lord Krishna's bamboo flute...

In a spirit similar to his many *jugalbandis* with the Hindustani flute maestro Hariprasad Chaurasia, where the music of the north and the south have repeatedly merged and complemented each other, Dr. Ramani has entered the orbit of a historic and global grand design. Like Chaurasia's emerging vision of making the melody of Krishna's flute resonate all around the modern world through his 'Vrindavan Gurukul', Ramani has his own dream child. The steadily proliferating centres of Ramani's Academy of Flute are making the Carnatic flute enticingly accessible to those citizens of the world who are gradually waking up to their inner melodies...

In an agreeable irony of history, this spontaneous north-south *jugalbandi* of the great Indian vision, has the power and charisma to unite even the East-West polarities of world culture. It surely has the blessings of Lord *Venugopal,* the greatest flautist of all time.

Living Memories...

With his guru, the legendary T R Mahalingam

With Lalgudi Jayaraman

At home with the home maker

An endearing image

Tuning a tanpura

With an American disciple

Breaking bread with Balamuralikrishna

On stage with Lalgudi Jayaraman

With the smaller flute

In penance

With tabla legend Allarakha

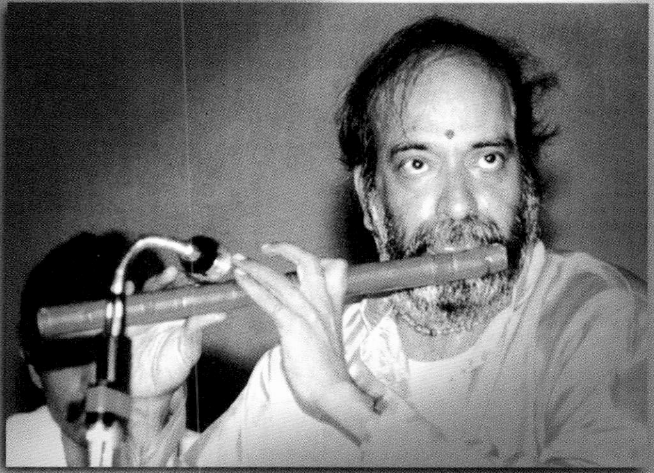

In concert

With Rajeev Gandhi & Narsimha Rao

With Lalgudi Jayaraman

With Ravi Shankar, Allarakha and Umayalpuram K Sivaraman

Being honoured by legendary film star Shivaji Ganeshan

Q. Who were the Carnatic maestros you accompanied at the beginning of your career?

A. *Palghat Mani Iyer, M S Gopalakrishnan, T N Krishna, Lalgudi Jayaraman...and many others.*

Q. When you began to perform jugalbandis with Hindustani Classical maestros, was it a spirit of challenge that prevailed, or was it all in friendly harmony?

A. *There was no harsh note of challenge. We tried to bring out the best in each other and explore common grounds. For example, there are many common ragas...one begins and the other takes over and expands on it and so on...Both parties learn a lot in the process.*

Q. You played many jugalbandis with Pandit Hariprasad Chaurasia. Who were the others you remember playing with?

A. *Pandit Ram Narayan...Dr N Rajam...Pandit V G Jog...Ustad Sultan Khan...*

Q. Ever played with vocalists?

A. *With Pandit Ajay Chakravarty in Calcutta. I must tell you, I have also played with Dr. Balamuralikrishna! We had an understanding; he sang fast notes, and I matched him in a slow tempo. It was very interesting.*

Q. Did you hear Pannalal Ghosh's flute?

A. *I never got to meet him, but I heard his recordings. I noticed he could hold his breath without a break for over a minute! And what depth of emotion! His contribution to the classical flute is tremendous.*

Q. Once, early in your career, you played with a German flautist?

A. *Yes. The Max Muller institute arranged a concert with this famous European musician, in order to show the difference between both systems.*

Q. Did you listen to any Hindustani music in your younger days for inspiration?

A. *Well, I used to enjoy listening to Ustad Bade Ghulam Ali Khan, Ustad Amir Khan, Ustad Bismillah Khan...they are all a delight to listen to.*

Q. Have you ever been asked to play for films?

A. *Yes, early in my career there were a few south Indian films I played for.*

Q. What about dance?

A. *I have admired Kalakshetra's achievements in dance. My favourite danseuse was the legendary Bala Saraswati. Once, long ago, I played for Rukhmini Devi...*

Q. You have been doing some research on Asian flute music? Do they have a legacy in flute?

A. *Their flute is largely folk-based. It is only in India where we have the flute that plays classical music.*

Q. In your lifestyle there is a lot of spirituality. Is that how your bhakti music compositions overwhelm the audience?

A. *The compositions of the saintly trinity of Carnatic music are themselves full of power and appeal. One just needs to present them with the right kind of bhava, emotions, and purity of mind and heart. As for lifestyle, I used to keep penance of silence, mauna, on every Thursday* *for many years in a row. I used to eat only once and visit the temple. This used to help my breathing and would also help in a cleansing process. I have also practised pranayam for better breath control. That was crucial.*

Q. You have had an open mind about the universality of music. You have studied Western flutes also. Did you ever get involved in fusion music?

A. *As Indians, we are truly fortunate to have such a great depth and vast legacy of music. Even for the pursuit of pure flute, I feel, one lifetime is not enough. Why go after something like fusion? More money? More popularity? Or, more titles? It is definitely not for me. Exchanging ideas and gathering knowledge from exotic sources is one thing; mixing the two in performance is quite another.*

Q. Your son Thyagarajan has already established himself as an eminent flautist. How is the younger generation in general responding to the appeal of the classical flute?

A. *Even my grandson Master Atul Kumar is maturing fast. A lot of youngsters are taking up the flute in right earnest. Even children. It is a happy sign. Then the various centres of my Academy of Flute in the West are expanding well. Today's generation has a lot more facilities and opportunities for learning and training. There are sponsorships, there are scholarships. And there is awareness...*

Q. Any message for the young aspirants?

A. *Have self-imposed discipline, devote time and be dedicated to your chosen art. Direct contact with one's guru is also very important. Have faith in God.*

RAM
NARAYAN

Held close to the musician's heart, and caressed by his gliding hands, this magical instrument comes enticingly close to creating the music of the human voice. And its earliest reference in Indian music dates back to the times beyond recorded history. Indeed, the saga of the sarangi is a major tributary to the river-like journey of Indian classical music itself! From the temples to the palaces, from the kings to the courtesans, from a rich tradition of loyal accompaniment to the recent elevation to solitary accomplishment...the sarangi has come a long way. And if it is a little fatigued in the course of such a long and meandering journey, it surely has found the right lap to feel at home, and the most loving caress in the world to rejuvenate its spirit. Yes, destiny appears to have placed the sarangi in the able and sensitive hands of Pandit Ram Narayan.

The time and place of Pandit Ram Narayan's birth are both touched with history and legend. He was born on a Christmas Day at Udaipur, in Mewar—the historic land blessed by the valour of Rana Pratap, the wisdom of Rana Kumbh, and of course, the poetry and music of Mirabai.

Young Ram Narayan's very first encounter with the sarangi was itself an indication of the power of providence. While his father played the esraj and the dilruba, no one had seen a sarangi before in the house of his birth. Until, a *sadhu* from distant Hardwar came for a short visit. *Ganga Guru,* as he was called, left behind an ageing *jogia sarangi* with multiple fractures and three precious strings. The strange and silent instrument hardly served any major purpose other than being a fond memento of the holy man...until one fine day, a five-year-old Ram Narayan decided that he would like to make friends with this toy.

Ram Narayan's father was indulgent enough to get the instrument repaired. He then took that opportunity as his first guru to introduce young Ram Narayan to the seven notes of music...on the sarangi itself. Since neither of the two had ever handled the sarangi, a rather maverick finger technique evolved in the process. And little did they realize that the seeds of a future sarangi playing *gharana* were being sown around their inspired overture to the *jogia* sarangi. Ram Narayan became obsessed with this tuneful toy and began to progress very rapidly, prompting his father to seek out established sarangi players in Udaipur who could take over the task of teaching his son further. And when the new gurus wanted the young boy to give up his strange and unique technique and relearn the conventional way of approaching the time-honoured instrument, the father requested them not to force his son to change his finger technique, but to move further along the same style. The young enthusiastic prodigy had already travelled a long way, and his father, a man of vision, had already glimpsed a bright, musical boulevard beckoning ahead.

Most sarangi players, those days, were not really ideal gurus. Their world revolved around the swirling, gleaming costumes of the court danseuse, their limited repertoire of musical gems were to be strewn around places where the focus was not always on the music. Young Ram Narayan realized soon enough that he had to move around in search of excellence, and his further progress would be an adventurous journey. He drew inspiration from his intimate deity Lord Dattatreya, who was known to have enriched his own music from several exotic sources.

Thus, after his father's initial thrust in the right direction, Ram Narayan's second real guru was a saintly sarangi player, who was not a willing teacher of music. He wandered around like a *ramta jogi* playing his sarangi around holy places like temples and gurdwaras. In the beginning, he may have been largely oblivious of the fact that a young boy was hovering around his spiritual orbit like a satellite, and was quietly imbibing some of his rare and soul

In front of the portrait of his departed wife

stirring art. Like an ardent mendicant, Ram Narayan collected enough gems from him to treasure for a lifetime. As his ordained journey into the world of classical music ran deep, his chosen instrument, the sarangi, began to flower in hitherto unseen shades and tones. He reached out to master vocalists far and wide, and learnt from Pandit Mahadev Prasad of Maihar. As his instrument began to sing, the ragas and the raginis began to dance around the voice-like tones of his hundred-hued *'Sau-rangi'*.

Inspired by the most elaborative *Raga Vistaar* of Abdul Vaheed Khan of the *Kirana Gharana,* Ram Narayan became his disciple too. His sarangi, in its unique playing style, became a rare golden goblet where musical nectars from diverse streams began to churn and brim over. From an eclectic and collaborative medium, Ram Narayan dreamt of elevating the sarangi to higher realms. From a subordinate instrument of accompaniment he saw the age-old sarangi's image go through a transformation. But all this was still ensconced in the realm of his private vision, yet to be realized...

Early achievers often tread a treacherous path. Their eagerness to cross milestones distract them from soaking in the experience of the journey. But with young Ram Narayan, this mirage was diligently avoided. He did not see an achievement as a pedestal, but only as a stepping-stone to surge ahead from, and learn further. Before he could complete twelve years of age, he was invited to teach music in a couple of schools at Udaipur, a rare honour indeed for someone who had himself dropped out of formal school after the very first day of attendance! Ram Narayan even earned a good salary from these music lessons, until his guru explained to him that such a job was detrimental to his growth and learning. With a mature mind, young Ram Narayan accepted his guru's advice and gave up the job the very next day.

After perfecting his art and instrument further, with sustained dedication, a seventeen-year-old Ram Narayan went over to join the Lahore radio station as a staff artiste. Radio being the major arena for music and musicians of the times, there couldn't have been a better meeting ground for exchanging ideas and finding one's place in the world. There were at least a dozen established musicians at Lahore Radio, and each one was handpicked in order to bring in colour and diversity to the repertoire. An eclectic Ram Narayan interacted with them all, and was enriched enormously. He gained adequate insight into the music of diverse origins, regions, cultures, and even *gharanas*. Like the fabled *Hamsa,* he gained the musical wisdom to separate the milk from the mere water.

The Partition of India disrupted and dispersed many lives. Many a stream lost its course and flow. Overnight, the euphoric days of Lahore became just a cherished memory in the hearts of many radio artistes. Ram Narayan shifted base to All India Radio, Delhi for a couple of years. Then, in 1949, his instrument guided him to seek their conjoint fortunes in the emergent 'city of opportunities', the bustling, bejewelled Bombay.

Living by its own rules and reveries, the film industry of Bombay has always been a world apart. Starry-eyed, aspiring talents from all corners of the country continue to converge here to grab their share of fame and fortune. Film-making throws up a constant carnival of diverse souls celebrating their dreams and

talents on the sprawling silver screen. And at the inner circle of this moving, magical carnival of Indian cinema, walk the music makers with their magic wands. To Ram Narayan, however, film music was never the destination; it was just the path his feet had to traverse, while his mind's eye was trained unwaveringly on his destined goal. The dream merchants dealt in myriad shades of human emotions, and each one of those was extracted by their music directors, from that one generous hundred-hued instrument. Many legendary names, from Raichand Boral to Roshan, enriched themselves and their film music with the emotion charged notes emanating from Ram Narayan's eloquent sarangi. The audiences may not have always consciously realized what pulled at their heartstrings with such power and precision, but within the combined effects of acting, lighting, and other cinematic crafts, the sound of Ram Narayan's sarangi soon became an indispensable element. In fact, much of the shine and glow inherent in the golden era of film music may have come from the sarangi.

For many years in Bombay, Ram Narayan led a dual life. One revolved around the crowded recording studios; the other converged on his private hours of *sadhana*. He had begun to realize, with increasing poignancy, that God

At riyaaz with daughter Aruna

had entrusted him with the solitary mission of elevating the sarangi to the status of a *solo* instrument on the glittering platform of classical music concerts. More than perhaps any other popular instrument, his sarangi responded to all the nuances and demands of the classical form. And he had perfected its style, which was to demonstrate to the world the versatility of his chosen consort.

After Ram Narayan gave his first few solo recitals, and the audiences began to acknowledge that the sarangi was indeed an instrument capable of interpreting the ragas with style and sincerity, there was no looking back. Except perhaps to remember the saintly Ganga Guru who had planted the broken *jogia* sarangi in his house long ago. The significance of his life's mission seemed to well up in sharp focus. Other music greats like Amir Khan or Bade Ghulam Ali Khan, had set aside their sarangis, and attained immortality as vocalists. Ram Narayan too could easily have taken to singing, but providence had scripted a path-breaking role for him, and ultimately, after a long-winding journey of musical adventure he had taken his appointed place on the platform of pure classical music, where the best percussion artistes were now waiting to lend accompaniment to *his* recital!

The voice-like quality of Ram Narayan's sarangi began to impress the classical music circles all over the country. Even the south Indian artistes appreciated his style, and many of the Carnatic stalwarts felt honoured to engage him in riveting *jugalbandis*. Radio programmes (and later, television) invited a new avatar of Pandit Ram Narayan; this time as the main artiste. Disciples flocked around him with new dreams and a newfound respect for the familiar instrument.

A number of Western tours revealed a wider audience for the Indian sarangi. In style, tone and temperament, it rivalled the much-revered cello and the violin, and was lovingly placed in the same class by the mature music world. Yehudi Menuhin wrote the foreword to a major scholastic treatise co-authored by Pandit Ram Narayan and Prof. Nell Sorel, titled Indian Music in Performance published by Manchester University Press. Further meaningful exchanges happened, and concerts and festivals echoed with applause for the Indian system of soulful melodies, and Ram Narayan never forgot for a moment that his sarangi's conquests were really the triumphs of Indian classical music...

That is why today, after almost seventy years of music *sadhana,* and after his historic achievement of according sarangi its rightful place on the concert platform, Pandit Ram Narayan is much more than just a traveller who has reached his destination, or a warrior who has won his battle. He is an institution of music. A high priest whose heart oscillates between the direct joys and sorrows wrought by life and music on the one hand, and the deeper significance of the fast changing attitude of the world and society towards the very religion of music, on the other.

His inspiring wife left this world early...his brother, the legendary tabla genius Pandit Chaturlal died young...disciples have been lost to the lure of apparent glamour... his own talented son Brij Narayan has chosen the sarod over the sarangi...yes, life has offered him many shades of mixed emotions counterpoised against those countless moments of pure joy gifted by his singing sarangi. He has loved music with his life. So he is most pained today by the drifting loyalties and the sliding

Remembering his elder brother, the legendary Chaturlal

standards of sincerity and commitment he observes all around. His courageous voice is laden with genuine concern for the immediate future of Indian classical music. That's why it rings so true when it attempts to pierce the veil of euphoria created by some charismatic stalwarts who have been playing to the gallery.

But then, he hails from the land of Rana Pratap. Agreed, the current trends do not look good to his insightful eyes. But instead of letting them moisten with despair, he decides to fill them with a vision. As his battle weary sarangi lies there, lost in a silent siesta, he pats it with his bare hands. "I shall take birth again on this soil, if need be," he whispers. " I shall battle yet again for the cause of the greatest music on earth...and *you* shall once again be my chosen instrument ..."

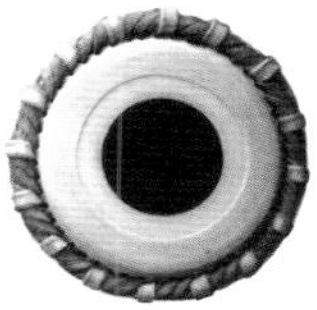

The inner joy of music

With Lord and Lady Menuhin and noted musicologist Raghava R Menon

Greeting Yehudi Menuhin

Living Memories...

With his elder brother, the tabla wizard Chaturlal

Greeting president R Venkatraman with his son, the talented sarod player Brij Narayan

Another happy moment with Yehudi Menuhin

Making a speech

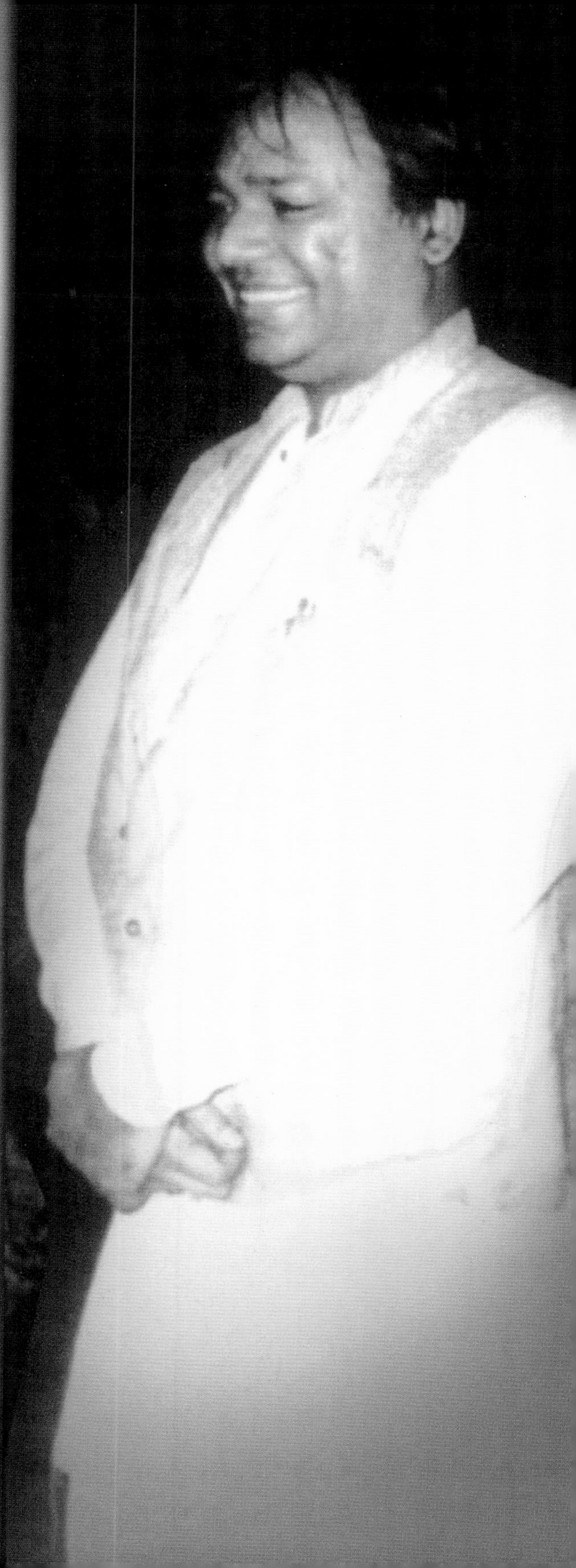

Standing tall

Q. Suppose you had not chosen the sarangi; is there any other instrument you might have considered?

A. *No. Sarangi is simply the best. The sitar, the sarod, even the veena have limitations. But the sarangi can produce all variations that our classical music may demand. There are as many as sixty different types of sarangi in various regions of India. Besides, it is one of the most original instruments in the history of music. Even the legendary Ravan played a simple sarangi. He used to tie a ghungroo to his bow to lend some taal...*

Q. A sarangi player did not enjoy a very high status in society until recently. Did your family approve of your decision to make it your chosen instrument?

A. *My father was very supportive from the beginning. He taught me 'sa re ga ma' on my chosen sarangi. And when his well-wishers had asked him with concern as to where would his son play the sarangi, he instinctively replied: on the radio! His utterance had come true before I was eighteen!*

Q. You played jugalbandis with many stalwarts from the south. What's your impression of Carnatic music?

A. *Carnatic music is very rich and has many things worth learning. Their saint musicians and vidwans have acted as 'godfather' to their music and shown very clear paths for generations to follow. They are rich in laya and taala. In fact much of the layakari that we see today is a gift from the south. Apart from Ravi Shankar, it was my brother Chaturlal-ji who had first learnt it from the Carnatic mridangam wizard Ramanadan Ishwaran. There was magic in those rhythmic patterns. I had once requested my bhaisahab to teach it to me, but he had very prudently advised me not to get into it because it could have adversely affected my 'swara-driven' music.*

Q. Has north Indian music given anything to the south?

A. *Not really. Carnatic music is basically written down and unchangeable. So not much can be imbibed from outside.*

Q. Who are the music greats whom you have heard and admired?

A. *Allauddin Khan, Abdul Karim Khan, Ali Akbar Khan, Bade Ghulam Ali Khan, Mallikarjun Mansur, Gangubai Hangal, Vilayat Khan, Bhimsen Joshi...and from the south, Allatur Brothers, MS Subbulakshmi, Palghat Mani, Palghat Raghu, Shivaraman, Mahalingam...Shall I tell you about this very touching incident about Mahalingam who was popularly known as Mali...*

Q. Yes, please do.

A. *Well, this hugely gifted Carnatic flautist loved his drink. So much so, that it virtually ruined his career. Once at a festival in France, he and I were to perform on consecutive evenings. But he was so drunk during his recital that he could barely hold his flute! Even the disciplined audience of the West had become restive, and catcalls had begun to float around. I was seated among the crowd, from there I went up on the stage and sat before him. "Play for me!" I told* *him, "forget the audience!" And he played with great effort, and played well. Later, after the applause had died down, he embraced me backstage, handed me his flute and said in a choked voice, "Keep this with you in memory of this moment. This was my last public recital!"*

Q. What a moment! And such an important lesson for artistes who indulge in vices of this nature...

A. *Yes. Even today whenever I look at that historic flute, I silently mourn its premature retirement!*

Q. What's your impression of the Western classical musicians?

A. *What impresses me most is their approach. The discipline and the seriousness are inculcated right from the beginning of their schooling. I had been invited to this institute in Switzerland. A huge place with hundreds of rooms, all devoted to various methods of teaching. The initial acceptance and categorization of students are done based on their natural artistic aptitude and also a scientific medical examination. The type of voice of a student would help decide the type of teacher who will take him under his wings. A violin player's shoulders will be checked to ensure that his bone structure and strength are suitable to hold the violin for long hours...and so on.*

Q. Their audiences are also very patient and disciplined...

A. *Yes. In fact some of my most memorable concert experiences are from the West. Once I was playing in a church. It was snowing outside the stone building, which had no heating arrangement! I myself was wearing just a silk dhoti and kurta. I knew I had to play something special to keep the audience warm and interested. I actually played for one and a half hours, and no one appeared to be bothered by the cold!*

Q. Amazing! What raga were you playing? Do you recall?

A. *Raga Shankara.*

Q. Does it have any special effect on the temperature?

A. *Well, it is actually a matter of 'sur' having the desired effect on you. Under the spell of music, feelings can undergo changes...*

Q. One has heard about Raga Deepak lighting up lamps and Raga Malhar bringing down the rains...are these really possible?

A. *Of course! Music has all the powers imaginable. But only those who are exceptionally gifted, or those who come with God's mission, or those who can immerse in deep sadhana, can actually reach such heights. Earlier musicians were totally dedicated to their art and learning. That's how they could create such divine music. I saw the great Thiraqua sahab doing rigorous riyaaz even when he was very old. When I asked him about it, he said there were still many things to be mastered so that he could continue with an advantage in his next life...*

Q. Kya baat hai!

A. *Whereas today, depth and dedication are rarely to be seen. Everyone is trying to impress. The fastest and the loudest are the ones who are popular! A raga is often replaced by the mere presentation of the scale! The aaroha- avaroha, gale ki taiyari, haath ki taiyari, gimmicky exchanges with the tabla player, sawal jawab...over emphasis on looks and attire...I see these as symptoms of deterioration...*

Q. Playing to the gallery?

A. Exactly! The real swaroop of the raga is scarcely presented. The shrutis are hardly recognized by the average musician today. Whereas such deep and vast work has been done by our sangeet sadhaks of the past...they considered music as the language of God!

Q. And today there's fusion...

A. *Fusion? I call it confusion! If there's no integrity and natural flow, there's nothing to be gained. Compare it with food and you'll know what I mean. There's food cooked at home. There's food cooked at someone else's home. And there's food bought at restaurants. I am happy only with my pure music. It is like my temple's prasad. Its taste is unique, divine.*

Q. Which of your pupils are carrying forward the Ram Narayan gharana ? Who are you grooming today in your style of sarangi playing?

A. *My daughter Aruna Narayan Kalle, and my grandson Harsh Narayan have shown a lot of promise. They have faith in my teachings; they will go far. There are some others too... While I keep visiting Europe and America on concert tours, I teach some very eager students there also. In fact, it is ironical that today I receive more honour and respect abroad than in my own country...*

Q. It is ultimately the triumph of Indian music, isn't it! Would you like to offer a message to the young generation of aspirant musicians?

A. *Keep your eyes and ears open. Pay special attention to old gayakis and styles. Have faith in your guru and genuine dedication to your art. Be prepared to spend some time in difficulty if there's no easy success. Perseverance will definitely be rewarded. Remember, hard-earned success is lasting success.*

Q. Pandit-ji, I must thank you and specially commend you for sticking your neck out and voicing your concerns about what's ailing our music and musicians of today.

A. *Somebody has to do this unpleasant duty. My love for our divine music is far greater than my love for my worldly popularity. So I have frankly aired my views, solely with the hope of seeing some drastic improvement.*

RAVI
SHANKAR

In a misty morning from mythology, Lord Shiva was singing to a cosmic ambience. The sheer impact of that divine music made Lord Vishnu melt. Brahma, the Lord of creation, noticed this rare phenomenon and quietly collected those molten emotions of Vishnu in his great urn, the *Kamandal*.

Eons passed by and then one day, this enormous celestial collection had to be released from that reservoir and allowed to descend onto earth. This, in fact, was the river Ganga cascading down the path created by the superhuman penance and endeavour of the royal ascetic Bhagirath...

There exists a present-day parallel to this mythological episode—that of creating a path for a divine music source to flow and transcend borders of country and culture. And in that context Pandit Ravi Shankar today compares favourably to the spirit of Bhagirath. While Bhagirath's efforts were aimed at liberating his own royal ancestors from the curse of an angry sage, Ravi Shankar has carved the path for the *Ganga* of Indian music to flow out towards more diverse and universal destinations. And he has done it by drawing courage and inspiration from his own musical genius, his own sense of destiny.

Significantly, it was Benaras, the eternal city by the Ganges, where Ravindra Shankar was born in the summer of 1920, and was able to soak in the aura of spirituality around the place very early in life. The 'baby' of the family of four brothers, young Ravi did not get to see much of his father who was a busy lawyer and statesman. Not that Ravi was allowed to brood over this deprivation. He enjoyed an enriching intimacy with his mother, and later, it was his elder brother, the legendary Uday Shankar, who engaged Ravi's vision with dramatic impact. Thanks to his pioneering pursuits, Uday Shankar was at the vortex of a relentless churning of creative activity and performing arts, including music, dance and ballet. Overwhelmed by the close proximity to such an epoch making creative explosion, a young and starry-eyed Ravi soaked in

every aspect of both classical and modern music, art and dance.

Ravi Shankar may not have been a child prodigy in the strictest sense, but surely he has been the child of destiny. Challenged and favoured by fortune, he has bravely made the most of the dramatic twists and turns of his life's course. Instead of merely being an enchanted boy, he began to imbibe the finer points of dance and music just by watching and listening. For five years he soaked himself in Indian classical music by listening to Timir Baran's masterful sarod, and observing from close the singing, the sitar, the tabla-tarang, the jal-tarang compositions of Vishnudas Shirali. He picked up the esraj and the sitar and began to play by sheer instinct and observation. And then he was inevitably sucked into the dance troupe of his 'hero' Uday Shankar and was soon well on his path to becoming an adept, playing challenging roles with flourish. He danced with grace and dexterity and played many instruments like the sitar, the sarod, the esraj...Every day then was like a new scene from a creative play.

Enter, Baba Allauddin Khan. The revered guru of classical music from Maihar came over to join Uday Shankar's troupe for a crucial musical interlude. The Maharaja of Maihar had graciously granted his state musician a year's leave so that he could travel with the troupe. The intensely emotional Ustad Allauddin Khan must have dearly missed his son, the young Ali Akbar, or at any rate, the great guru wanted a worthy disciple to be around, to make him feel at home. Whatever the mystery, the maestro took an immense and instant liking to the promising young Ravi. For the first time, Ravi Shankar began to receive focused education on how to refine one's vocal chords correctly, and how to strum out real music from an instrument. Mesmerized, he waded headlong into the deep and vast ocean of Indian classical music.

It was a short but enchanted voyage into the unfolding riches of Indian classical music and it created a deep impact on the young man. So much so that the seeds of a pivotal decision in the womb of future were sown sometime during this one year period, after which Baba Allauddin had to return to his native Maihar at the end of his contract with the troupe.

For about a couple of hectic years after that, Ravi Shankar kept touring the world with his Dada, earning fame and applause as a dancer. He even began to choreograph his own solo items and his flowering talent earned rave reviews in the western press. This, however, did not last long. The winds of war began to blow across continents and this euphoric voyage of the young cultural ambassadors from India had to change course. Having created unprecedented ripples in the world of creative dance, Uday Shankar returned to India and began to plan a cultural centre at the hilly Almorah. And it was time for an eighteen-year-old Ravi Shankar to confront his private moment of reckoning at the crossroads of life.

Fortunately, Ravi was able to put his highly eventful globetrotting stint as a talented dancer in the right perspective. This short but concentrated period enriched and matured him far beyond his age. He already had a rare and panoramic vision of the world of art and entertainment. He was exposed to the dance and music of diverse cultural and stylistic genres. His young mind had a continued exposure to the indulgent world of high life and glossy glamour. A lesser person, unaware of his calling in life, might have strayed too far in the wrong direction. Ravi's deep love for music lead him gently by the heartstrings and after some inspired soul-searching, he surrendered to the vision of Baba Allauddin Khan. The history of Indian music might have etched that moment on its scrolls.

His fashionable silk and satin were replaced by coarse *khadi* work clothes, his long luxuriant hair was cut short and scruffy, his suave bearings and urbane air of confidence gave way to the demeanor of a resolute student. Packing just the barest of essentials in a tin trunk, Ravi Shankar landed up at Maihar, a place in the back of beyond, where Baba Allauddin Khan was bringing up his disciples in the ancient *gurukul* way of life.

Visibly stunned by the young man's transformation, but secretly proud and impressed by his yearning and resolve to totally dedicate himself to the deep and difficult pursuit of Indian classical music, Baba Allauddin embraced Ravi like the loving father he had scarcely known.

It was a difficult life at Maihar, sleeping with mosquitoes, cockroaches and scorpions on one hand, and waking up to the strictest routine of *talim* and *riyaaz,* on the other. But Ravi took it all with a deep sense of penance and providence. Baba Allauddin gave his highest and best to his favourite disciple, and displaying remarkable grasping power and application, Ravi Shankar matured speedily as a musician worthy of that affection, trust and generosity.

The legendary Ali Akbar Khan, the son of Baba Allauddin, was slightly younger than Ravi, and the two of them often learned together like two brothers, inspiring each other to greater heights, the celebration of which the music world was to

Posing with an eloquent picture of the celebrated Uday Shankar

enjoy years later as many electrifying *jugalbandis* between the best of sitar and sarod.

Ravi's respectful distance from Annapurna, the attractive and talented daughter of Baba Allauddin, however, was nullified by some zealous matchmaking by relatives of Ravi, who engineered an early marriage between the two. And from a pledged 'son', Ravi suddenly became the son-in-law of his guru. Everyone approved and rejoiced at the happy merger between two talented young music makers.

After seven years of rigorous learning and deep exploration of the depths of Indian classical music in the strictest *guru-shishya* tradition, Ravi Shankar was ready to surface and look for his place in the sun. One fine morning, with Baba Allauddin's tearful blessings he left for Bombay.

After a few years of creative music compositions in plays, ballets and films, and countless concerts of pure classical music, Ravi Shankar was invited to Delhi to join All India Radio as its youngest ever director in the External Services division. Then, having switched over to the Home Services within a few more years, he founded the chamber orchestra, *Vadya Vrinda,* which brought into play an unprecedented array of instruments, both Indian and western. It was during this period that the composer in him began to visualize the big canvas of world music, while the pure classical musician journeyed inwards with his chosen instrument, the sitar. As his popularity soared, he travelled to all corners of India ushering in new waves of interest and excitement in the rich tradition of Indian classical music. With the sure feel of a true pioneer he combined the unique qualities of both his gurus: the deep

At the central courtyard of the Ravishankar Centre in New Delhi

introspective effect of Baba Allauddin's music and the great appeal of grand presentation learnt from his *Dada* Uday Shankar.

With his charm and eloquence, he began to explain the finer points of his music even to uninitiated audiences who found it inviting and rewarding enough to attend his recitals. As his audiences grew in numbers and diversity, it became increasingly clear and compelling that he should now embrace the momentous task of taking the unique and soul-satisfying music of his motherland to the rest of the world. Bhagirath's heraldic conch shell, transcending millennia, had found its echo in the strains of Ravi Shankar's sitar. And the *Ganga* of Indian classical music was poised to break through its age-old confines and flow out into the unexplored territories of the shrinking world.

It was time to relinquish his prestigious position at All India Radio, and embark upon extensive concert tours to Europe and America. As he went to all those places he had earlier visited as a young dancer, doors began to open, and an awakening towards Indian music was slowly but surely being apparent in the music circles of the West.

Many music greats from the Western world made acquaintance with him. The burgeoning world of jazz and rock found Ravi Shankar's Indian music curiously appealing, and through it some of their exponents found the soul in their own musical quest.

Ravi Shankar's world vision and universal temperament proved highly conducive to many collaborative efforts with other music legends, which, apart from his own solo recitals, have become part of music folklore around the world.

Among many of his celebrity admirers and collaborators is the great violinist Yehudi Menuhin who, after his first ever exposure to Indian classical music through a Ravi Shankar recital, said that Columbus might have been just as moved after discovering America! Similarly impressed, one might say, were other greats from the West, including jazzman John Coltrane, Dave Bruebeck, Jean Pierre Rampal, Mstislav Rostropovich, Philip Glass, and of course, George Harrison.

With an amazing inherent feel and understanding, Ravi Shankar has not only composed music suited to Western instruments, but also been ideally inspirational to the virtuoso musicians of Europe and America. Yet, the most discernible feature of all those compositions was the Indian spirit, which shone through all their performances. The London Symphony Orchestra and the New York Philharmonic have many commissioned pieces composed by a collaborative Ravi Shankar which have honoured and enriched their formidable heritage, resulting in lasting friendship with Andre Previn and especially Zubin Mehta.

Success in this monumental mission of taking Indian music beyond the shores of this vast country might have been achievement enough for one lifetime. But Ravi Shankar's immense creative prowess and energy have inspired him to play many diverse roles in one panoramic epic of an eventful life! And, ironically, this very spectrum of his versatility and its fruition in many diverse artistic spheres, boggle the minds of those who try in vain to see a complete portrait of him on a single canvas...

The recorded music industry, both Indian and global, have treasured his countless chart-

bursting albums...concert halls around the music world have reverberated with his memorable recitals...young generations of diverse cultures have found freedom and inspiration in his music...citadels of art and culture have showered upon him their highest honours and titles...universities and institutes have presented him with doctorates and enriched themselves with his visits and lectures...states and royalties have decorated him with the loftiest of awards...students and disciples mastering a diverse range of musical instruments have launched into their illustrious careers with his teachings and blessings...accompanists like the tabla players are grateful to him for the platform and creative recognition he brought them...landmark films in the history of movies have been touched with the magic of his music scores...major world festivals and fund-raisers have drawn upon his charisma and magnetism to ensure their success...floodgates of cultural exchange have opened up in the wake of his pioneering pursuits...multitudes beyond region and religion have been touched and moved by his electrifying recitals...and bedazzled women of talent and beauty have made great sacrifices to get to know the man...and of course, the music critics and culture custodians have eventually expanded their collective vision in trying to fathom him and his work....

All this, and so much more...in just one life? Does this incredible record of God's favourite child of destiny ever have a false note on the flip side? He perhaps doesn't voice them, but his private domain has often been tormented by unbidden tremolos. Childhood deprivation, a broken marriage, vicious criticism, contrived controversies, prolonged estrangements, cruel bereavements, emotional traumas, even physical setbacks including a delicate heart condition and impaired hearing have all kept their tryst with the envied achiever. But then, quietly and manfully he has taken it all with a spirit of dignity and penance, and has sublimated everything into the ethereal music he has been able to make throughout his trailblazing career. And his wonderful sense of humour and honesty, his innocence and integrity have shone through his angelic smile.

Today, in what appears to be the autumn of his personal life, everything around him seems to be falling beautifully into harmony. Millions of admirers across continents, a cordon of true friends, a passionately loving and caring wife, a reunion with his estranged celebrity daughter Norah, a galaxy of famous disciples, the brilliant doting daughter Anoushka taking charge of his great name and legacy, and the idyllic, hermitage-like Ravi Shankar Centre gearing up to be of long-term service to Indian music and world peace...

Amidst that tanpura-like fluid resonance, Ravi Shankar presides with his sense of destiny and his luminous mind, still shimmering with waves of creative energy and inspired ideas...

Within enticing reach lies his loyal consort, the curvaceous, gleaming sitar. And he knows, just as the whole world of music does, that anytime he might pick it up, and with a caressing, meditative overture, begin to sublimate a life-long musical quest with the magical confluence of just a few notes of a chosen raga...Notes that can as easily wrench the heart as they can moisten the eyes with inexplicable joy...and cleanse the soul.

This indeed is the divine music of the *inner world*. And *Bharat Ratna* Ravi Shankar has lovingly taken it to the outer world...as a priceless gift from India.

Living Memories...

The music, the magic

The legendary guru Baba Allauddin Khan

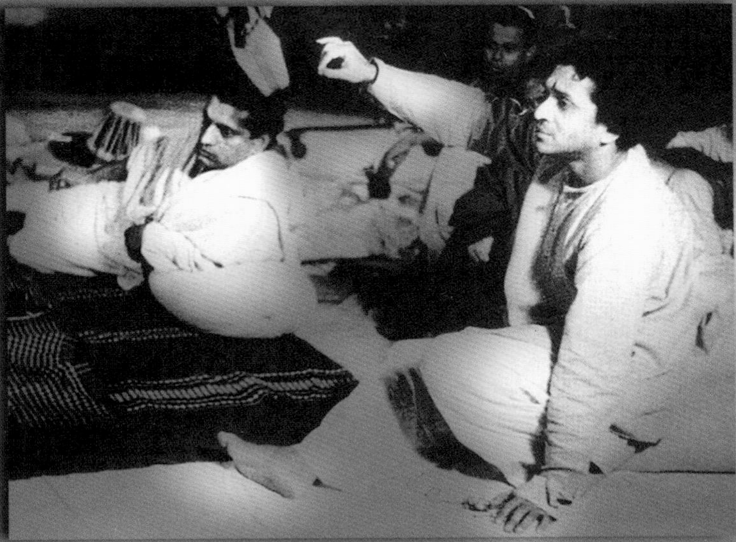

In action as music director for an early Satyajit Ray film

Basking in marital bliss, with wife Sukanya

The stealer of hearts

At the French Embassy after receiving the 'Legion d'honneur'. Seen with wife Sukanya, daughters Norah and Anoushka

The talented duo, Norah Jones and Anoushka Shankar

With Hollywood legend Marlon Brando

Talent unlimited within one frame! With Allarakha, Ali Akbar Khan, George Harrison and Bismillah Khan

The Shankars with the Queen of England and the first couple of India

All smiles. With Sue Jones, daughter Norah Jones, son Subho and grandchildren

With his first wife, the deeply talented Annapurna Devi

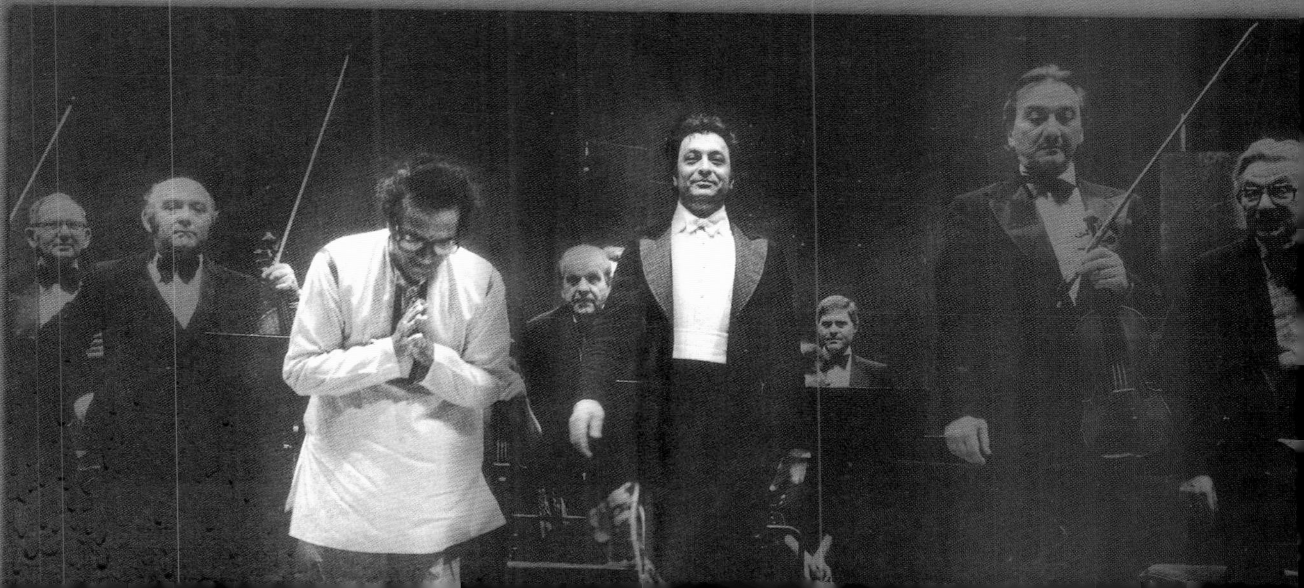

aking a bow with the famous conductor Zubin Mehta and the members of the London Symphony Orchestra

Q. Pandit-ji, people often describe you as the musical bridge between the East and the West...How do you react to that?

A. *Well...in a way it is true. But on the other hand, the way they try to depict me most of the time is quite wrong. They say I have mixed the two, I have encouraged fusion and many such things which hurt me sometimes. Because that is one thing I have not done. Words like fusion irritates me no end, because it is just a commercial gimmick taking a bit of this and a bit of that and making a cocktail...*

Q. Any incident or moment you cherish from your involvement with Satyajit Ray's Pather Panchali?

A. *Well, after doing the music for several Hindi movies like Chetan Anand's Neecha Nagar and K A Abbas's Dharti ke Lal and many documentaries and even a few Bengali features, getting involved with Satyajit Ray's trilogy was a different experience. It was a wonderful memory. I remember he showed me the rushes, and immediately I came out with the theme tune (sings it aloud), I sang it to him and he was overjoyed.*

Q. But this doesn't appear in the film on sitar. Does it?

A. *It appears on many different instruments at different times at different pitches, depending on the mood...including sitar and flute...*

Q. Similarly, any other film memories from, say, Meera or Anuradha...

A. *Anuradha was a film I enjoyed working on tremendously, because of two reasons. Hrishikesh Mukherjee showed such great feel for music, and the story was so beautiful, and yes, I was very friendly with the heroine...*

Q. Leela Naidu?

A. *Yes... and I poured out my heart into the music. And finally, although the songs were unconventional and distinctly classical, each song became so popular...*

Q. In fact, I suppose it was for the first time that such classically rich songs were received so well by the common public...

A. *Exactly. It was extremely rewarding. Then I also did some good music for Godan, but the film unfortunately did not do too well for whatever reason. Then I did Kabuliwalla and Kala Mati with Tapan Sinha, one of my favourite directors, he's been so sensitive...*

Q. Any memories you cherish from Gandhi ? You had an Oscar nomination for its music...

A. *Gandhi was a fantastic experience, although I wish I had done the entire music alone. But Richard Attenburrough thought George Fenton should collaborate with me and do the Western orchestrations etc. and I agreed. It was a truly great film.*

Q. One amusing question: If you had picked up the sarod and Ali Akbar Khan saheb had picked up the sitar while you began your learning under Baba Allauddin, would the two of you have reached where you are today?

A. *I am sure it would have been the same. After all it is not the instrument that makes the music; it is an extension of your body. The music is*

made by your mind, your entire being...

Q. An obvious question: Do you sing silently in your mind while playing your instrument?

A. *Always, always. It is always inside and the endeavour is to bring it out. It is happening simultaneously or just a split second later...*

Q. Has it ever happened that you have conceived something in your mind but the instrument was not able to bring it out? Pardon my audacity...

A. *Oh yes, it does happen. It is a technical aspect...when you are a little out-of-practice, or you have neglected your sadhana, it is quite likely that your mind reaches a point but your hand falls a little short. It is your own fault in a way. But when you are in your element your hands are your slave...they take you wherever you want to go...*

Q. Then, maybe the opposite too happens: your hands might suddenly produce something beyond your conscious effort?

A. *Of course, and it surprises you! Whether you call it conscious or subconscious, sometimes certain things come out of your hands, which make you exclaim, 'Wow! What was that?'*

Q. There must be a certain chemistry between the conscious and the subconscious mind, the result of which transcends both...?

A. *Exactly. It may transcend many times during an inspired recital. And yes, there's also this delicate aspect of how instruments behave under certain light and temperature conditions...then the sound and the equipment are a factor...sometimes even the vibrations of a certain venue, very subtle and perhaps inexplicable, but it so happens that despite your best efforts that magic does not happen. Maybe* *the audience is happy, and you are even being applauded, but privately inside, you know there's something missing...*

Q. Is it fair or even possible to compare a vocalist with an instrumentalist in the context of Indian classical music?

A. *Absolutely possible. But you know, a vocalist has always enjoyed an edge according to our shastras...*

Q. Yes, one has heard adages like 'uttam gana and madhyam bajana...'

A. *Yes, that may be a rather extreme interpretation...but on the other hand, yes, 'gana' is really the main thing...because that is what is actually happening; we are singing inside...we may not be using the voice. That's why when you compare a vocalist with an instrumentalist it is ultimately an appraisal of how good or talented the individuals are. Today we do not have an Amir Khan or a Faiyaz Khan or a Bade Ghulam Ali Khan amidst us...*

Q. Whom did you hear in your younger days? Sorry to interrupt...

A. *Oh, I have really been lucky. Starting from Vishnu Digambar...I have had the rare opportunity to hear all the great legendary voices... But during our times of assimilation, we used to always notice: Oh, this man's asthayi-antara is fabulous...or, this man is doing bol-taan in such great laya...or this ustad is really wonderful in pure sur...we never expected the good points of A in B...or those of B in C, each one was given the highest respect even if he had just one special quality in which he excelled. But today it is not so. The audience wants everything in everyone. We could easily tolerate a harsh vocal quality or even some out-of-tune patches, provided there was something great to compensate for it, or something else worth learning.*

Q. In very recent concert circuits, either due to the audience mix, or paucity of time, we don't even get to hear complete ragas any more...?

A. *See, there are two sides to every such issue. Many people think that unless you play on for an hour or two, the raga is not complete...but I differ. I have heard many of the old greats and they never sang or played for too long. They would start one raga, dwell on it for fifteen to twenty minutes, and then begin another one...and so on. This proves that you need to show the cream of the raga and not get caught in tedious repetitions and meaningless variations like that of a computer. The real test is when you have been listening to a raga for over an hour...yet you feel it has just been going on for a mere ten minutes and you earnestly want it to continue...the barhat is there, the vistaar is happening...there's sur, there's emotion...the aesthetic part is really the essence. Instead of trying to impress with speed and taiyari...if you can bring tears to the eyes by striking just one magical 'sur', that is so much more, and that is really the core of our music. This quality was there earlier much more than what is visible today, especially in the Dhrupad era of olden times, before Dhrupad sadly began to lose its way...*

Q. Have jugalbandi recitals ever really satisfied you?

A. *Jugalbandis have always been there...in the olden days between two sons of an ustad or between two brothers as they have grown up learning together with a similar style and a*

shared sense of understanding between each other...but whenever it was something else it has been more like a fight or a contest. I think the only good jugalbandis that I have known have been between me and Ali Akbar Khan, and that too for a limited span of only ten to twelve years. The great understanding and love between us have taken it to great heights. But after that, as musicians are in a state of constant evolution, we have grown far apart in our respective paths...and even after trying hard, it could never be the same. As for other jugalbandis that I have heard, frankly, I have found them inadequate, even a little silly sometimes...

Q. If you believe in rebirth, who do you think you might have been in your last birth?

A. *(Laughs) I wish I really knew...but yes, sometimes I like to sit and imagine and I think definitely I have been immersed in arts. Maybe music, maybe dance, maybe even painting...I have this strong intuitive feeling that I have surely been involved in artistic pursuits.*

Q. Here's a related question: what would you like to be if you were to take rebirth?

A. *Hmmm...again I would like to be born as a jaatismar so that I can remember and continue with whatever I already know, and (laughs) instead of starting from ABC, I would like to start off from the doctorate level...and this sort of thing happens, mind you...like that boy from Jaipur...or even the gottuvadyam player - what's his name - yes, Ravikiran. When he was three years old he was brought over to meet me, and he already knew all the ragas and the talas...it was amazing...and they said, it was his grandfather, a great ghotuvadyam player of his time, who has been reborn as Ravikiran!*

Q. Did you ever consciously feel that God has put upon you this special responsibility of spreading the appeal of Indian classical music to the rest of the world?

A. *(A brief silence) Whether I had the word 'God' in my mind or not, I am not entirely sure, but definitely I have felt very strongly that I am the person who can do it and who should do it...and by God's grace I think I have done it. Because at that time, in the mid-fifties, I do not think there was anyone in the horizon who was articulate enough to explain the finer points of Indian music, especially to the Westerners. The nuances, the differences, the depth and the spiritual qualities of our music...so I took upon myself the entire responsibility of it. And I am glad that I did so, because it opened up a whole new world for the West in terms of appreciating our music.*

Q. Yes, and had it been presented wrongly or inadequately, it would have had a different effect altogether?

A. *Absolutely. And because it happened the way it did, many great musicians, and even many young and upcoming musicians also, got the opportunities they deserve. Even at this very moment, if you just check, you will find at least ten to twelve top musicians residing abroad or touring the world.*

Q. When you smile on stage, it appears like you are God's own child. But does that famous smile ever hide any pain or any unfulfilled desire...

A. *(Smiles) Maybe the smile that comes out when I am making music is of that moment of fulfillment, and which is as true as the tremendous amount of unfulfilled desire I also have. For instance, I used to wonder about Baba when he used to say that he had just about begun to understand music. How could he have said that? But believe me, today I feel exactly the same. Sometimes it comes in a flash of light that there's so much more to our music, which I have not been able to achieve, and that is often a source of sorrow. Then there's this other dimension, where, in creative terms I am full of ideas, in ballet, in films, which need the big canvas and many other people's participation, which is not always forthcoming, because I haven't learnt the art of gathering people together and organizing things. That too is an area where I feel quite unfulfilled.*

Q. Your compositions for the virtuoso Western classical instrumentalists have always had a unique flavour of Indian ragas as their soul. Was this a conscious effort?

A. *Absolutely. Because that's exactly what I have always tried to do, by shirking away from this 'fusion' element of taking a bit of this and a bit of that and having an unholy mixture. I have never done that. Because there is so much of everything in our own music, not just the spiritual or the deep meditative aspects, but also so much joy, colour, playfulness, everything is there and I have kept them alive in my compositions. I may have used Western instruments or Western musicians, but the basic core and appeal have unerringly been truly Indian. In fact, my goal has always been to take the audience along with me deep inside, as in meditation, to bring tears to the eyes, and to feel totally peaceful and cleansed.*

Q. Would you like to make a mention of some of your favourite or memorable concerts from the many that the world remembers? Like the 'Concert for Bangladesh' for example, or the one at the Kremlin...?

A. *As you said, there really have been so many...but yes, even among those some do stand out. Like in the West, there have been those in the churches, and then, the Monterey Pop Festival which was a special event and quite miraculous...then some fantastic performances in the Royal Opera House in London...while in India I remember so many of those Music Circle programmes in Bombay, where I performed in the presence of a galaxy of great masters in the audience...then there's the one recital I specially remember which was in a temple courtyard in Madras in the presence and honour of the late Shankaracharya of Kanchi. It was noon time on a hot, humid day, and Alla Rakha and I were performing in the open, our attires were soaked with sweat. And you know that sensitive instruments like the sitar and the tabla get out of tune and tone even under strong electric lights, but on that auspicious occasion, everything played perfectly. That was a miraculous experience...*

Q. Any other miraculous experiences you have had during your long musical journey?

A. *Plenty of times. Sometimes when I have become one with my instrument, for instance, there have been these wonderful experiences of continuous goose flesh, almost like an orgasmic feeling, and these have been some of my memories of the highest bliss...and it didn't matter where I was at those times...*

Q. You are known to have taken the numerous awards and accolades that have been showered upon you rather lightly. But even then, does it not bother you that some of your significant contributions have not been widely given credit for? Like, for example, the 'Sare jahan se achcha' tune?

A. *Yes, of course. But unfortunately the concept of copyright is still not prevalent in this country. It hurts me that the fact that this tune was composed by me, was made public only about three years ago, while it was actually composed way back around 1945, and has been so popular ever since. Even this tune you hear every morning from Doordarshan...then there's 'Suswagatam' which also has been so popular...but then, to bring these issues up myself makes me feel rather small...*

Q. Do you think Anoushka's generation will take Indian classical music to even greater heights? What's your gut feel?

A. *It remains to be seen really. I am actually quite confused. Because even until a couple of years ago, I was so confident that our music has enough strength to survive any outside onslaught...but all of a sudden this surfeit of fashion, modelling, television shows, and 'Bollywood'...all of which have come on so strong...and practical reasons like the virtual disappearance of sponsor support for classical music functions have got me really frightened! That's why once again I have begun to talk about the need for sponsors and corporate houses to support classical music and culture. There's so much of young and wonderful talent floating around...but they are not getting enough programmes and opportunities to sustain their efforts and ambition...it really gets me terribly worried when I think of the immediate future...*

Q. But what would your advice be to these young aspirants? What would be your message?

A. *See, it is very well to tell them, do this, do that, 'sadhana karte raho', have patience and perseverance...but I also sympathize with their problems: times are so fast and demanding, that* *everything is wanted in a hurry. There's so much talent but not enough application, so much information but not enough wisdom...how does one make them understand and encourage them? We all will have to put our heads together and think of some solution...*

Q. But even then, do say something. A message coming from Pandit Ravi Shankar will surely mean a lot to them...

A. *Well...I would like them to realize that while a desire for quick success is understandable, it is possible only in fields like say, modelling. But for anything which is deeper and classical, be it music or dance, it would require a little more time and a little more patience. The rewards can then be well worth the effort and sacrifice...But then, will the young sit and listen to such advice today? It's difficult...*

Q. I must still say, I feel there is a cultural resurgence already on course...and with the blessings of people like you who have started it all... this has to go forward...

A. *It will have to...and it should...yes. Because talent is there in great abundance...and it has to surface in a conducive atmosphere. Let's hope and pray...*

Q. If God sat in audience before you and asked you to play just one complete raga, which one would you play? Would it be one of those lovely new ragas you created...or whatever the mood of the moment would dictate?

A. *My God! Well, Yaman Kalyan has always been among my favourites...then there's Khamaaj...but then, as you said, it will perhaps have to be the mood of the moment.*

And indeed, what a moment that would be! Perhaps, I will pour my heart out with a burst of offering of Raag Mala!!

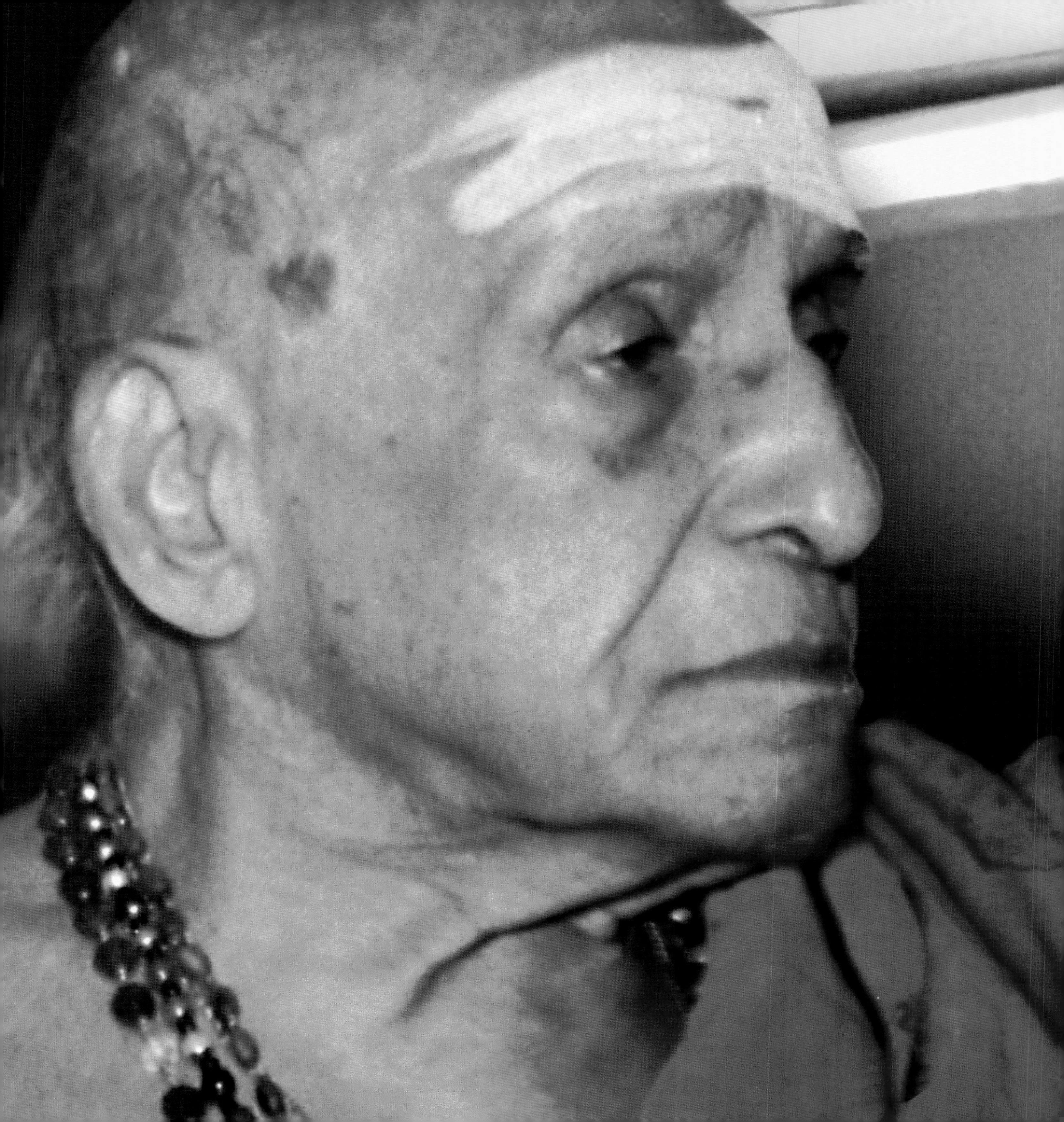

SEMMANGUDI SRINIVASA IYER

If man is the measure of his world, there are men whose stature defines the visible horizons. There are men, who, merely by their colossal presence, mark the era and etch the arena of events.

Assigned a life and a role, they pursue their potential. And in their own strife and struggle, in their own triumph and despair, in just living their own eventful life, they realize one fine day that they have transcended their active existence...and have become a symbol. Like the awesome wingspan of the ageing eagle, or the expanding canopy of the shady banyan tree, they have become a metaphor of grandeur and glory. From the combating gladiator, they have suddenly become the story-soaked arena itself. They are not the whizzing blizzard any more; they are the serene sky far beyond the passing storm.

If Semmangudi Srinivasa Iyer does not talk much today, it is not because he wears the imprint of ninety five cycles of the Indian seasons on his aged bones; it is because he's humbled by the awareness that as a chosen messenger, he has just finished delivering the message of God...by living an exemplary life dedicated to the religion of music.

Like *Pitamaha* Bhishma of the *Mahabharat,* Semmangudi has defended and glorified his cause and calling with such valiant dedication, that in the end it ceases to matter whether he has been on the side of the victors. His valour itself has been his victory. Walking tall amidst treacherous winds of change, he has guarded and guided contemporary Carnatic music through a difficult path of evolution.

Srinivasa Iyer was nurtured in the very cradle of Carnatic music, the chosen village of Semmangudi, in the Tanjavur district of south India. Born on the 25th of July, 1908, he was the third son of his eminent and cultured parents, Radhakrishna Iyer and Dharmasamvardhini Ammal. By the age of five he began to display remarkable talent and a compelling affinity to *swara* and *laya.* His maternal uncle and cousin were

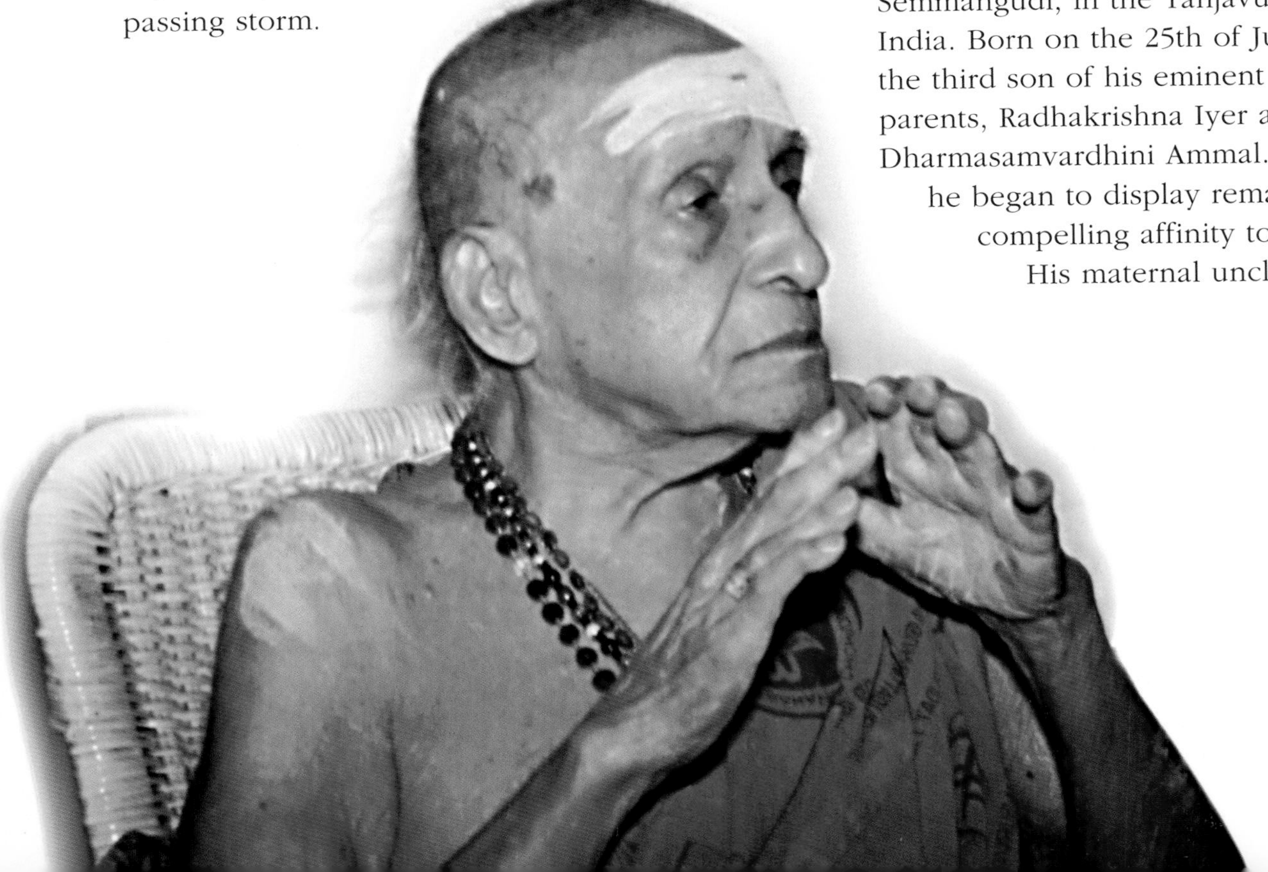

celebrated violinists, and that gave his parents the confidence that a career in music could be just right for young Srinivasa.

Soon after his ninth birthday, Semmangudi Srinivasa Iyer was initiated into formal music training under his cousin Semmangudi Narayanaswami Iyer. This was the auspicious *Vijaya Dashami* day of the year 1917. This later led to further fortuitous opportunities to learn under three more stalwarts of Carnatic music. First, it was the celebrated gottuvadyam maestro Sakharama Rao, followed by two *Sangeetha Kalanidhi* vocalists, Umayalpuram Swaminatha Iyer and Maharajapuram Vishwanatha Iyer.

Most of his learning was under the tradition-rich *gurukul* system, where music was imbibed wholeheartedly like a natural element. The *guru-shishya* relationship was sacred and symbiotic. There was a spirit of worshipful service to the guru, reciprocated by parental affection and constant access to his wealth of knowledge and wisdom. Semmangudi's monumental achievements over a long and illustrious career received its rock-solid grounding during his *gurukul* years under these four masters presenting a wide spectrum of knowledge.

When he was eighteen, his *arangetram,* the first public performance, was arranged at the revered Nageshwaraswami Temple of Kumbakonam, where auspicious *arangetrams* of many great artistes have been held since then. The audience comprised just a precious handful of well-wishers and music lovers. But the resident deity must have been pleased with the radiant young singer displaying remarkable talent and ardent devotion to his chosen art. The performance was blessed with a shower of heavy rains and applauded by lightning and thunder! A resounding success, by all standards.

Semmangudi's music *sadhana* progressed with arduous dedication, and he gained performance maturity by providing enthusiastic vocal support to his guru, Vishwanatha Iyer, in a number of memorable concerts. Blessed with an eclectic and holistic outlook, young Semmangudi did not miss any opportunity to attend concerts of contemporary stalwarts, including Ariyakudi, Chembai, Naina Pillai and the celebrated flautist Sanjeeva Rao. He imbibed the finest musical nuances of even the nagaswara exponents Rajaratnam Pillai and Karukurichi Arunachalam, by attending frequent temple festivals. Since the modern media for music propagation were yet to find their feet, attending as many live concerts within accessible distance as possible proved very rewarding.

As his fame began to travel fast across the music circles, young Semmangudi's life took an interesting detour. He was invited to Kerala and was offered the coveted position of *Asthana Vidwan,* resident musician, at the Travancore Palace. The Maharaja of Travancore, a great artiste and patron of fine art, music and spirituality, honoured him with great appreciation and affection. The senior queen, who was an accomplished veena player, showered motherly affection on the young and radiant musician.Within a couple of years he joined the Swati Tirunal Music Academy in Trivandram, and rose to become the principal of that prestigious institution of culture.

It was around this time that Semmangudi must have realized his ordained role in the history of Carnatic music. While his talents as a vocalist were flowering handsomely, and his maturity as a frontline musician was bearing fruit, his sense of history and legacy was taking

root. He was growing into an institution, a huge tree, rooted in tradition, with branches reaching to the future, and casting a shade of security onto the field of music with his imposing presence. Students and disciples began to gravitate around the emerging stalwart.

Semmangudi did not merely teach at the Swati Tirunal Academy; his vision for the future of Carnatic music was enriched by his profound sense of inheritance. The grand treasure house of the timeless compositions of Maharaja Swati Tirunal was available in an archival state, as if waiting to be revived and accorded currency. A large portion of the Maharaja's lyrical creations was musically silent. Along with other masters like Harikesanallur Muthiah Bhagavathar, Semmangudi plunged into the historic project of setting appropriate music to the inspiring lyrics. The dedicated task had to run parallel to his busy schedule as a teacher and a performer. Two publications were finally harvested from all the hard work, releasing music notations for over two hundred Swati Tirunal compositions. Furthermore, in the same spirit of commitment, Semmangudi tried to include at least a couple of such compositions in his own concert performances. Many creations such as 'Deva Deva' set in Raga *Mayamalavagowla,* and Pankajalochana set in Raga *Kalyani* attained immense popularity among the masses. Bhavayami Raghuraman, a major work based on the epic of Ramayana was adorned by a sparkling garland of beautiful ragas and embellished with a rich set of *chittaswarams.* Striding over historic chasms, these have now become timeless gems of Carnatic music.

A man of destiny, Semmangudi was obliged to play his assigned role in the emerging mass medium for music. While it was not easy to stay

At a recent felicitation function. Seen with young talents Sanjay Subramanyan and Shruti Sadolikar

away from the flourishing music academy, Semmangudi had to respond to the demands of changing times. Taking a leave of absence from the principal's duties of the academy, he went on to serve All India Radio, Madras, for over three landmark years, as the chief producer of Carnatic music.

The enormous contribution of Semmangudi Srinivasa Iyer to the field of Carnatic music has encompassed all possible faculties of an individual. As a guru and teacher, he made many promising youngsters blossom, and also nudged many luminaries of the current generation into the orbit of fame and fortune. He has been like a father to the likes of MS Subbulakshmi through his advice and affection. Many of his disciples have done *gurukulavasam* with him, and many more have learnt from him at the Swati Tirunal Academy. He has also responded with warmth and grace to a parade of musicians who have approached him for casual lessons or just to learn some of his choicest compositions. Semmangudi himself has gone over to learn specific compositions from the legendary Ariyakudi, T Brinda and GN Balasubramaniam...

Almost all possible titles and awards have been heaped at the feet of Semmangudi Srinivasa Iyer during his long and exemplary performing career of almost seventy five years, studded with over twenty thousand concerts. At age thirty-nine, he was the youngest artiste to receive the *Sangeetha Kalanidhi* from the Music Academy of Madras; today, at ninety-five, he is the oldest living kalanidhi of Carnatic Music.

Leaving behind his years of fruits and flowers to history, Semmangudi Srinivasa Iyer today is like the colossus tree whose sheer presence provides an expansive circle of soothing shade for music lovers. Standing out and standing apart, he observes the changing winds of the current music world. He absorbs the heat and dust of the 'noise pollution' in the music scene, smiles at the futility of 'forced fusion'. As the Pitamaha of Carnatic music he shields the lovers of pure, genuine music against the ominous dark clouds and passing storms of contamination. His abiding faith in the strength, sanctity and continuity of the best of tradition has been in luminous evidence throughout his life...it will merge with the larger legacy of Carnatic music when he takes his final bow.

Long ago, when the earlier Sankaracharya of Shingeri had met Semmangudi, he had foretold, "You will be the grand old man of music! You will live a hundred years!"

The good wishes of millions of Indian music lovers have been at work to ensure that the prediction proves to be a blessing...

Living Memories...

Being conferred the title of 'Rajya Seva Niratha' at the Travancore palace

The 'Pitamaha' of Carnatic music

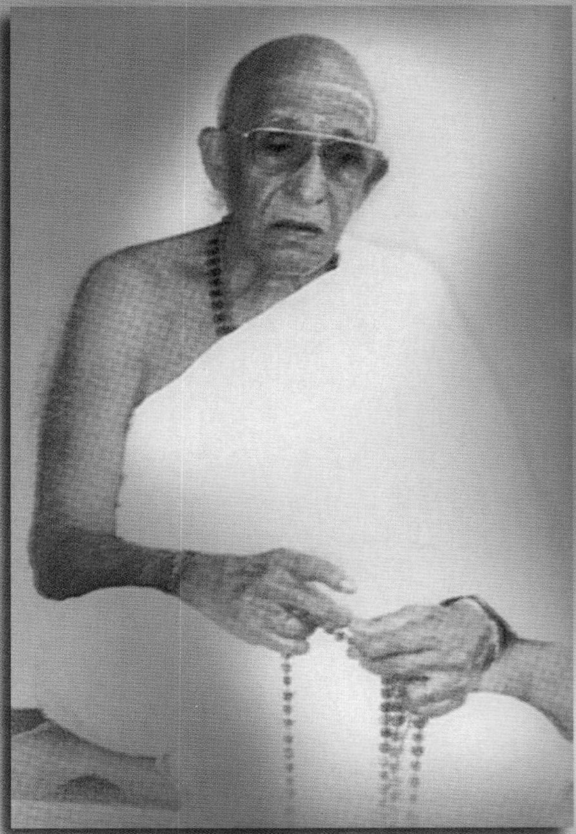

Reflecting on the spirit of music

The venerated stalwart

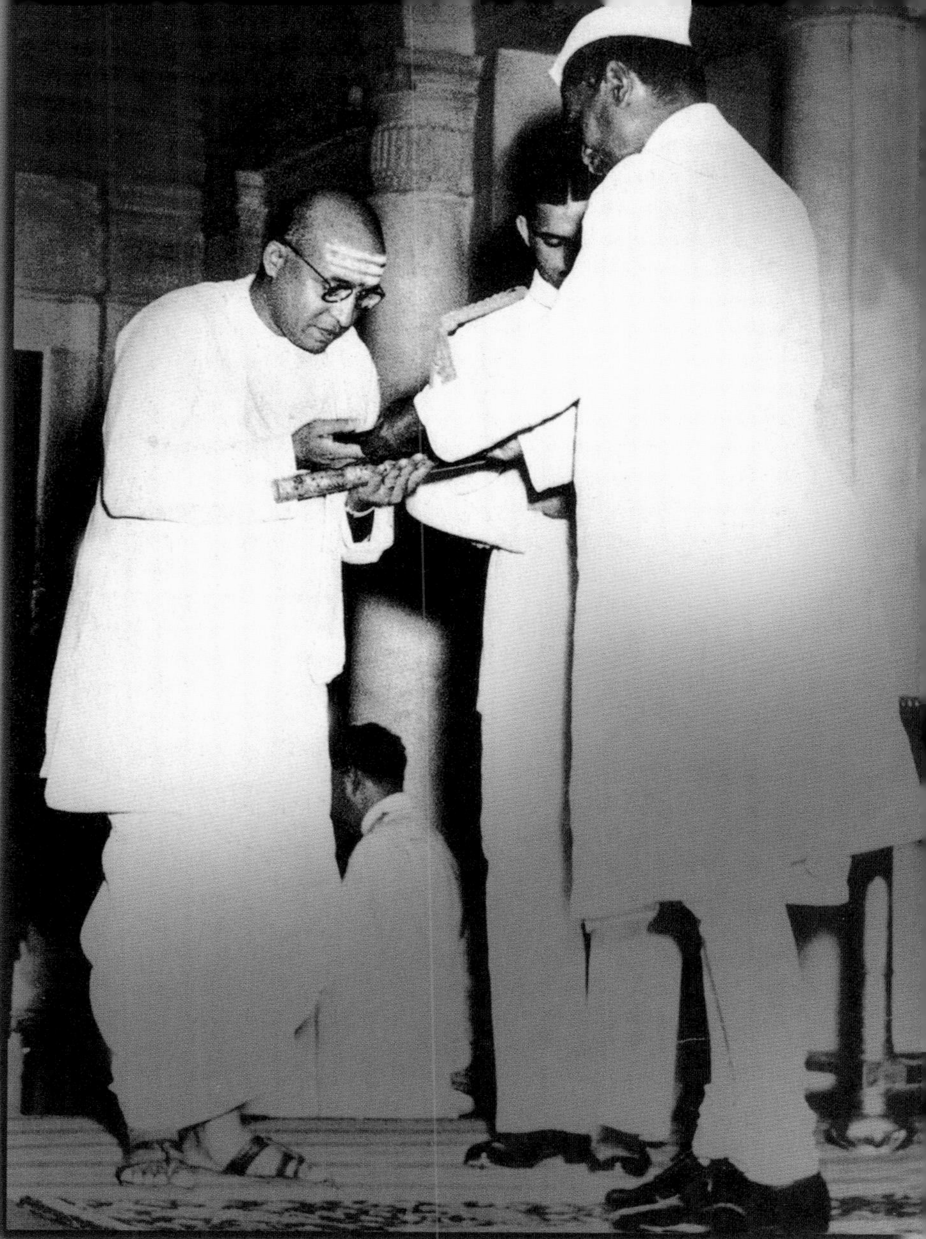

Receiving a national honour from India's first president, Dr. Rajendra Prasad

With Kishori Amonkar

Moments before receiving the first Shanmukhananda National Eminence Award

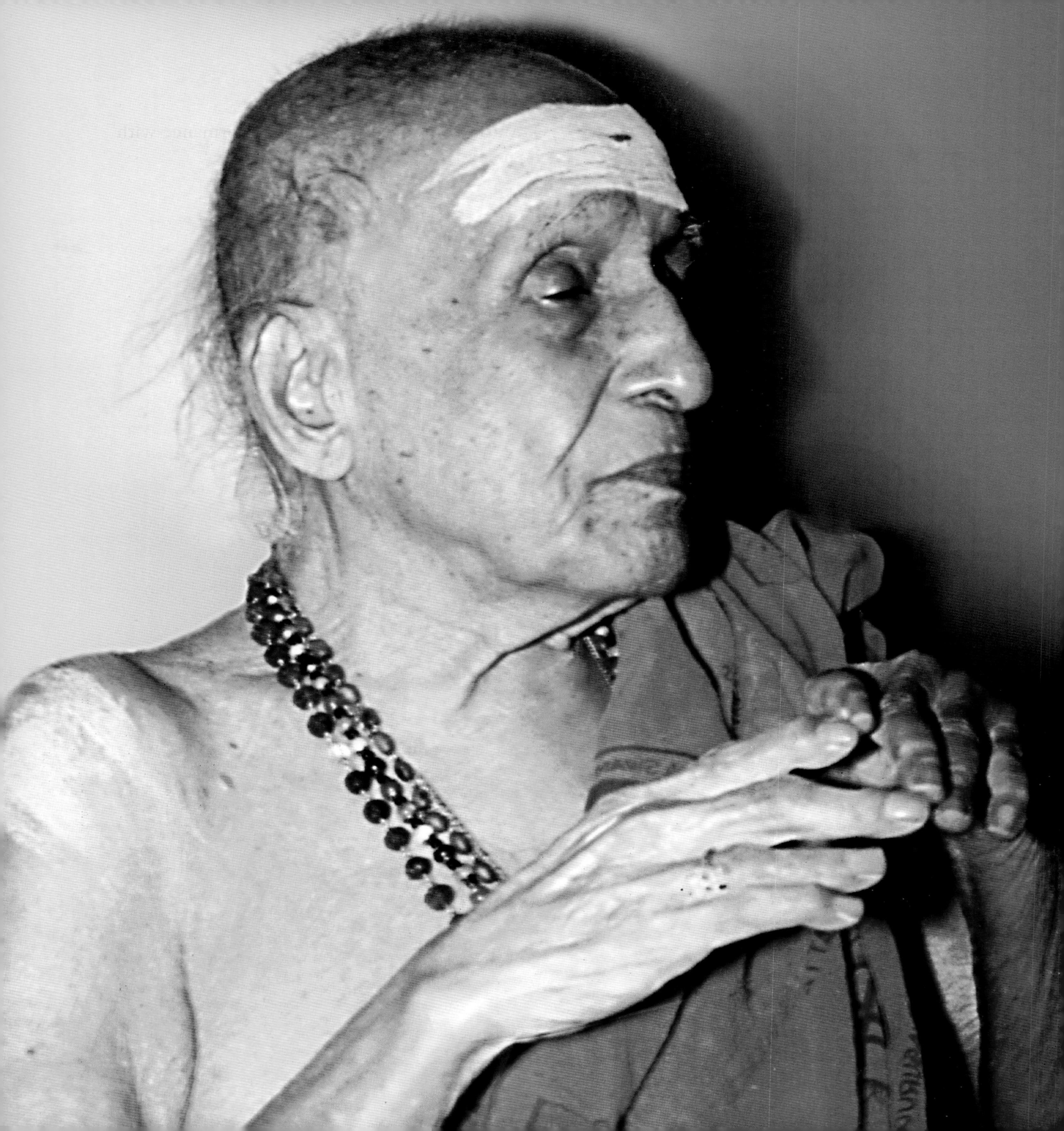

Q. You haven't been performing in public for quite a few years now. How do you feel about it?

A. *Forget singing, I am not even able to talk much to people these days. I think I have done enough for the world of music. Now I prefer to be like those three monkeys of Gandhi-ji. Speak nothing, hear nothing, see nothing. (Smiles).*

Q. No more desires or dreams?

A. *I am satisfied with life. At ninety-five, all I want now is a link with God.*

Q. Any special memories of the Maharaja of Travancore?

A. *He gave me a lot of affection. He was a great human being with a king-sized heart. I remember, when Sardar Patel went to ask him for his state, he said, "Take the state; just leave the temple and our culture for us..." Patel said, "If all the kings were like you, things would have been so great!"*

Q. There was some untimely downpour during your arangetram?

A. *Untimely for me! Because, I myself could not hear what I was singing, due to the loud thundershower! (Smiles) But then, the heavy rains ensured that no one could dare to leave in the middle of my performance!*

Q. From over 20,000 concerts of yours, could you recount one or two special ones for us?

A. *Well, off hand I remember a recent and unusual function, where a lovely portrait of Thyagaraja was unveiled by the beautiful danseuse Dr Saraswathi. Then your Dr Balamurali played the viola! And I sang.*

Q. And what about that special performance with the mangoes? Was it an exaggeration?

A. *(Smiles) Oh yes, those heavenly Salem mangoes! I was young, and I sucked up more than one hundred mangoes without too many breaks! Obviously my voice was out of action for many days.*

Q. Recently you were the first recipient of the National Eminence Award instituted by the Shanmukhananda Sangeeta Sabha, Mumbai. The Sabha president commented in his welcome speech that you deserved the Bharat Ratna award more than anyone else. How do you feel about it?

A. *The great Paramacharya of Kanchi had called me 'Sangeeta Thatha', the Grandfather of Music. That was enough for me! And recently again, the present sage of Kanchi called me 'Bhishma'. I gently reminded him that Uttarayan isn't too far...(Smiles). I am also known as 'Kairasikaran', which means, all the projects I was associated with always did well. All these fill up my cup of satisfaction...*

Q. What do you think of the growing encroachment of fusion in Carnatic music?

A. *If indeed it is growing, we should be worried. I do not think the purity of classical music should ever be compromised.*

Q. Any other point that worries you about the way music has changed over the decades?

A. *See, with the advent of the microphone and all that, more people are able to listen to music. But to include quantity, we are perhaps sacrificing quality. The great appeal of full-throated singing has virtually disappeared... But music itself hasn't really changed. The way it is*

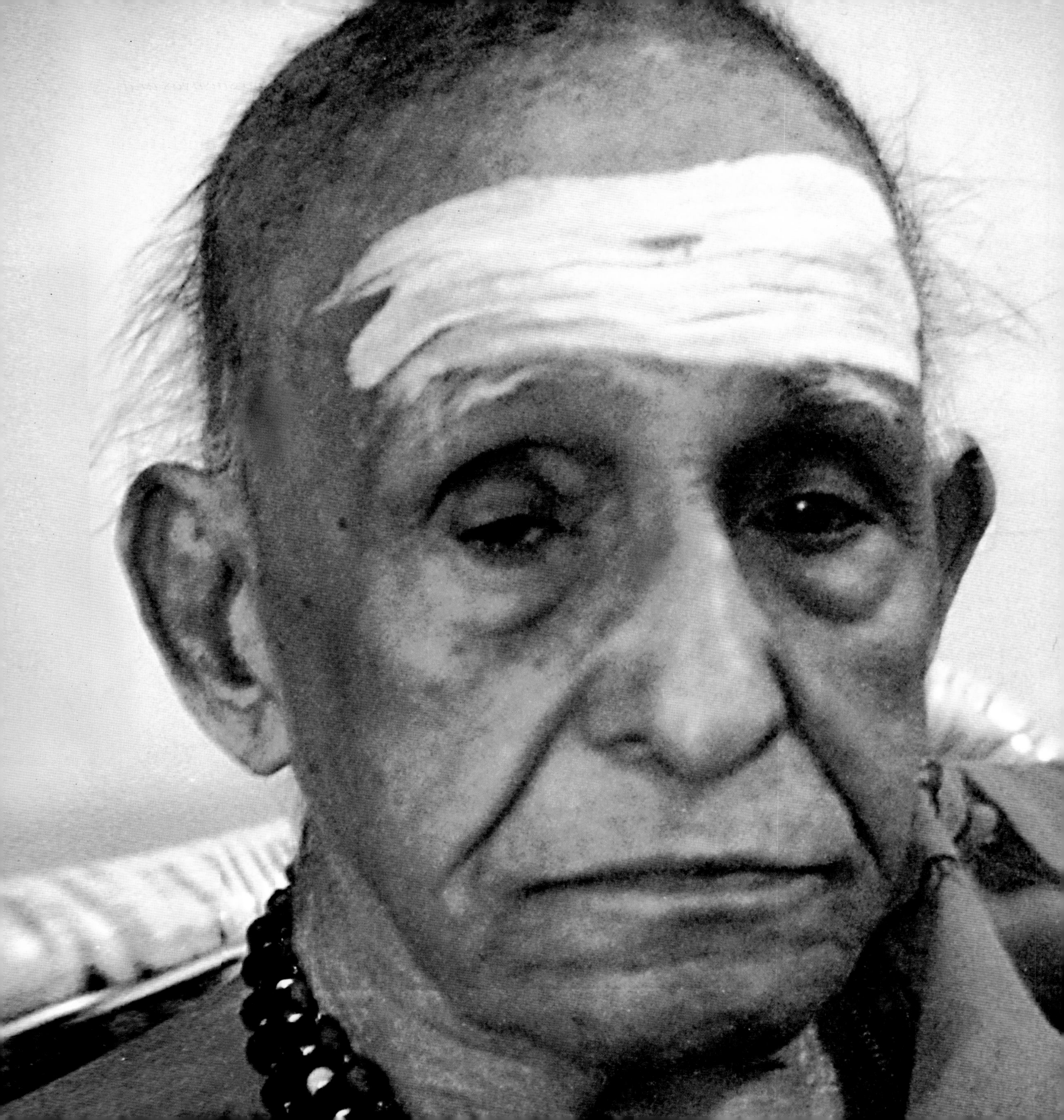

expressed differs from time to time or person to person, and this variation only makes it more interesting and enjoyable. The musicians from the distant past strictly followed what their gurus taught them, practised hard and reproduced it flawlessly. The present day vidwans are intelligent enough to give importance to their own way of handling the same basic music. It is like taking different paths to the same destination...

Q. Any change in the attitude towards performance?

A. *(Thinks) Well...despite the fact that the earlier generation vidwans were equally talented, their earnings were not much. Today, I notice that it has become a trade. Ample rewards, high remuneration, more 'sabhas', more 'kacheries', artistes are busy all 365 days of the year. Foreign tours too have become a fashion...*

Q. How has all this affected the performance and the maturity of musicians?

A. *In those days, life was less hurried. Music was taught only in the gurukul system. Which also meant that the day the guru gets complete confidence in his disciple, only then does he commence his lessons. Until that day the guru would not allow the pupil to touch the thambura! And then, unless the disciple practises properly, the guru would not add an alphabet to his knowledge! Perfection had to be achieved through stringent sadhana. Even if the ghandara (ga) or the madyama (ma) is sung, the raga's identity should be hundred percent clear! Until then, the shishya cannot learn the next lesson. Of course, those days there were less number of concerts, so there was ample time to teach and learn and practise. Nowadays, cassettes and records have become teachers! Just for name's sake a student goes to a well-known master and proclaims that he's all in all for him! I pity such shishyas and such gurus!*

Q. You talked about the variations brought in by individual singers in the same traditional compositions. How does one know where to draw the line?

A. *Take 'Theleyareru Rama' for example. How many times it has been sung by various vidwans, yet it is appreciated and enjoyed because of the subtle individual touch. The songs of the 'Trinity' have been sung for years, and have been glorified and appreciated by one and all at all times. It always gets a new flavour when presented by different musicians in different styles. This is exactly what is required! What the composers wanted to express in their songs should be clearly understood while singing. So that the emotions and the moods of the composition are maintained, for every new audience to encounter and appreciate.*

Q. Any message for the coming generations of musicians?

A. *Be deeply dedicated to your music, and totally devoted to your guru. (Recites in a soft, sonorous voice) Gurur Brahma, Gurur Vishnu, Gurur Deva Maheshwara...Gurur saakshat Param Brahma, tasmayeeshri Gurave namah!*

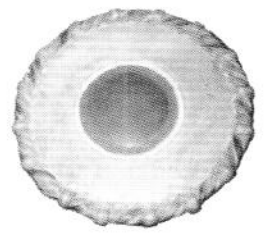

(Blurring our vision of 'Living Legends', Semmangudi Srinivasa Iyer passed away even before the printing inks could dry on these pages. Having transcended this world, he shall continue to make divine music for some heavenly audiences.)

SHIV KUMAR SHARMA

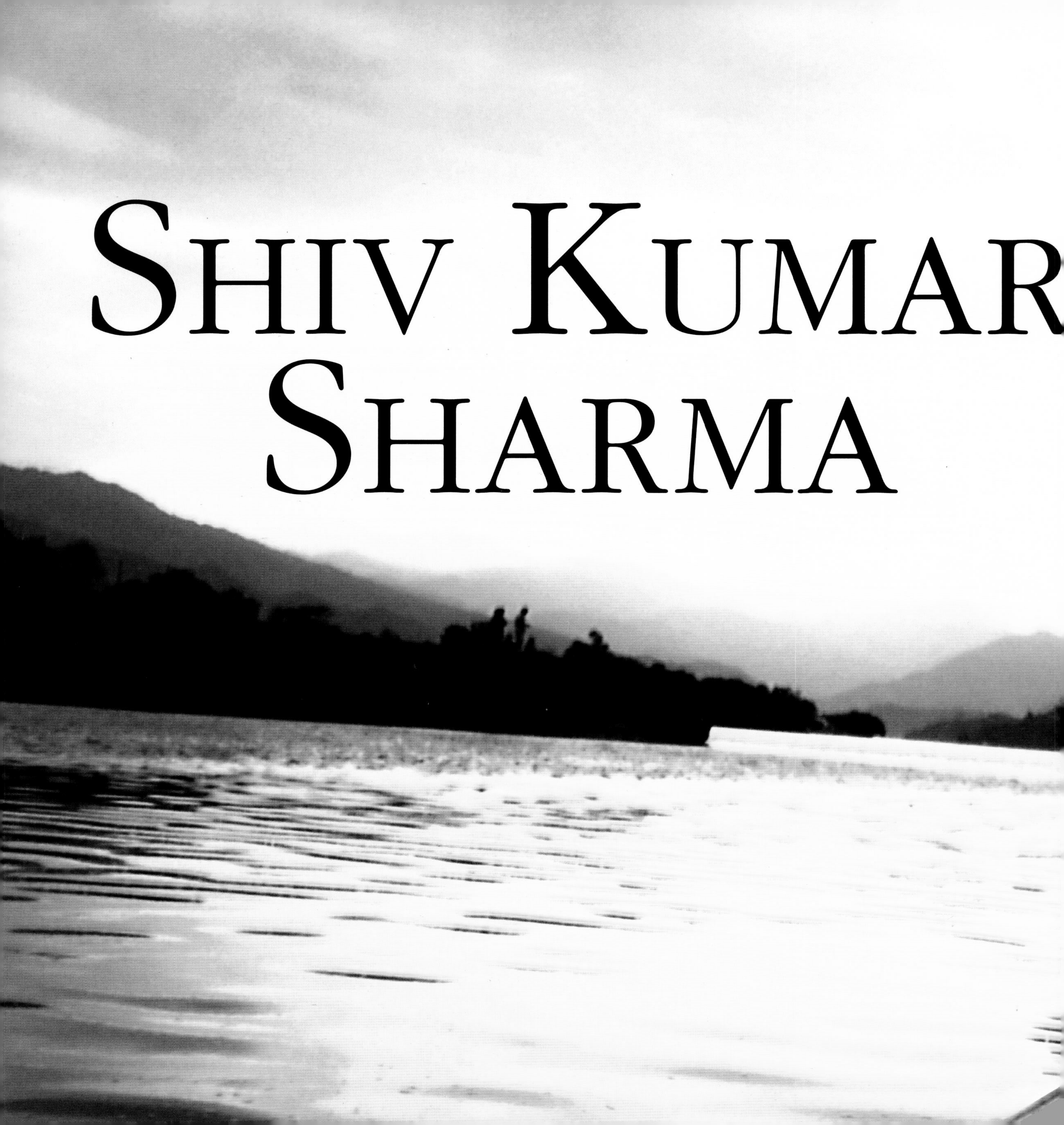

When Pandit Shiv Kumar Sharma was a lanky young lad of fourteen, his father had suddenly and ceremonially handed him a mysterious looking box wrapped in muslin, and had declared that from that day onwards this would be his musical instrument! Providence unfolded with the unwrapping of the gift, as Shiv Kumar stood staring at the strange Kashmiri santoor with shock and disbelief! Later, his father solemnized the moment further with a whispered prophesy, "Mark my words, son," he said, "Shiv Kumar and the santoor will become synonymous one day!"

What could a young adolescent do to change the face and fortune of an age old, traditional instrument played until then only in the context of Kashmiri Sufiana music? The answer lay in the fire of vision and conviction enkindled in Shiv Kumar by his mystic musician father. Pandit Uma Dutt Sharma, as if through prior knowledge, had already gifted his son the heredity, the *samskaras* and the environment to grow up and inscribe an exclusive chapter in the history of Indian classical music.

Shiv Kumar Sharma was born in Jammu, amidst such natural beauty and serenity that even the fleeting breeze there was palpably musical. A panoramic backdrop of meditative mountain range, including the lofty Vaishnodevi in the distance, the meandering indolence of the river Tawi, the fragrant garland of pine trees...everything was harmoniously orchestrated to provide a perfect setting to the large and beautiful house of his father, the *Raj Purohit* of the royal temple of Jammu. The versatile Uma Dutt Sharma's abode itself aptly complemented the idyllic natural environment. Rooms reverberated with philosophical discussions, prayers and Vedic chants, and from dawn to dusk, there was someone or the other singing or playing a musical instrument in some corner of this enchanted house. Shiv Kumar's graceful mother, like the quintessential Indian mother, often sang folk and secular melodies in her soft, beautiful voice. But it was Shiv Kumar's imposing father who ushered in a deluge of classical music in the family. Not content with merely the inherited duties of Royal Priest from his own saintly father, Uma Dutt found time to give passionate expression to his 'first generation' musical pursuits and learnt vocal music, the tabla, and many other instruments from various and far-flung sources, all by his self-willed efforts. He then went on to become a music teacher, and a young Shiv Kumar saw music students all around him, learning, practising, and even staying with their guru.

Shiv Kumar had heard that his father was overjoyed when, after ardent prayers to Lord Shiva, he was blessed with a son, more than a decade after Shiv Kumar's elder sister had been born. But later, as a growing child, Shiv Kumar could himself sense an even deeper joy and pride in his father when he began to realize that his son was born with music in his blood and breath.

A deep, meditative nature and a spiritual calm helped young Shiv Kumar imbibe all the Vedic teachings and rich Indian traditional values quite early in life. His romantic and sensitive soul found pure music in brilliant sunsets, dark monsoon clouds, and the canopy of bejewelled night skies...as he was constantly in quiet and solitary communion with nature and God.

Long before the santoor was handed over

to him, Shiv Kumar had, very naturally begun to formally learn music from his resident guru, his father. Completing the cycle of melody and rhythm, as it were, in his musical maturity, he soon acquired proficiency in both singing, and playing the tabla, under the affectionate guidance of his father. Since there were various other musical instruments strewn around the house, Shiv Kumar made easy acquaintance with each of those as well. As for soaking in the best of classical, folk, film and even Western music, there was the radio, in addition to his father's large collection of records. Academic studies in school and college were given just a cursory attention, while he enjoyed huge popularity among fellow students because of his musical skills and conquests. Everyone watched him starry-eyed as, even before he was ten, the beats of his tabla would often be heard over Radio Jammu! And soon, through the radio exposure, an adolescent Shiv Kumar had become a favourite tabla accompanist for stalwarts like Ravi Shankar, Radhika Mohan Moitra, Nikhil Banerjee, Nissar Hussain Khan, Illias Khan, Bhimsen Joshi, Hirabai Barodekar, Siddheswari Devi, and Begum Akhtar, whenever such artistes were in town. It was, in many ways, a fairytale childhood and adolescence for Shiv Kumar Sharma, placed in an ideal home and idyllic environment. Receiving that quaint santoor from his father, and feeling its weight on his young shoulders on that historic day, paradoxically, must have been Shiv Kumar's first major experience of discord and challenge!

Listening obediently to the conviction-powered voice of his father and guru, if not to the distant drums of destiny, Shiv Kumar began his courtship with the hundred stringed Kashmiri instrument. As he continued with his training of classical music from his father his exploration of

Shiv Kumar on stage with his favourite, Zakir Hussain

the santoor as an instrument of expression of that music ran parallel...with the understanding that the two will have to meet and merge perfectly one day for Shiv Kumar to realize his mission in life.

Housing an intricate pattern of strings and bridges, the santoor may appear like an acoustic labyrinth. But as Shiv Kumar began to know it intimately, he realized that, intrinsically, the instrument offered a good balance between rhythm and melody. It was a melodic instrument made to sing by striking it with percussive sensitivity. Shiv Kumar's goal focussed into vision, and he decided that he would need to virtually re-engineer the traditional instrument to take it beyond its technical limitations. His calling in life was to proudly enter the highest *darbaar* of Indian classical music with santoor in hand.

Shiv Kumar picked up the santoor from its traditional wooden stand, and quite like a symbolic gesture of *'god lena'*, adopting a child, he placed the instrument of his destiny gently on his own lap. As with a cajoled baby, a great deal of harsh vibrations vanished immediately. Then he set out to improve the tonal quality. Changing the number, the composition and the interrelation of the strings and the bridges, he embarked on a patient and challenging journey through the ebbs and tides of despair and determination. Years passed in his penance like efforts at making the instrument play the *alap* without which the rendition of his classical ragas would remain elusive. He spent many hours discussing and crafting his ideas and requirements with santoor makers in Srinagar. Finally, it was a combination of insight and inspiration, technology and technique, probe and practice, that eventually convinced Shiv Kumar that it was time to face the skeptical classical music world with his soul-mate, the maturing santoor. And from then on, his every recital would aim to be, at once, a new step into the ascents of classical music, *and* an assertive statement by the latest member of the elite club of classical musical instruments...

His first day of reckoning came unexpectedly. After being a regular on Jammu radio with both his santoor and tabla, there was a sudden invitation to perform at the prestigious Haridas Sangeet Sammelan in Bombay. Keeping his excitement in leash, Shiv Kumar laid out a condition: he should be allowed to play both his tabla and his santoor at the festival! The organizers argued with an adamant, teenaged debutant, the youngest among the galaxy of stalwarts slated to grace the occasion, but finally they decided to grant Shiv Kumar just thirty minutes to play whatever he wished. On D-day, when the curtain went up, many critical eyebrows went up with it, as the lanky lad from distant Jammu began his tabla solo, while an exotic instrument waited beside him under wraps.

His tabla solo received enough applause and encouragement to use up the allotted thirty minutes. Then, with the assured demeanour of a pioneer, he placed the santoor on his lap, tuned it, and without looking at the wings, began to play for the august gathering, the familiar Raga *Yaman* on his hitherto unfamiliar instrument. When he raised his face to face the audience after a full one hour's devoted performance, there was thunderous applause as the full glare of the arc lamps lit up his face and future! In view of the public demand, the organizers requested him to continue, but already having overshot his allotted time, Shiv Kumar bowed to the audience and walked into the wings. A star was born, and an instrument had announced its first cries of arrival within the portals of the lofty arena of classical music. Among the many who rushed to the greenroom to pat his back was the great Allah Rakha Khan, who had come to proudly congratulate the young musician from his own homeland Jammu! Genius embraced genius, and despite the age difference, a lifelong friendship had begun in that enchanted evening.

The next big performance was in Calcutta, at the All India Music Conference, where Shiv Kumar played in front of another huge and appreciative gathering, accompanied by the legendary tabla maestro Anokhelal. He won many laurels that night, including the prestigious Enayat Khan medal!

The Himalayan task of establishing his santoor on the classical pedestal, however, had just about begun. Many more peaks remained to be conquered. The problem was that although the general music lovers were exalted by the new sound of the santoor and its young talented exponent, the classical pundits and music critics remained skeptical and offered only mixed or patronizing reactions. Some even advised the 'promising youngster' to abandon the 'wrong' instrument and choose either the sarod or the sitar to realize his potential and promise. An introspective Shiv Kumar could rise above his feeling of hurt and see the point they were making after all. The seamless continuity of the notes, the perfection of the *meend* in the alaap of a raga still hovered just beyond the reach of his instrument. The *tapasya* had to go on...

The facility with which the new santoor created various moods, however, had been amply demonstrated, and V Shantaram, the doyen of early Indian cinema, invited Shiv Kumar to play some important pieces for his *Jhanak Jhanak Payal Baaje,* marking the *mahurat* thereby of a long future relationship between Indian film music and the santoor maestro in the making...

After graduation, back in Jammu, Shiv Kumar had to make a decisive career choice. This time his father's advice could not guide him. Because, for the first time in life, he braced himself to go against his father's advice. There was apparent career security in the two offers that were available to Shiv Kumar. One, of a music producer for the local radio, and the other, of a music teacher at the Jammu music school. While his *pitaji* would have been happy if he chose either, Shiv Kumar had to refuse both, because he had a creative

mission, and a routine job would surely make him feel stifled. Was the young man getting carried away by the sporadic concert invitations and the growing adulation, to think that a performer's career was the best choice? Debates and arguments came to a head, and when his father defied him to go and prove his worth in a big city, Shiv Kumar too grabbed the moment in a defiant fist, and declared that he would certainly try! All the heated pride had to finally melt down to tearful smiles and brave-faced parting, as with baggage and blessings, young Shiv Kumar left for Bombay. He must have held his santoor close to his heaving chest wherein his musical dreams had waited long enough to face the real world.

Bombay, the famous city of struggle and opportunities, provided both to Shiv Kumar in ample measure. After some initial hardship, his musical talent and the unique appeal of his santoor in creating both emotions and atmosphere were soon recognized by film makers. Furthermore, his pleasant personality earned him serious offers to play lead roles as an actor! His deep commitment to serious music fortunately kept him from being swayed by easy glamour and other urban distractions. He continued to burn the midnight oil over his task of perfecting the santoor, while his diary began to fill up with recording studio schedules and classical music concerts. He struck a ready friendship with fellow musician Hari Prasad Chaurasia, who had come to Bombay to establish his own instrument, the flute, and before long, they began to share a common sense of purpose in a common field of music, cementing their relationship with mutual respect, affection and warm companionship.

With a steady increase in earnings, a certain measure of security and comfort had set in. And it was enough to weaken Shiv Kumar's resistance towards parental appeal to get married and start a real home in his chosen karmabhumi. His charming bride Manorama, his parents' choice from hometown, brought a touch of domestic bliss and Bombay began to appear like a good place to settle down and ride the crest of his growing success as a versatile musician.

With the comfortable lifestyle and lucrative recording assignments in films, playing for topmost music directors from SD Burman to Ravi Shankar, a dark cloud of slumber and complacency had begun to glide in. His life's pledged mission of serious classical music was put on the back burner. Distant concert circuits were neglected and organizers were left with the impression that Pandit Shiv Kumar Sharma was losing interest in his crusade of pioneering the santoor's advent onto the centre stage of classical music. But the situation was soon met with timely awakening and remorse as his promise to his father echoed around his indolence, and Shiv Kumar soon returned with vengeance, determined to take his musical *tapasya* further, by carving out his own path.

Once the focus of his life's mission was regained, it was sharper than ever before. Just the rough edges needed to be ironed out in order to permanently end the oscillations, which still put a question mark on the santoor's status in the classical music field. While some great musicologists like Thakur Jaidev Singh of All India Radio, and international stars like Pandit Ravi Shankar, or even the most respected Dhrupad stalwart like Ustad Rahimuddin Dagar were very impressed with the santoor's classical potential, there were others, some diehard skeptics, including those that guarded the last bastion of the 'National Programme' slot of the All India Radio. So after years of careful research and *riyaaz,* when the technique to play the *alaap* was perfected, Shiv Kumar accepted the invitation to play santoor solo, to be measured against a top class vocal recital, in the presence of an eminent panel. And finally, the thunderous applause from that critical audience blew away all remnants of doubt. And All India Radio's prestigious national programme slot from then on has been repeatedly graced by Shiv Kumar's solo classical recital. And till today the santoor is a favoured instrument with various radio stations airing serious classical music.

In jugalbandi with Hariprasad Chaurasia, accompanied by Yogesh Samsi

The forward march of the santoor thereafter shattered all mental, physical and geographical barriers. As if in extended celebration of its elevated classical status, the instrument's all-round potential and unique qualities were being embraced by the expanding horizons. While, energized by the sound of santoor, thematic music albums like "Call of the Valley", "Antardhwani" "Elements" and "Soundscapes" were creating recorded music history, live concerts featuring enchanting *jugalbandis* and solo recitals of the Indian santoor maestro, were setting the world's far-flung auditoria on fire...creating fresh waves of audience interest towards Indian classical music.

Providence, whether one notices or not, plots well and casts well too. From that old Kashmiri instrument handed over by a visionary father to his prodigious son, the santoor in the last fifty years has claimed an entire chapter in the rich narrative of Indian classical music. And the protagonist, destiny's man Shiv Kumar Sharma has been chosen perfectly to pioneer the phenomenon. The santoor, in its new avatar, presents a gentle, soul-soothing sound quality and indeed, it is a perfect complement to the spiritual, saint-like persona of Pandit Shiv Kumar Sharma. Providence, evidently, has brought them together to serve a certain purpose in this era of fragile world peace, stressful lifestyles and strained human relations. Saints and spiritual greats like Swami Muktanand and Satya Sai Baba have lauded the promise of nirvana in Shiv Kumar's santoor...doctors and healers like Dr Keni of Mumbai and Richard Willis of Switzerland have been using his music to cure and comfort patients...and the young generation in growing numbers is reaching out to it to aid relaxation and concentration.

With Shiv Kumar's relentless tours for ITC's Sangeet Research Academy, reaching far-flung venues of India, and his commitment to SPICMACAY's vision of creating tomorrow's generation of music lovers... his widening sphere of carefully chosen disciples from diverse countries...his string of memorable conquests in the major arenas of cultural events and music festivals...his world renowned galaxy of friends and collaborators...and with countless lovers of his art poised in grateful exaltation...Pandit Shiv Kumar Sharma's ordained presence in the annals of Indian music shall forever be celebrated with the enchanting strains of the santoor...

Efforts to know the man intimately, however, will require a pure and spiritual vision, and a sense of identification with nature and eternity. You may have to begin with a scene even earlier than the one when Shiv Kumar had touched his santoor for the very first time...you may have to begin with *that* magic moment when his father, lovingly and expectantly, had drawn the sign *'Om'* with honey and saffron, on the tongue of his smiling, newborn son...

Living Memories...

That well-known profile

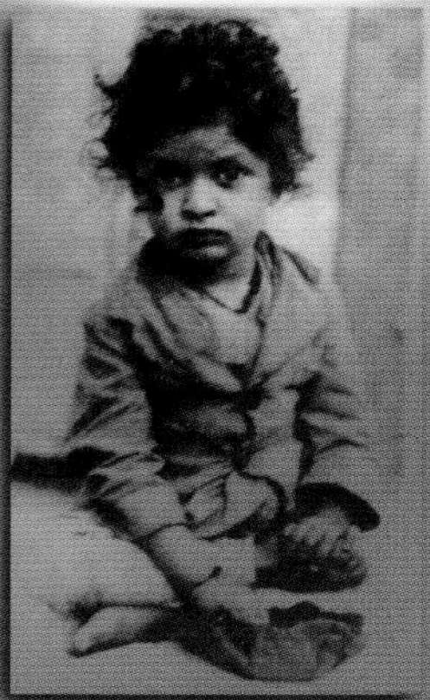

In Jammu as a two-year-old

Great friends. With Hari Prasad Chaurasia and Zakir Hussain

With collaborator Hari Prasad Chaurasia at a New York studio

With son and disciple, the talented santoor player and music composer Rahul Sharma

A congenial moment with Zakir Hussain

With Ravi Shankar and Hariprasad Chaurasia

At the launch of his book. With co-writer Ina Puri and the legendary actor Dilip Kumar

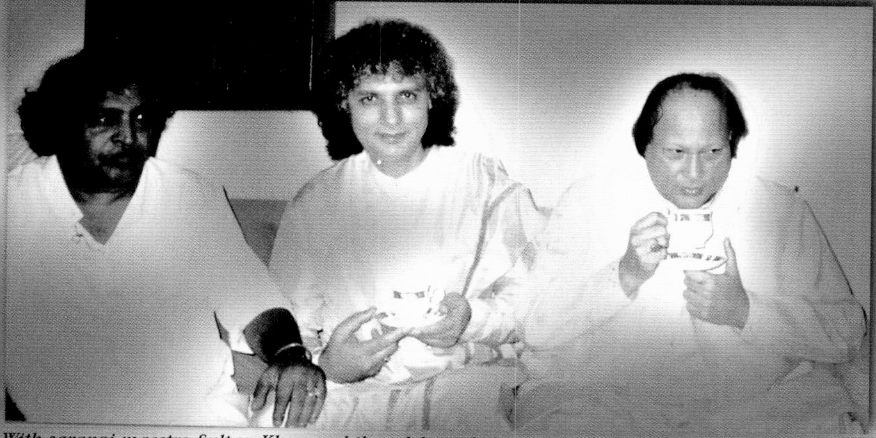
With sarangi maestro Sultan Khan and the celebrated singer Nusrat Fateh Ali

With senior disciple, the talented Satish Vyas

Family bliss. With wife Manorama, sons Rohit and Rahul, Rohit's wife Mayuri and their daughter

With the instrument synonymous with his name

Q. You began with an extraordinary sense of balance between melody and rhythm. Can you elaborate a little on this 'balance' factor?

A. *If you consider melody and rhythm to be like two wheels of a chariot, you will realize that for the vehicle to run smoothly, the wheels need to be in perfect balance and alignment. My extensive experience in vocal music and tabla playing early in life may have given me that edge where I have an instinctive feel about it. And later on I tried to turn a certain weakness of the santoor into a strength. Unlike many other stringed instruments, the santoor's tuning can be fixed, so that when you strike at a certain spot you get exactly the same note everytime. I have taken advantage of this in creating an ideal balance between rhythm and melody. People say emotions could be expressed through melody only and not rhythm. My experience says emotions could be expressed through the combination of melody and rhythm. Not melody alone. When you create a perfect balance between intricacies of rhythm and the emotional aspect of melody, then the music created is quite different. That's what I have tried to do. That's why perhaps, when I am trying to create something very intricate from a musician's point of view, even a layman is enjoying it! All because there is a balance. In rhythmic intricacies also, there is an emotional, aesthetic expression.*

Q. When you are playing your santoor without the tabla accompaniment, the rhythm factor is still in play?

A. *Yes. In fact, even when I am playing my alaap or jod there's a rhythm element present there.*

Q. I feel it is because of the nature of your instrument and your own musical sensibility...

A. *Yes, the lay listener may not be aware of the rhythm aspect, but actually because of that the music may be appealing to him.*

Q. The spirituality in you and your music is quite palpable. When were you first aware of it yourself?

A. *I have been very spiritual since childhood. Without prompting, I would repeat 'Om Namah Shivay' for hours at a stretch. Sometimes I would be drawn towards a remote Shiva temple and sit there all by myself. Such things came from within...*

Q. A hundred-stringed musical instrument named Shatatantri Veena is mentioned in ancient Sanskrit text. Does our santoor have other such reference points from distant history or geography?

A. *Yes. The Persian santoor, the German hackbrett, the Chinese yang-qin, the Hungarian cymbalon. And there are more variations in modern-day Iraq, Iran, Tibet, Kazakhstan, Vietnam, Switzerland, Greece, Italy and Ireland. I have personally had the opportunity to exchange notes with many exponents of such comparable instruments. And yes, it is quite possible that the santoor as we know it can trace back its origin to the Shatatantri Veena.*

Q. You had gone ahead with some plans to create a gurukul kind of institution for your students...?

A. *Unfortunately, I got cheated out of my land and investments, and I lost a lot of my own money there...*

Q. Oh! So what are you doing about it now?

A. *Well, (Smiles) I have not stopped teaching. My students still come to learn, from all over the world. The only thing is, I wished to provide some of them with a place to stay so that they wouldn't have to worry about lodging and boarding. But that was not to be.*

I still teach as per the guru-sishya parampara, without charging any fee. But I give priority to those who want to become professional musicians. Those wanting to learn as a hobby etc. are passed on to some of my senior disciples. As for the revival of my 'gurukul' plans, I am not very good at running after grants and donations, or pulling strings at government levels or whatever; my temperament does not allow me that.

Q. But suppose someone takes it up on your behalf?

A. *(Smiles wistfully) Who will take up such a task for me? It was my own responsibility. I tried, but it did not happen.*

Q. Journey with a Hundred Strings is a truly wonderful autobiographical book you wrote in collaboration with Ina Puri. When did you decide that it's time to pen your memoirs?

A. *It was during the celebration of my sixtieth birthday.*

Q. Any message or advice for aspiring musicians from the younger generation?

A. *My first advice would be never to offer advice unsolicited (Laughs). Still, if you insist, I might cite my son Rahul as a case worth watching. He is from the younger generation and he has himself chosen classical music as his career. He took his time, and I did not advise him to take up the santoor either. Today he already has a young fan following for his santoor and he is composing music for films too. Besides, he also involves himself in collaborative projects with other musicians like Richard Clayderman. The point is, today the world has become so small that you cannot but be aware of what's happening elsewhere and use that awareness in finding your own level and path. My advice to the young generation would be to do what its heart dictates. But yes, without forgetting one's roots, without distancing oneself from the rich culture, values, heritage and spirituality that India has to offer...*

Q. If you believe in reincarnation, what do you think you might have been in your past birth?

A. *(Nods). Definitely, I believe in rebirth. And if not a musician, I must have surely been a spiritual person. In fact, I have met people who are aware of their previous lives, their relationships with us...they used to visit our home and meet my father. I too have met some people who have told me a few things. This is a deep and fascinating subject.*

Q. What would you like to be in your next life, if you take rebirth?

A. *(Smiles) I am trying not to come again. But then, for that I need a few answers. Who am I? Where have I come from? Where am I going? Who's residing in this body, taking different identities in different lives? Until these answers come, maybe another life is needed. And then it is once again unthinkable without music.*

Q. Santoor?

A. *Maybe. Maybe something else. But music, for sure.*

T. H.
VINAYAKRAM

The ghatam is not just an empty earthen pot. On the concert stage of Carnatic music, it is the sacred womb of possibilities, the reservoir of percussive potential.

At repose in your lap, it is the repository of your wisdom, the extension of your physical being into the elemental awareness of Earth, Air and Ether...merged with the memory of the Water and the Fire that have gone into shaping it like the world.

At play, it wakes up Mother Earth's latent energies. Bathed in ripples of pure rhythm, she is poised to create new life on her surface. As your hands and fingers perform the primitive dance on the gliding arena, she warms up to the human touch, shivers in ecstasy. If your palms sweat, she smears it on her brown body. If your fingers ache, she absorbs the pain like offerings. The interplay heightens further with the tidal rise of your rhythm. You feel like the creator, suffused with his own creation. Your creative *kundalini* is awakened as your spirit enters the ghatam and plays it from within. You become your own ghatam, the epicentre of a cosmic storm. And then, alas, the audience applause reaches you like a faint, distant thunder...shattering the trance!

Things do not quite happen this way every time the ghatam is played on the performing stage. It takes a rare master like Thetakudi Harihara Vinayakram to make the ghatam float on its own sound waves and become the microcosm of the world.

Like many chosen souls, Vinayakram's life too had an unusual beginning. He was born along with his twin sister, named *Raman* and *Sita*, in the family of a great Carnatic musician with spiritual leanings.

Newborn twins had a high mortality rate those days in that kind of environment, and Raman did not look healthy enough to survive. Even astrologers said that the girl will survive; the boy might not. And Raman's feeble health seemed to endorse the grim prediction. To break the twin tangle, his healthier sister Sita was sent away to grow up in the custody of their musician uncle. And Raman was 'given away' to his father's *ishtadev* Lord Vinayaka, in symbolic adoption, with prayers for survival. Lord Vinayaka 'took him in his care' and Raman eventually lived and thrived by the extended name Vinayakram!

Life, however, was by no means easy, and nothing could be taken for granted, even as he grew up to be a boy showing rare musical talent. Vinayakram's father, TR Harihara Sharma, who used to teach music and play the mridangam for a living, had permanently damaged his finger in an accident. The sole breadwinner of the family, with a wife and six children, he had to switch over to playing the single-stringed *morsing!* An insignificant instrument compared to the 'mother of percussion', the morsing could not help him fight poverty with much success. He looked to his sons to help augment the family earnings by ascending the concert stage as soon as possible. He began to teach Vinayakram the basics of the mridangam, his estranged first love, which he himself could not play any more. But then again, another practical consideration pushed his plans further away from his desire. Professionally, it made more sense to add a ghatam to the family repertoire, whereby a combination of two artistes could get invited to perform in a given concert, instead of just one. So, Vinayakram's tender hands had to switch over to the hardened clay of the ghatam...often

Teaching at the Jai Ganesh Tal Vadya Vidyalaya

turning red and swollen at the end of the long hours of his daily practice. But then, the rare boy who could survive against great odds by bonding together the diverse Ram and Vinayaka into his own unique name, was not the flame the gale of adversities could easily put out! The ghatam was hard and heavy, but soon it became his best friend and helped lighten the financial burdens. Under his father's loving guidance, young Vinayakram seemed to pack in ten years worth of concentrated learning within a single year's time. The most intricate rhythmic compositions were clay in his dynamic hands.

His first public performance, again, was touched with a hint of the miraculous. Chosen to accompany a great vocalist, VV Sadagopan, at Turtugudi, a coastal town, the father and son duo reached the venue early, with several other musicians. The eleven-year-old 'Vikku' was eager to go to the beach with the others and try his luck with the oysters, which were sold there. But his father would rather have him sit at the guesthouse and practise on his ghatam. Soon, a vendor walked into the lane, and sold Vikku six shells for half a rupee! Prying open the six oysters was like pushing open the doors of fortune for the excited little Vikku! And then, inside the last shell waited a huge gleaming pearl, worth a thousand times more than the eight *annas* that were invested! More than its monetary value, it was a true omen and a harbinger of luck, as Vikku Vinayakram's budding talent shone like a pearl that evening at his crucial debut public concert!

Vinayakram's father revealed later that the gem compatible with his astrological rashi was indeed the pearl! Lord Vighnesh's blessings shone brightly on Vikku's fortune and he began to be recognized as the rising star in ghatam accompaniment in major Carnatic concerts. Vinayakram's loyalty to his ghatam increased day by day as he practised for endless hours, and even did some research on the genesis of the percussive instrument. The ghatam really had an ancient history, with a mention as far back as the *Valmiki Ramayana,* and also in a *shloka* associated with Lord Krishna! Closer to our era, the tribal women of Rajasthan, with their wrists adorned and armed with elaborate bangles, have been playing on their multipurpose earthen pots whenever their colourful skirts have swirled around on the

desert landscapes under the moonlit skies. Young Vikku's romancing the ghatam had acquired an epic sweep. His bonding with his quaint instrument was complete.

He began to play with many stalwarts of Carnatic music, both for cinematic scores and stage concerts. Great contemporary legends like GN Balasubramania, Ramanuja Iyengar, Allatur Brothers and TR Mahalingam were all pleased to have young Vikku with his ghatam in their stage concerts.

Then came that momentous evening which proved to be a prelude to his becoming an internationally recognized percussionist. The *'Pitamaha'* of Carnatic music, Semmangudi Srinivasa Iyer encouraged young Vinayakram to accompany him on stage. It was the best of occasions and the most prestigious of venues to showcase one's talents in front of the most discerning audience. It was the annual festival of the Music Academy, Madras. Young Vikku may have been a trifle overwhelmed, but the large hearted stalwart Semmangudi Iyer urged him on to give a spirited performance. He allowed Vikku a longish solo bout of *thani avartanam*, and the audience applauded heartily. The great MS Subbulakshmi sat in the front row and wondered if this wonder boy would agree to play for her concerts as well. Semmangudi, who was already showering his blessings on Vinayakram and his ghatam, was willing to mediate. Inviting Vikku and his father Harihara to his own residence the following morning, Semmangudi Iyer formally inquired if Vinayakram would like to play with a female artiste like MS Subbulakshmi. With respect, gratitude and spontaneity, Vinayakram said yes. Soon, Subbulakshmi's husband Sri Sadasivam

Soft hands working hard on the ghatam

thanked Vikku for his decision, and handed him their detailed concert schedule for the next six months! For Vikku, this was a very agreeable surprise, because amidst prevailing uncertainties, it meant the promise of a clear, fixed income for a period.

Indeed, Semmangudi Srinivasa Iyer and MS Subbulakshmi are the two angelic benefactors Vinayakram always remembers with mellow warmth of gratitude. Although Vikku's very first scheduled tour of America with MS was cancelled at the eleventh hour, owing to the sudden war with Pakistan, it was rescheduled for the next year, and the music centres of the West, playing host to the exotic feast of Carnatic music from India, were duly conquered. Including the UN headquarters in New York.

With Vinayakram's growing success providing the stability, his well-knit family experienced the added impetus to contribute its might to the service of Carnatic music. His two brothers gained expertise in the violin, mridangam and ghatam. His father continued teaching music with renewed vigour. They proudly watched Vikku become the greatest and the busiest ghatam maestro in the eventful Carnatic music arena.

Soon it was time for yet another major leap ahead, both for Vikku and his ghatam. L Shankar, of the three famous violinist brothers, introduced friend Vikku to the Western jazz guitarist John McLaughlin. After being a percussion accompanist in India for as long as a quarter of a century, Vinayakram burst forth on a rapidly expanding horizon! On an equal footing, he joined the four-member international fusion group named 'Shakti'. John McLaughlin with his guitar, L Shankar with his violin, Zakir Hussain with his tabla, and Vikku Vinayakram with his exotic ghatam...created major waves on the global fusion scene. Each member was given full liberty and was able to exhibit and develop his talent to the maximum, at the same time, the spirit of coordination fused and blossomed with each season.

'Shakti' literally demonstrated the *power* of collaboration between diverse forms and polarized entities and drummed away a few myths. The north and the south made music together through the tabla and the ghatam. The East and the West embraced, as did melody and

percussion. Rehearsed structure courted free improvisation. And many vocal critics of fusion music were made to eat their words of discord, as *Shakti* toured the world with resounding success...

For Vinayakram again, Shakti brought in more than just global recognition; it helped him gain popular access to the north Indian music arena as well. Stalwarts of Hindustani classical music, like Shiv Kumar Sharma and Hariprasad Chaurasia invited Vinayakram to play alongside them, and the audiences were delighted.

Overseas tours continued and kept getting more hectic. Balancing it out between concerts and family demands became increasingly difficult. In the faces of the frenzied international fans, Vikku began to see the quiet beacon of the smiling faces of the near and dear ones waiting in India. Shorter trips began to replace long drawn itineraries after that, as Vikku had to give more time and attention to his immediate home quarters, and of course, to the extended courtyard of Carnatic music.

The world at large, however, had no intention of leaving the percussive wizard alone for long. Vikku also performed with another fusion group named J.G.Laya, which included pianists and other percussionists. Amidst their sporadic tours, Zakir Hussain introduced Vikku to the globally famous Mickey Hart, and their explosive chemistry soon precipitated into the percussive triumph 'Planet Drum'! The global sales of the album by this name soared to a crescendo, and also won a Grammy award for its special creative achievement. It was the first time ever that a south Indian artiste had anything to do with a Grammy. Back home, there was another round of applause, as the 'insignificant' percussive instrument was finally recognized by India's Sangeet Natak Academy, who saluted Vinayakram and his ghatam with a long overdue award.

As far as Vinayakram's family was concerned, it was the ghatam that kept alive the mridangam. Vikku's father's tryst with the mridangam continued, taking a different form as he wrote his scholastic treatise on his first love, the mridangam, which he could no longer play on. His dream school was inaugurated in 1958, to teach the mridangam and other percussive

arts and instruments to young musicians. With Vinayakram's brothers plying the violin and the ghatam, the next generation also began to echo the percussive legacy with an exalted sense of belonging.

Buttressed by talented percussive pillars all around him, and inspired by his earlier experience with collaborative efforts, Vinayakram launched his own percussive group, naming it *'Sapthaakshara'*. Like the seven *swaras* of music, the seven auspicious syllables of percussion contain in them the entire *tala* and *laya* of the universe! Sapthaakshara is a splendid ensemble of young and talented performers like N Ramakrishnan, N Rajaram, A Ganeshan, V Umaganesh, V Umashankar and V Selvaganesh...led by the master himself. The artistes make their special music as they weave together their percussive magic with their classical instruments, including the mridangam, the khanjira, the geth, the morsing and the ghatam. A winner of the prestigious UNESCO award, this 'Tal Vadya Group' has been holding audiences in a rhythmic trance at concerts in a number of Asian and European venues.

Straddling the music world, holding his clay pot in close proximity, Vikku Vinayakram has never lost touch with the basic mud and soil of simple living. His child like innocence, saintly simplicity and genuine humility have endeared him to the entire world of music. He has helped open up many a window around the sacred temple complex of Carnatic music, whereby winds of alliance can enter and exit, carrying fragrances from either side. He is effusive in his praises for the human side of his fellow musicians as well. Along a unique professional

Enjoying an outdoor session with his senior students

career and a family life of dramatic ups and downs, Vinayakram has always kept his faith in man and god.

At the age of eleven, he had begun to support his father's family by playing the ghatam with his tender hands. Today, after repeated *'thani avartanams'* of personal glory, he is back holding the supportive reins of his father's percussive school at Chennai. His father's dream of passing on the power and magic of his 'lost' mridangam to the next generation is surely being realized.

As for the 'ghatam' of Vikku Vinayakram's life, it is both full, and empty. Full of joy and gratitude towards the god of life and music. And empty of all starry airs and achiever's ego.

Living Memories...

The young 'Vikku'

Giving his Ghatam a rightful place on the Carnatic concert stage

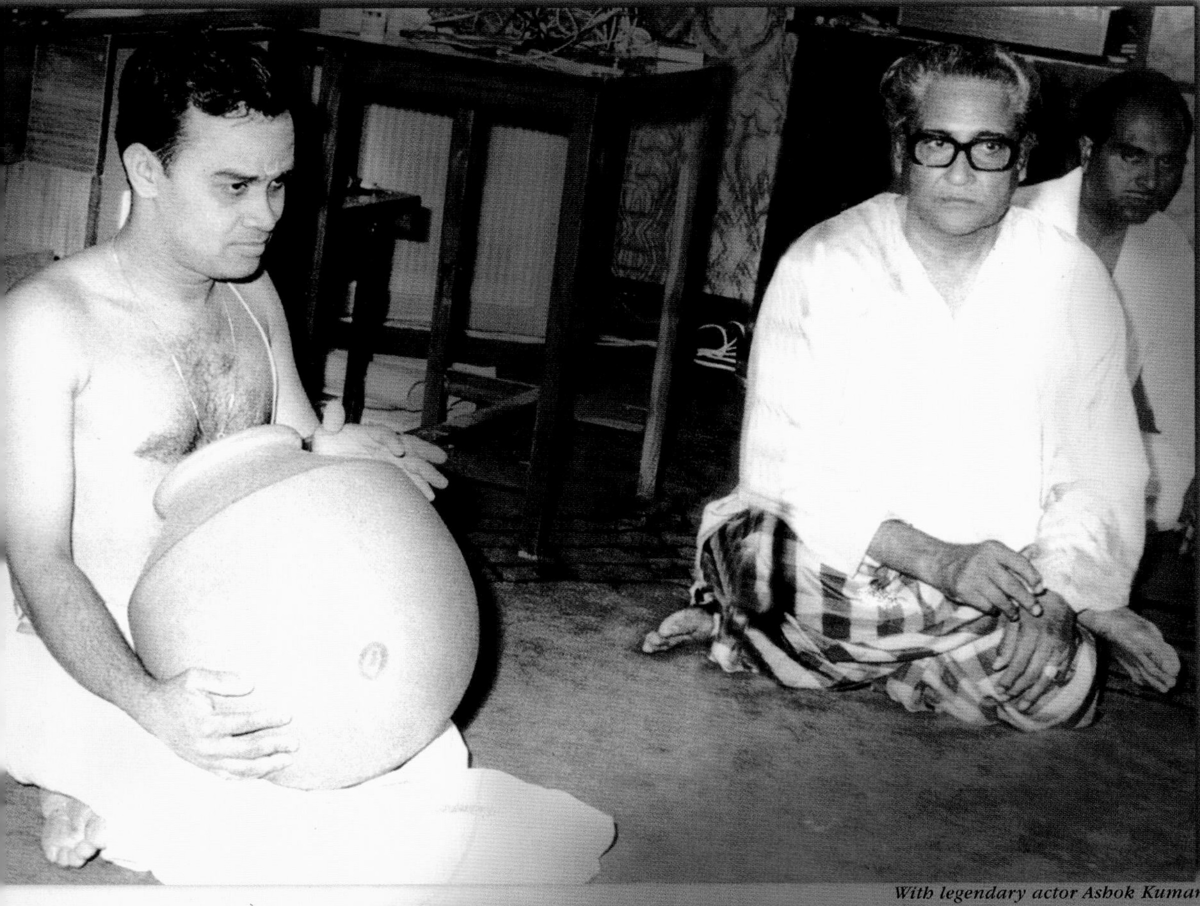

With legendary actor Ashok Kumar

With mrudangam legend Palghat Mani Iyer

A very early start to the career

Vikku and his percussion troupe, "Sapthaaksbara"

With actor chief minister MG Ramachandran

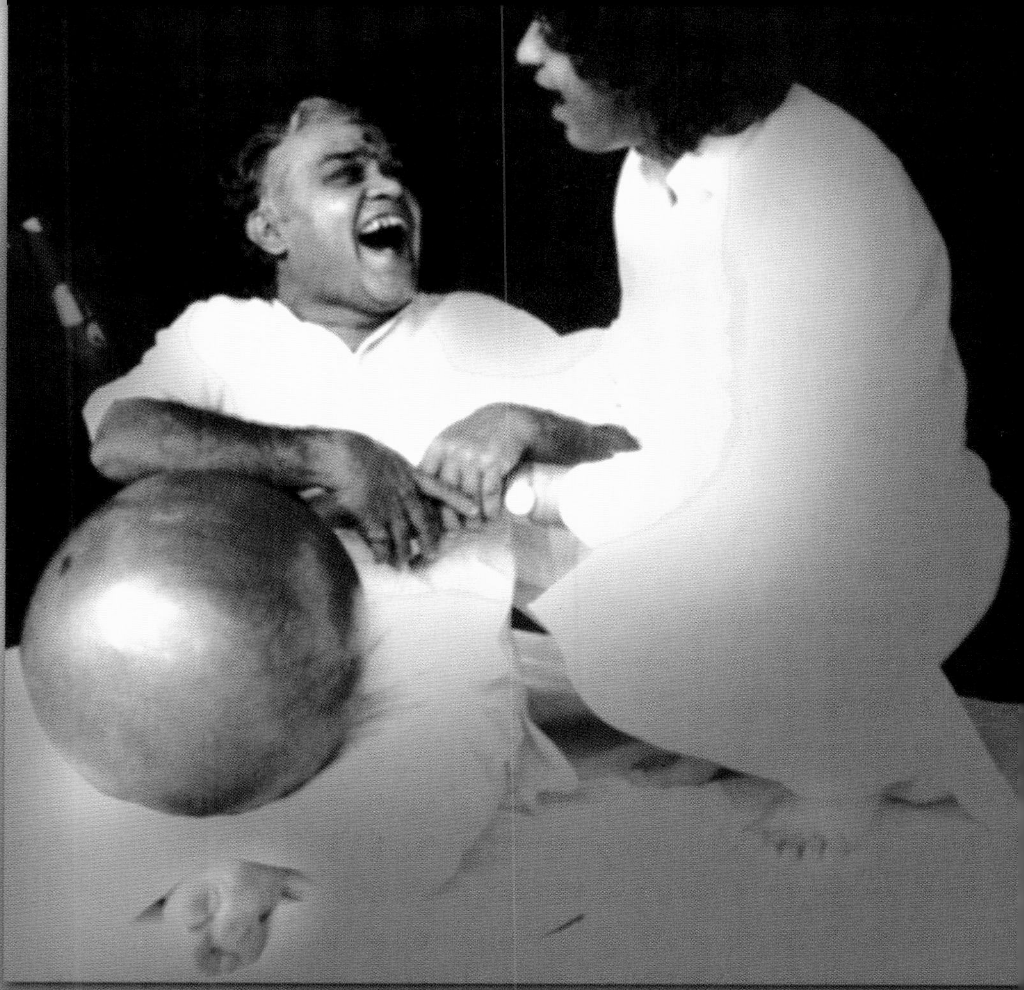

Frolicking with Zakir Hussain

At the centre of the first ever Carnatic music team invited to perform at the UN beadquarters

Q. Is the percussive ghatam as simple as it looks? How's it made?

A. *Basically it is clay. Fired with some metal filings. Five types of metals, panch dhatu, may also be added. Each individual ghatam varies from the next, both in size, and in pitch (picks up different pieces and demonstrates). This is from Germany, this one is from Athens, and these are products of pure Indian soil...And that other ghatam that you see there among the deities, is worshipped by me regularly. It was made auspicious by the touch of the Saint of Kanchi.*

Q. Rama and Vinayaka are deities from diverse pantheons. That makes your name somewhat rare...

A. *I was born as Raman, and was then 'adopted' by Vinayaka. Hence, the rare combination.*

Q. You learnt the mridangam first. And then, switched to the ghatam?

A. *Mridangam, as the mother of all percussion, should be learnt first in any case. I switched to the ghatam later because that gave our family members a chance to perform more and earn a little more within the limited scope of concerts.*

Q. More importantly, I feel you were destined to be associated with the ghatam, isn't it? It is a very eloquent and symbolic gesture when you throw up the ghatam in the air in moments of performing triumph?

A. *Perhaps. (Smiles)*

Q. Zakir Hussain's tabla and your ghatam have had a long and exciting history of association? It must have been a rare chemistry?

A. *Absolutely. Even at a human level, Zakir has been a wonderful person to associate with. He's like a brother to me. I remember, once in the middle of one of my earlier foreign tours, I was required to rush back to India because my mother was critically ill, and the promoter refused to allow me. Then Zakir, himself an exemplary, loving son to his mother, sympathized with me fully, and persuaded the promoter to agree. He even helped me with the extra airfare. Thanks to his gesture, I could see my mother in her last moments.*

Q. You have played with MS Subbulakshmi. How was the experience?

A. *Simply wonderful. Those days there was this odd attitude among male accompanists who were reluctant to play with lady artistes. But when MS expressed her desire to have a young ghatam player like me to accompany her, I felt honoured. My first air-travel, my first tour abroad, were all due to MS and her generosity, appreciation and affection. I shall never forget this.*

Q. How was your experience with the pioneering fusion group 'Shakti'?

A. *It got me recognition and fame beyond all expectations! I shall always remember John, Shankar and Zakir with great warmth and gratitude.*

Q. But you have opted out from the group when it was revived later as 'Remember Shakti'?

A. *My son Selvaganesh has taken my place. What could be better than that?*

Q. You have had many interesting experiences abroad...

A. *Yes, some were providential, if not miraculous. (Looks amused) Once, on my way to USA, I had taken a break at Germany for a concert with a veena player. Then, after a long car ride to the airport, I missed the onward flight. Just wandering around, I drifted into a music shop where I was stunned to spot a ghatam! An old German lady had made it, and after the shop owner requested me to test it and endorse its quality, he was keen that I accept the piece as a present. Since it was a small ghatam, I was able to take it along in my lap on my flight. When I reached my concert destination in America, my original ghatam was found broken! There was no other replacement, and the small new ghatam I carried, saved the day for me! Curiously enough, it was also of the same pitch!*

Q. What inspired you to launch the Tal Vadya group named 'Sapthaakshara'?

A. *Like the seven 'swaras', the seven basic syllables of our percussion too are auspicious.*

'Ta, Ti, Tum, Nam, Sha, Dhin, Ta' have immense mystical power and beauty. My group brings together many percussive instrumentalists to explore this and also experiment with new compositions to present a rhythmic experience to the audiences.

Q. You are the principal of the Jai Ganesh Tal Vadya Vidyalaya. Do you enjoy teaching?

A. *I like my disciples everywhere. I have earlier taught formally at the Centre for World Music, California, for some time. And of course this school in Chennai is my father's lifelong dream. As you can see, we begin teaching students at a very young age. I am happy that public interest in the percussive arts is steadily growing.*

Q. You had some miraculous experience at Athens?

A. *Oh yes. There again, my one and only ghatam broke into pieces, despite all care and protective packaging during air travel. There was no hope of finding another ghatam before the concert. I telephoned home to my wife to share my grief. Her brother, who is very spiritual, asked her to pray silently before god, and took her to the Saint of Kanchi, who gave her a coconut. Looking at the coconut, my brother-in-law was sure that I shall find a ghatam! As it happened, Zakir was to join us from London before the concert, and L*

Shankar and I went to receive him at the airport. There, as we saw him approaching us from far, we sighted a perfect ghatam! He was holding it on his head with his arms turned up, like the laughing Buddha! He had found it with some stranger in London, who had happily loaned it to him, simply because, the ghatam was gifted to him many years ago by some 'TH Vinayakram'! It was a mind-blowing experience to have been reunited with one of my own ghatams, when it was desperately needed!

Q. Amazing! Any message for the young, aspiring musicians?

A. *Well...have faith in God. Have faith in yourself; never doubt your abilities. Work hard as per your guru's instructions. And cultivate good behaviour towards every human being. Success will be yours.*

UMAYALPURAM
K. SIVARAMAN

His nimble fingers were making magic on the *mridangam* for the last one hour, and the sprawling audience was held in thrall. The slender, attenuated fingers, which could belong only to an artist, resembled two groups of acrobatic dancers trapped in rhythmic frenzy within their moonlike, circular arenas, on both ends of the percussive instrument. It was an intense and intricate interplay of contact and detachment, sound and silence, yet Umayalpuram Sivaraman himself looked more poised and relaxed than his captive audience! His senses, however, were actually in the realm of a yogic state of awareness, and that's when he noticed that tall, white man with golden hair, jostling gently for a foothold at the fringe of the rapt gathering. So, he had arrived again! Except, this time, something must have prevented him from coming on time, because the performance, alas, was very close to conclusion. Soon, as the excited audience began to disperse, almost reluctantly, the white man still stood his ground, as if rendered immobile by the abject dejection of having missed the major part of the concert. On an impulse, Sivaraman beckoned to him, and after a hesitant moment, the two men approached each other.

"Where are you from?" asked Sivaraman, "I have noticed you so many times in my audience!" The white man answered with a shy, reverential smile, " I am from Belgium." Then, as if to legitimize his presence, he muttered, " I like Carnatic music, and I am crazy about your mridangam!" Both men instinctively extended their hands in silent bonding, and then the real craziness of the situation gradually came to light. " For twelve years, I have been following your music, and attending this concert every year in India. This time I missed the venue and could rush in only too late!" A flattered Sivaraman enquired, "Who, really, are you?" Again, the shy smile, " I am a music lover. I am also a humble musician, who plays the saxophone."

Inevitably, the two men became friends. And later, when Sivaraman happened to visit Belgium, he realized that the 'humble musician' was none other than Fabrizio Cassal, a widely respected jazz artiste of his country! Somehow he had drifted into the universal orbit, the *tala* cycle, unleashed by Sivaraman's magical mridangam. Like many musicians and music lovers from distant shores, he too had his tryst with *Nada Yoga,* through this percussive force, which has a ripple effect on time, space, and events that guide the movements of men and matter.

Umayalpuram K Sivaraman was born almost seven decades ago in a small village of Tanjore, the cradle of Carnatic culture, where countless music vidwans have been born and brought up. Heir to the glorious lineage of the *sishya parampara* of the great saint Thyagaraja,

Sivaraman's father, Dr P Kasivishwanatha Iyer, is a medical practitioner and an accomplished musician himself. Evidently, he had recognized the inborn talents of his son, and had decided to nurture it with great intuition and foresight, in line with the traditional *gurukul* discipline, under the best of gurus.

Even as an infant, Sivaraman was utterly at peace with *tala* and *laya*. His father used to pick him up from the cradle, drum on his body with gentle, loving fingers, and Sivaraman would fall asleep with a smile on his face. In his waking hours, as he grew up to be a toddler, Sivaraman would drum his fingers on every object that would produce a pleasing sound! Impressed, his grandmother, presented little Sivaraman with his first percussive instrument, a real khanjira! Their house at Kumbakonam, where his father used to practice medicine, was a visitors' haven for all types of artists and musicians. A three-year old Sivaraman would move among the guests freely, playing away at his khanjira with great aplomb. It was time to find him a guru, thought his father, but providence beat him to it! A patient whom he had just treated, turned out to be Sri Arupathi Natesa Iyer, a mridangam player! The doctor remembered hearing his name before, and so he requested his grateful patient to take his five-year old son as a disciple!

By the time he was ten, Sivaraman's *arangetram,* or first public performance, was held in the precincts of a famous temple in Kumbakonam. It was impressive for the indulgent audience and encouraging for the ten-year-old prodigy. Seven years passed like a fast, *teen tala* beat for young Sivaraman under the guidance of his first guru, who then blessed him and passed him on to his next source of learning! Sri Tanjavoor Vaidyanatha Iyer, another stalwart of Carnatic mridangam, who had shaped even Palghat Mani Iyer into greatness, taught Sivaraman some of the finest nuances of the percussive art, for a year, before he passed away. Then it was the legendary Palghat Mani Iyer himself who accepted Sivaraman as his disciple for just a short while in Madras, but it was providential and touched with magic. Mani Iyer showered the cream of his knowledge on Sivaraman like a blessing, and remembered him

with the warmest affection evermore. Sivaraman then came back home to learn under his fourth teacher, Kumbakonam Rangu Iyengar, whom even Palghat Mani Iyer considered to be the greatest guru of all. He pursued his academic education at the Town High School of Kumbakonam, which had earlier produced the world famous mathematics wizard, Ramanujam. By the time Sivaraman completed his graduation in Arts, he had literally lived with the mridangam for almost sixteen years! He had already earned enough experience by accompanying many Carnatic musicians, and now, on his guru's advice, he went over to Madras where the concert arena was much wider and brighter.

Always a believer in holistic education, Sivaraman joined the law college in Madras to acquire his law degree. The art-loving principal changed his class timings from the evenings to the mornings, so that Sivaraman could easily perform at concerts and music festivals. After his law degree he went on to study international law, although all his lawyer friends advised Sivaraman not to get involved in the law profession, showering on him prophetic good wishes that he would become the greatest mridangam artiste in the country.

Madras was the ultimate challenging arena for any aspirant musician. The great Carnatic stalwarts were all there, including his guru Palghat Mani Iyer, to test him thoroughly, whether as rival or accompanist, as the case may be. Sivaraman saw all challenge as inspiration, and simply thrived in this environment. He had learnt his lessons well from the best of gurus, and had earned their heartfelt blessings. He had educated himself holistically, and had meditated deeply on the instrument itself and its playing technique. He had endless respect for tradition, yet he was open to exploring modernity and progress. He diligently developed his talent and attitude, which put him onto the path to becoming the greatest living mridangam player.

His attitude to his beloved mridangam has matured through a deep understanding of music itself. Sivaraman has seen the mridangam not just as a percussive device. To him, it is the 'king of percussion, *and* the queen of melody'! To his musical sensibility, it is nothing less than a *Naad Vadyam*! There are so many overtones on the right side, so many *gamakas,* or grace notes, on the left side! There is nothing lacking in the mridangam; it is the supreme percussive experience! It is this attitude that inspired and fuelled his will to undertake some practical developmental work on the instrument.

Sivaraman has been perhaps the only Carnatic *vidwan* who has explored, researched, and placed before the expanding world of percussion, the techniques and nuances of the mridangam in a continuous and systematic manner. Anticipating the difficulty in availability of the ideal varieties of seasoned wood like neem, jack, sandal and ebony, he has introduced the fiberglass mridangam. He has analyzed and experimented with the ingredients of the all-important black patch on the right side, he has researched the use of tanned and untanned skins and hides, evolved new patterns of rhythmic designs, and also devised a mechanical contrivance to eliminate human error in moulding skins for the mridangam on both ends. Above all, he has been able to merge the modern with the traditional technique of playing the instrument.

An acclaimed wizard of solo performance, Sivaraman has also enthralled audiences from diverse music spheres with his memorable duets or *jugalbandis*. He is the only Carnatic percussionist who has involved himself in more than sixty-five *jugalbandis* with famous north Indian artistes including tabla maestros. When Kishan Maharaj embraced him after a thrilling collaboration, there was an electric atmosphere of great ecstasy all around! Sivaraman played no less than fifteen duets with the dexterous Samta Prasad. At the end of their last *jugalbandi* at a concert in Hyderabad, the hefty Samta Prasad bodily hoisted Sivaraman in unbridled joy and exaltation!

Sivaraman, through his inborn talent and hard earned wisdom, regards music as the power and means for uniting countries and cultures. From interstellar dimensions to intra personal levels, he creates complete cycles of emotions with his fluent mastery of *tala* and subtle control over *laya*.

With the blessings of *Vakdevi Saraswati*, Sivaraman's unique eloquence on the mridangam, with its tuneful tones, often creates the illusion of a stringed instrument! Every stroke of his hand, like the diction of his speech, resonates with rare clarity. Rhythm in his hands, is like clay, with which he can playfully mould images that get enshrined in the memory of discerning listeners. When he underplays, it is like a whispery lullaby. When he takes the lead, often to the concealed delight of even the main artiste, he creates an electrifying spell of subliminal drama, a glorious bout of tension and resolution, which is the hallmark of all great art.

Sivaraman's unique sense of perfection in accompaniment is a philosophy in itself. At a tender age he was told by his father, that the mridangam accompanist should be the first *rasika*, the prime admirer of the principal artiste. Then your mood, your talent, your

Sivaraman with his musician wife

knowledge, your *nada,* everything will automatically merge with the music, and the performance as a whole will rise to great heights. Sivaraman has himself realized that when emotions merge, one can play with any form of music, accompanying any musician of the world. That's how, perhaps, he has successfully accompanied, without rehearsals, both familiar and exotic music makers alike. Music of the north, or that of even the West, have only meant new directions for his collaborative talent. From Ravi Shankar and Ram Narayan, to Pandit Jasraj and Hariprasad Chaurasia, every stalwart of Indian classical music, who has ever shared the concert platform with him, has commented that Sivaraman's *swara* is great! His mridangam sings!

And on his home ground of Carnatic music, Sivaraman's accompaniment has set the standards for the era. His supportive presence on the platform has often provided, what some critics have termed as the *'Siva-Raman Effect'*, assuring grandeur, glory and success to the concert itself! He has earned the blessings and warmed the hearts of all the stalwarts he has accompanied during all these eventful decades! Starting from Ariyakudi Ramanuja Iyengar, Palladam Sanjeeva Rao, Musiri Subramania Iyer from the yesteryears, spanning entire generations of stalwarts, down to the living legends, Semmangudi Srinivasa Iyer and Balamurlikrishna, he has merged his *tala* and *laya* with the divine swaras of the entire galaxy of luminaries from the Carnatic music universe.

Carnatic music is an expansive, cohesive, continuing tradition. There have been giants like Tanjore Vaidyanatha Iyer, Palghat Mani Iyer, and Azhaghanambia Pillai who have embellished the fluent tradition of the mridangam with their brilliance. Umayalpuram Sivaraman has crowned it all, with his lifelong contribution to the art and craft of mridangam playing. He has codified the paradigm and has developed demonstrable methods by which all possible combinations have been worked out and applied.

A prophetic philosopher at heart, Sivaraman has complemented the brilliant timing in his sense of percussion with his grand sense of Time. As advocated by the epic poet Kalidasa, Sivaraman has shown the wisdom of combining the essence of the past with the cream of the present, to lend directions for the future. And having found directions he has himself walked the path...with a pioneer's gait and an explorer's enthusiasm.

The rich harvest of his research and realizations has been distributed freely and lovingly to diverse forums and institutions of the world of music and percussion through his insightful articles and his innumerable and memorable lecture demonstrations. His professional recordings of concerts and thematic features like the 'Drums of India' and 'The Garland of Rhythm' are some of the treasures for the current and future generations of percussionists. The ever-approachable and ever-adorable Umayalpuram Sivaraman has appreciated the music of the entire multihued world, and has zealously accepted invitations to perform and collaborate with other musicians...spread across the continents.

After he has been honoured with almost all possible music awards and titles including the Padmabhushan, along his marathon musical journey spanning vast landscapes, the Music Academy, Chennai, in its recent Platinum Jubilee concert, has conferred upon Umayalpuram K Sivaraman the ultimate title of *'Sangeetha Kalanidhi'*.

His greatest honour and recognition, however, has been a moment etched in memory. After one of his many electrifying concerts with the great Semmangudi Srinivasa Iyer, he was complimenting the greatest living vocalist of our time with some heartfelt words of gratitude and adulation. The grand old maestro returned the compliments by telling Sivaraman how marvellously he had played. Then suddenly, the unanimously acclaimed *Pitamaha* of Carnatic music, did something quite unexpected. Silently, he gathered Sivaraman's hands in his own wrinkled palms...then placed and held them over his two eyes.

Sivaraman knows, there might never be a more eloquent statement than that silent gesture. Even from a thundering mridangam.

Living Memories...

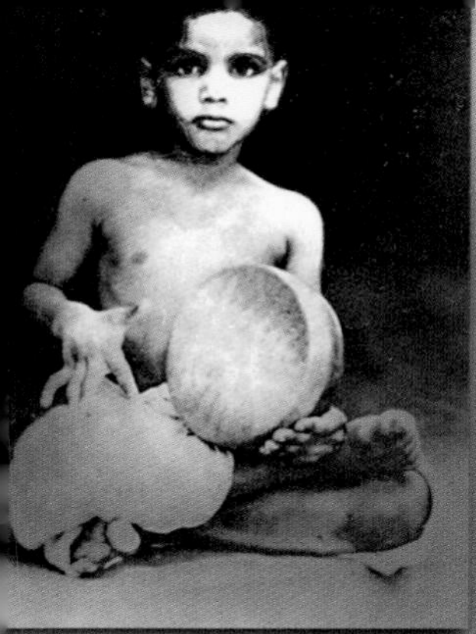

Playing the khanjira presented by his grandmother

With film star and chief minister Jayalalitha

The young couple

On stage with compatriots Balamuralikrishna and N Ramani

As 'mrudangam consultant' to the legendary actor Shivaji Ganeshan

With tabla maestro Allarakha

Dazzling under the spotlight

Sharing the microphone with film actor David Abraham

The 'spiritual guru'. With a famous European jazz band

With president APJ Abdul Kalam and violin maestro N Rajam

Being honoured by chief minister MGR

With former president Shankar Dayal Sharma

Accompanying Ravi Shankar at a recital

Q. Is there anything that resembles the gharana concept in Carnatic music?

A. *It is important to refer to the historic background of the north and the south. About five centuries ago there lived a great scholar named Haripala. In his writings we find the oldest ever reference to Hindustani and Carnatic music as separate terms. Before the Muslim invasions, there was just one music throughout. That's how, in Dhrupad, you may find many similarities with Carnatic music, for example, the pakhawaj instead of the tabla, for accompaniment. Since north India was more exposed to outside invaders, and their culture and music mixed freely with Hindustani music, this could have inspired the creation of several gharanas. As for the south, it almost remained intact, with very few invaders from the north, and therefore Carnatic music retained its composite form in all the four states, Kerala, Tamil Nadu, Karnataka and Andhra Pradesh.*

Q. How does the music evolve from guru to shishya?

A. *The guru teaches everything according to his knowledge. But the disciple learns and imbibes according to his manodharma. He has to give full vent to his shravana, his act of listening. When you hear, say, the same Shankarabharanam by different exponents from the past and present, the disciple can pick up different threads and create his own impression and interpretation of the raga. That's how the raga gets embellished and flowers. In mridangam playing, for instance, there are only two schools. The Tanjavoor, and the Pudukottai. While the Pudukottai school is characterized by denoting the appropriate bols or percussive fraises for the lyrics, the Tanjavoor style concentrates on tonal beauty, embellishment and the elevation of the music to a high degree of excellence and aesthetics. Today, the Pudukottai school is slowly getting absorbed within the more popular Tanjavoor school.*

Q. The genesis of mridangam is very ancient, isn't it?

A. *Three instruments are considered most original and sacred along with their presiding deities. Lord Krishna and his flute, Devi Saraswati and her veena, and God Nandikeshwara with his mridangam. The shastras even mention that when Shiva danced his cosmic dance, Mahavishnu played the mridangam! Music is nada yoga. It is said, when the yogi reaches his highest state of trance, he enjoys the taste of nectar in his tongue. He enjoys the sound of the veena and the Vedas. And the nada of the mridangam.*

Q. Tell us something about the construction of a mridangam?

A. *'Mrit' plus 'anga' makes 'mridanga'. Earlier it used to be made of mrit, or clay. Then different types of wood came to be used. Jack wood, neem, ebony, sandalwood, red sander and a variety of palm trees. It was auspicious. We used to cover our mridangam with a saffron cloth, to protect it from pollution! Then there are the skins or hides on both ends. The black patch that gives tonal beauty, in the olden days, used to be taken from riverbeds and mixed with rice and applied on the right side, while it was cow dung ash and jaggery on the left side. Now, the black patch is*

Happy memories of being honoured by MGR

available in stones. A combination of iron and manganese ore are finely crushed into a powder and mixed with cooked rice and applied on the right side, while for the left side one uses the cream of wheat (rawa).

Q. What made you think of the fiberglass mridangam?

A. *While more than two-hundred-year-old wood used to be ideally chosen earlier, today you do not easily get that kind of seasoned wood. Plus, the skilled artisan families are becoming increasingly rare. So I thought, why not try fiberglass and also standardize the measurements etc. It has worked rather well. I am contemplating setting up a factory for instruments like khanjira, tabla, mridangam and drums in fiberglass.*

Q. You say that the syllables of the mridangam are sacred and auspicious. Could you elaborate on it a little?

A. *As you get up in the morning, our shastras prescribe certain objects to be seen which are beneficial. Such as the cow, the mirror, the palm of your own hand, the mridangam...*

The auspicious and the beneficial qualities of the mridangam extend into its dynamic form as well. The percussive fraises emanating from both sides of the mridangam are known to confer great power and goodness to the performer and the listener. For example, the very first four letters that are taught to the students of the mridangam are 'tha, dhi, thym and nam'. These very letters can be the quintessence of the Vedas: "tat twam asi" or, "that thou art". Likewise, in music, " Sa re ga ma pa dha ni " confer the same beneficial effects on mankind. All that I play on my mridangam, as taught by my revered gurus, are traditional and authentic. Of course, my own manodharma in mridangam playing has presented a new concept, which is known as the 'Sivaraman effect'.

Q. An accompanist on percussion automatically gets to encounter different kinds of musicians and their music. You must have had the best of alliances.

A. *Indeed. I have, first of all, been lucky to be born in an era where my shravana, my sense of hearing, has been suffused with the divine music of an astonishing number of great musicians. Then, I have myself been blessed and honoured by encounters and alliances with so many stalwarts from as diverse sources of music as one can imagine.*

Q. Most of it is common knowledge. Tell us about a few unusual ones?

A. *Do you know, a great scholar musician, Kallidaikurichi Shri Mahaveda Bhagatar, an authority on Muthuswami Dikshitar compositions, who also happens to be my music guru, sang for me for ten years, without expecting anything in return! Did you know that once in Delhi, Ustad Amjad Ali Khan played along with my mridangam, instead of the tabla, for one and a half hours. For the last eight years I have been a guest artiste for Aka Moon, a famous jazz band in Belgium whose members consider me their spiritual guru...Steve Coleman came to Chennai for a whole month to exchange musical ideas with me, and later I was invited to the Chicago Festival. Pandit Birju Maharaj requested me to play my mridangam with his Kathak for one hour...My experiences are really diverse because I regard all music as great and divine.*

Q. You have recently surprised everyone by making music for a fashion show?

A. *Yes, I took it up as a challenge. (Smiles) I discovered kinetic movement in their walk, in the liquid flow of the fabrics, I regarded the visuals like a graceful dance form, and composed music for it. At the end of it the participants confessed that they lost their sense of time, it was such a spiritual experience for them. So, I don't think I have gone away from my music; if anything, I have expanded my horizon. One should never remain static; one should continuously evolve. Every opportunity is a gift of God, and should not be rejected without a thought.*

The guru, amidst his senior disciples

Q. People look forward to the 'Sivaraman touch' in mridangam learning...How optimistic are you about the future?

A. *My wife is deeply involved in music. My two sons play the mridangam and the violin, even my five-year-old grandson is learning mridangam and music. My daughter-in-law is learning the veena. And, of course, I am particularly proud of my spread of disciples from India and abroad, to whom I pass on my 'touch' without discrimination. Even ladies learn the mridangam these days...A few ladies learnt the mridangam and the khanjira from me. A rich legacy must surely be passed on to the next generation. That is my mission in life.*

Q. Do women have the kind of strength and stamina to play the mridangam?

A. *They are the real 'shakti'. They shape men, families, societies, nations... One needs more spiritual energy than physical power.*

Q. Some people lament the decline in interest in classical music from the younger generations?

A. *Where is the decline? There are a hundred schools of music today. Music academies, institutions are thriving. There's growing media support, sponsorship, seminars, festivals. Today, festival organizers of Carnatic music receive thousands of applications from musicians who wish to perform! Plus, there's growing interest abroad in our kind of music. I am currently interacting with some American university students, and producing a fusion of Hindusthani, Carnatic, Jazz...so that even on a saxophone you can produce swaras and ragas... I give them notations and they reproduce everything wonderfully!*

Q. How do you begin teaching traditional Carnatic percussion to the students?

A. *First I tell them, you don't beat the mridangam, you 'play' the mridangam. Next, you should learn to relax. From your shoulders to your elbows, to your wrists, to your fingers, you've got to relax. When you have got a relaxed body, you won't tire even after six hours of practice. I teach them tala, I teach them vocal music, and finally I teach them how to accompany and embellish the music. In accompaniment, you have to be like a dharmapatni to the main artiste. You have to adjust and reach the pinnacle of excellence in execution. The same musician may display ten different moods in ten different venues; you have got to sense it, and harmonize with it quietly, sensitively. I also teach them the holistic* *approach to percussion. In fact, one of my projects is an elaborate treatise on tala itself. For each tala, there's a star, a gem, a colour to wear for clothing and so on...everything is interconnected. Every tala too has an appropriate rasa, which can be expressed through this wonderful instrument. There are so many finer points...heard, and unheard.*

Q. Have you ever suffered from ego clashes during a performance?

A. *I have been fortunate enough to be liked by all my collaborators, vocalists, as well as instrumentalists. They have appreciated my attitude of adjusting to their strengths and weaknesses, of constantly embellishing their music further, and raising the performance as a whole to greater heights. Once, I told a senior legendary stalwart, that I was enjoying performing with him so much, that I did not want the thani avartanam, the solo percussion bout. He, of course, decided to announce that to the audience so that everyone present could appreciate my attitude! The applause I received instantly was far greater than what the thani avartanam would probably have fetched me! Similarly, whenever I have requested greats like MS Subbulakshmi, DK Pattammal and ML Vasanthakumari, not to do 'namaskar' to me, but to bless me instead, they have said, of course, they would bless me and my family. But they must do 'namaskar' to my art, my talent. That's the kind of response I have always enjoyed from fellow musicians. There has never been any question of ego clash, and nor shall it ever be.*

Q. Do you believe in reincarnation?

A. *I do. (Smiles) And I look forward to be born again as a 'mridangam vidwan' with even better qualities, and the same heart and desire to enhance and pass on all my knowledge to the future generations...*

ZAKIR
HUSSAIN

The attack was timed with deadly precision. The aircraft was flying high at forty thousand feet and its earliest possible touchdown was a good thousand miles away. The body of the beautiful and newly crowned Ms Universe was eased out flat in a supine position by the shocked airline staff. She was still warm and gorgeous, except, her heart was not beating! Her companion, a celebrity make-up artist, looked helpless and was in tears, even as the anxious voice of the captain had begun to peter out after having repeatedly requested the passengers to keep calm. Since there was no doctor on board, the chief steward recalled his training days, and tried to revive the celebrity victim, but his nervous attempts at resuscitation proved futile. Everyone was grappling with a sinking feeling of hopelessness. Some had begun to pray for the departed soul.

The biggest celebrity on the flight, however, was in deep slumber in the very first row. With his halo of silvery curls around his calm, handsome face, and looking much younger than his seventy years, Ustad Zakir Hussain had been catching up on some lost sleep perhaps. But suddenly, as if prompted by some inner voice, he woke up, and after a quick appraisal of the gloomy situation at hand, sought out the head steward and whispered a request in his eager ears.

A pair of tabla was hastily pulled out from his cushioned bag and placed near the head

of the lifeless Ms Universe. Then the world-renowned wizard of percussion rolled up his sleeves and made space for himself to squat on the floor. He closed his eyes for a moment or two, touched his ears and his heart fleetingly, and placed his hands, which were insured for a million dollars, on his tabla.

He thought of asking everyone to remain quiet, but already there was such a heavy air of silence, that one could hear nothing but the faint drone of the speeding airplane filtering in. Holding their breath, the passengers were staring incredulously at the maestro, clueless, but sensing some impending drama. Zakir Hussain began with a light touch on his *baanya,* the left tabla, and with a movement that resembled a cobra about to strike, he gradually created a semblance of stifled heartbeats. Slow and laboured in the beginning, the beats picked up rhythm and momentum, sounding like real heartbeats, amplified manifold, and moving steadily towards a shattering impact! The effort looked magical and superhuman...and soon the effects of it went beyond realism, as his right hand began to impact the edge of the right tabla, with sharp, spirited, empowering strikes, pushing each 'heartbeat' to explode with life! Those who were bending close in the inner circle of the audience moved back instinctively. They had literally held their collective breath for an unnoticed length of time...until they saw a sudden glorious smile replace the taut, animated expression on the maestro's face! Then, as they looked down, they found Ms Universe looking at them with large, fluttering eyes, as if she had just woken up from her beauty sleep! She was greeted with a thunderous 'welcome back' to the mortal world as everyone began to clap like children. Within breathing distance, she found the well-known face of one of the world's favourite musicians staring at her like an angel! A jet-set spiritual guru seated in the rear, explained quietly to his disciples, that the beauty queen's spirit must have been hovering with deep attachment around her hour-glass figure, when the crafty tabla maestro managed to pull it back into the body with some percussive wizardry...

The above episode may well sound incredible, but it is not impossible. It was a candid attempt at foreseeing the manifestations of Ustad Zakir Hussain's genius in the future... After all, even with his already Himalayan past achievements in music in general, and the tabla in particular, he appears to belong to *the future.* A future that he continues to shape with his electrifying performances, and inspiring presence in today's unified world of music.

Zakir Hussain, the eldest son of the great Ustad Alla Rakha, was born into a lineage of gifted musicians, who had migrated from

Jammu to the metropolis of Bombay. Long before he can himself remember, a toddler Zakir had made his intention of becoming a tabla player amply clear, by beating on idle pots and pans around the house. When the disciples of his father would practise on their tabla, Zakir would sometimes walk in and play the invader's drumbeat inviting an instant surrender.

After the initial span of indulgence, young Zakir would be gently shooed away. But when this persisted over a period, one fine day Ustad Alla Rakha was compelled to show his young son how the 'real thing' should be played. Zakir himself does not remember the specific date or time when his physical and spiritual tryst with the tabla was flagged off with his father's blessings.

While there is no doubt that Zakir was a young genius who arrived with his gilded baggage of percussive instinct and musical intuition, it is equally true that his sense of commitment and application made him devote most his adolescent waking hours to learning and practising the art and craft of the tabla. If there was any divine inspiration, it was worshipped with honest beads of perspiration. He would sit alone and practise, and Ustad Alla Rakha would walk in and out of the room, suddenly correcting a mistake he might have noticed, suddenly throwing him a teasing challenge, and suddenly again rewarding Zakir with a happy nod. This kind of regular yet informal interaction went on to form the bedrock of Zakir's learning process. The disciple had to call his guru's attention to his needs, sometimes even by making a contrived mistake or two.

Thus, without thinking that he was doing something earthshakingly unusual or special, or that he was being consciously groomed to take the name of his father to even greater heights, young Zakir kept himself immersed in music. He plumbed the depths of Indian classical music as naturally as a fish would explore the ocean. And unlike many other budding musicians of that era, he did not miss out on a good, formal school education either.

Zakir was always aware of a mind of his own: realistic, analytical, and pragmatic. His subtle and intuitive musicality was steadily enhanced by these complementary qualities. He was proud and happy to be a student at heart. He could therefore listen to other music greats without judging them, and thus imbibe qualities and styles he liked or enjoyed. If he was critical, it was only towards his own self, his *riyaaz,* his learning, his performances.

By the age of twelve, Zakir had begun to play the tabla professionally. He gained confidence by playing at private functions before small gatherings. Both as a tabla player and a young boy, he was treated casually, and at best, patronizingly at the elite business houses where he would play for invited guests who would sip at their wine, or puff away at their cigars after dinner. Zakir would return home late, perhaps with a hundred-rupee note, or sometimes, carrying just a packet of assorted food leftovers, but a lot richer in worldly experience and stronger in his resolve to make his mark in music.

Without latching on to his star father's coat-tails, he began to slowly but steadily carve out his own path by responding to travel and concerts at far-flung places. At times, when he could not afford a reserved seat, he would be armed with an old newspaper, which could be

spread over the floor of the train compartment, if he failed to find a seat. No false ego, or cocky notion of being a great *ustad's* son, could deprive him of the valuable human experiences that go to enrich the mind of a youngster who climbs his own ladder.

Soon, Zakir had begun to accompany some great musicians of the land. Pandit Shiv Kumar Sharma, among many others, was to play an important role as a future collaborator in many concerts, tours and recording achievements. As a curious coincidence, both Zakir's and Shiv Kumar's affectionate mothers, unknown to each other, sat side by side in the front row of the audience, when a fifteen year old Zakir gave his first public performance with Shiv Kumar at a Bombay auditorium!

The year 1970 was a major landmark for a nineteen-year-old Zakir Hussain, as he made his American debut. America was to be the land that would give him his wife, his family, and a greenroom behind an expanding stage platform, which would eventually span the entire world...His performance in the first American concert was with none other than his father's long time collaborator, Pandit Ravi Shankar!

Ravi Shankar, despite the age difference, found magic in Zakir's accompaniment as well! The freedom and encouragement that he gave to the tabla accompanists, sometimes by going to the extent of laying down his sitar and keeping time with his hands while the tabla player got to play solo, had already revolutionized the age-old equation between the main musician and his accompanist in the Indian classical music arena. The justification and success of this pioneering endeavour was once again in full view of the appreciative music world! A privileged audience witnessed two exceedingly charismatic musicians light up the stage with their envied appearance and gifted genius. Their instant chemistry, and the manifestation of it in melody and rhythm, must have been a sight for the gods. Ravi Shankar was at the peak of his career, and Zakir was at the peak of his youth...and it was evident that achievers of Himalayan magnitude have many peaks along their long career span. This was also a collaboration that symbolized and underscored many salient aspects of Indian classical music, within the ambience of a grand Western venue. Because of their age difference, it was a meeting of the present and the future, melting away the generation gap. Because of Ustad Alla Rakha's long association with Pandit Ravi Shankar, this concert was also a statement of glorious continuity. Young Zakir must have glimpsed in the older man, an inspiring, glowing idol of what a versatile genius with a universal musical vision could achieve. And Ravi Shankar must have held the younger man in an affectionate gaze, proud and secure in his belief that the world shall continue to be romanced by brilliant musical ambassadors from his motherland. The performance extracted a thunderous applause, and ended with an essential cultural statement as Zakir bent down to touch Ravi Shankar's feet and was gathered lovingly in a fatherly embrace, the sweat beads on both faces gleaming under the arc lamps...

Zakir's American debut opened up the floodgates for an avalanche of musical accomplishments. In India, he straddled the diverse arenas of north and south Indian classical music by accompanying stalwarts from both regions, and as an emerging world musician, he bridged the great East West divide. With an uncanny grasp of music in any form he could easily understand each one among the wide and diverse range of musicians he accompanied. In the midst of growing adulation and a young fan following, Zakir's self-assessment continued with unabated honesty. He would sit for hours and scrutinize his performance recordings, detecting faults and areas of improvement.

He played with the great Kathak exponent Pandit Birju Maharaj, and other classical dancers began to wish for his accompaniment. He became the leader of the Taal Vadya Rhythm Band, the group that later evolved as the Diga Rhythm Band. Spreading his wings, Zakir joined forces with the British guitarist McLaughlin, Indian violinist L Shankar, and ghatam wizard Vikku Vinayakram to form the 'East-meets-West' super group 'Shakti'. As a bandleader, he toured the world with 'Zakir Hussain's Rhythm Experience'.

The recorded music industry, both in the East and the West, owes enormously to the versatile and disciplined talent of Zakir Hussain. Way back in 1980, when his first recorded album for HMV with Pandit Shiv Kumar Sharma was to be released, the santoor maestro defied convention and compelled HMV to put the accompanist's photograph beside his own on the jacket cover. Two years later, HMV's very first live recording of classical music took place in front of a 2500-strong audience at Bombay's Rang Bhavan, where Zakir and Shiv Kumar kept the audience so enthralled that there was no ambient noise except for a series of well-timed audience applause! HMV's first-ever double album 'When Time Stood Still' acquired its name from the headline of an ecstatic review where a leading music critic showered unprecedented praises on the sublime music produced by Zakir and Shiv Kumar.

Zakir's exemplary talent in providing inspired accompaniment to any great musician of the world is almost telepathic! And it is rivalled only by his other great talent of playing electrifying and utterly inspired solo tabla. Reversing the conventional equation between melodic and percussive exponents, today, even respected musicians feel privileged to provide simple melodic accompaniment to Zakir's riveting solo performances on the tabla! Planet Drum, an album co-produced with Mickey Hart in 1992, fetched Zakir his first Grammy for "Best World Music Album". His debut solo album "Making Music" had earlier won accolades as "one of the most inspired East-West fusion albums ever recorded"! One of his many historic achievements was a musical celebration of India's fifty years of independence, where Pandit Shiv Kumar Sharma, Pandit Hariprasad Chaurasia and Ustad Zakir Hussain bonded in a magical combination to present the concept of India's 'unity in diversity' through the river-like journey of classical music down the ages. Such a sublime presentation would have been unthinkable without Zakir.

As his musical mind began to seriously transcend the conventional confines of percussion, Zakir gave vent to the creative artist in him in a variety of ways. He composed several albums with the cream of global musicians like George Harrison, Van Morrison, and Joe Henderson, and also performed with the New Orleans Symphony and the Hong Kong Symphony. He took charge of arranging the grand opening music for the 1996 Atlanta Olympics. Many film makers had this exciting idea of inviting Zakir to perform for their soundtracks. Apart from doing a commendable job there, Zakir then ventured into complete music direction for those film makers whose style, theme and content presented him with challenge and inspiration. At the 1983 Cannes Film Festival, Zakir got nominated for an award as composer and music director for the film Heat And Dust. The other landmark movies, which used Zakir's versatile musical talents are, Apocalypse Now, In Custody, and Little Buddha. Zakir's acting talents have been showcased in movies like Heat And Dust, and more recently, in a series of highly successful advertising endorsements for India's famous Taj Mahal tea.

Always experimenting, always pushing the limits of his creativity, Zakir has gradually matured into a complete and well-rounded creative colossus. He has also pushed himself constantly to allow the simple and humble human being in him to manifest. Otherwise, for someone constantly riding the crest of creativity and basking in starry-eyed mass adulation, there is always the danger of being deified and losing touch with one's true self. It is a matter of good fortune for the current generations of young musicians, that their idol Zakir Hussain remains exemplary in his every action and gesture, both on and off the performing stage.

Extremely eloquent in his speech, Zakir can articulate his own philosophy, and his reflections on life and music with great facility and flourish! Ustad Alla Rakha's great sense of humour often surfaces in Zakir's spirited story-telling among friend circles. Setting up home in a culturally and geographically distant American town, Zakir has never lost touch with his Indian core. Indian cultural nuances, Indian *tameez-tehzeeb,* find enduring and endearing expressions in his behaviour.

An incessant flow of titles, awards and accolades from an early age has not unduly coloured or burdened his self-appraisal. His disarming charm and genuine humility are a perfect foil for his commanding dexterity on his tabla! Musical power and pride may brim over his intensely energized finger-tips during a performance peak, but his face glows with a shy and embarrassed smile, when the lion's share of the audience applause gets directed at the 'accompanist' Zakir Hussain. And when accompanying someone as senior as Ustad Ali Akbar Khan, for instance, Zakir squirms at the use of the prefix 'ustad' before his own name.

With all the world as his stage, Zakir is truly a global citizen of music. He has travelled the continents and has responded creatively to the people and the music of many countries and cultures. He has imbibed much, but perhaps, has contributed even more. His underplayed acts of charity and philanthropy are in the grand tradition of his great guru and father Ustad Alla Rakha, who took his final bow at the turn of the millennium. *Abba's 'barsi'* is observed by Zakir and his talented brothers, as a majestic tribute to the kind of music he has left behind. In this annual function, many major musicians and almost all the top percussionists are invited to participate and perform, in an exalted spirit of belonging and musical brotherhood...

Going back to the 'future', Zakir himself perhaps would not approve of such a fanciful projection with which this chapter begins. Neither will he admit as yet, that his talent with the tabla has reached such a steady pinnacle of perfection that he'll have to seek future challenges only on a different plane. But then, only when the rose realizes that it cannot perfect its beauty any further, that it discovers fragrance...

Like, when all dreams surrender at your feet, only miracles beckon.

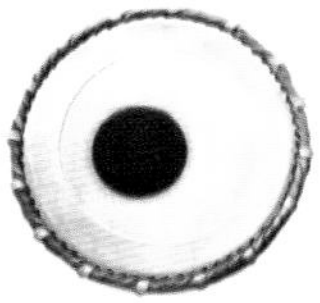

Living Memories...

Youthful and adorable

The young ustad

As an adolescent, with Ravi Shankar

Man and wife

With 'abbajaan' Allarakha, Kishan Maharaj and Shiv Kumar Sharma

Demonstrating the finer points of tabla playing

With father Allarakha, tabla nawaz brother Fazal, the sarangi wizard Sultan Khan and the legendary danseuse Sitara Devi

Trying a different percussion

With Amjad Ali Khan, Jasraj and father Allarakha

With friend and admirer Moon Moon Sen

With Ravi Shankar

In his elements among fellow percussionists

With celebrated sitar maestro Vilayat Khan

With much respected sitarist Nikhil Banerjee

Q. How is the guru-shishya relationship changing in a faster world?

A. *Those days, the guru would keep testing the patience and dedication of the student before investing time and energy on him. So you had to be humble, patient, you had to realize the importance of the knowledge you were going to acquire. Today's students may not understand that, because the guru is willing to sit there and teach you. What comes easily loses its importance. Yesterday's gurus took a long time to teach even one raga—but then, they made sure that the student learnt to appreciate it, honour it, cherish it and protect it. Protect its purity.*

Q. As a young boy you wanted to be like your father?

A. *Of course. But then, you realize you cannot be what he is. So you learn to be different. Having imbibed all that's great in him, you may strive to be a bit different, a little better if possible. This is a very significant aspect of Indian classical music. Bade Gulam Ali Khan's style was not like his father's. So, the style of the Patiala gharana changed during his time. Amir Khan's style was not like his guru's. So, Kirana changed. These people gave the gharana system a boost. Took it forward, rather than let it stagnate, and perhaps fade away...*

Q. Then there are instances where the son takes a deviation. For instance, Pandit Ram Narayan's son took up the sarod.

A. *Sure. It doesn't have to be the same, exact pursuit. Among Thirakuwa Khan saheb's sons, one became a novelist, one became a singer, and only one played the tabla. As long as you are in the same creative field your father lived in, you can maintain it, or you can expand on it.*

Q. What about your children?

A. *It's the same thing. My elder daughter is a film maker. My younger daughter is learning dance. I have told them it's not important for me that you become a doctor, or an engineer, or a computer programmer. Just do something creative with your life. I don't expect you to earn millions of dollars and support me in my old age. Just go out and follow your creativity - whatever it is!*

Q. Your father's stature and presence must have been so imposing when you were young. Did that stifle your desire to go and listen to other tabla greats?

A. *In my father's time, the opportunity was very limited. Travel was neither fast nor easy. Since my time things began to change. Today there's television, radio, discs, cassettes...*

Q. So, did you form any opinion of the other greats?

A. *Whether they were good or bad?*

Q. Yes. And whether some special quality in someone appealed to you?

A. *Well, basically I listened because I enjoyed them. I never tried to judge them. After all I was a student; how could I even think of judging masters? If I liked something, I tried to follow it, that's all! People like Chaturlal-ji, Kishan Maharaj-ji, Kanthe Maharaj-ji, Shamta Prasad-ji, or Ahmad Jaan Thirakwa sahab, they were such great musicians, such great players, one just loved listening to them. Even today, when I am* *listening to, say, Swapan Chowdhury, or Anindo Chatterji, or Anees Pradhan, or even my brother Fazal...and if I like something, I say, "Hmmm...that's good! Let me see if I can do it?" It's the learning process, you see. It's always there.*

Q. What do you think of the newer generations of tabla players?

A. *I know of about eight or ten tabla players, who are as good as me, if not better.*

Q. That's incredible! What about other kind of musicians?

A. *I am not truly an expert to analyze that.*

Q. But you have played with so many musicians; what do you like about the current crop?

A. *What I like is their hunger for knowledge. And they have the access. Plus, today's gurus are willing to teach them day and night! What knowledge I acquired in thirty years, today someone may get it in three years! Even before he is technically perfect, he has the knowledge. So, the moment some proficiency is achieved, the show begins!*

Q. But that's facility. What about dedication?

A. *This hunger for knowledge is evidence of their dedication. No one can stuff information into your head unless you want it, unless you value it and use it in your own enrichment. That's why today you find so many fabulous performers like, say, Kala, Amaan, Ayaan, or whoever. But if you go back in time, and take the example of the great sarod maestro Ustad Ali Akbar Khan, you will realize, that at these people's age, he probably was still trying to unravel just two or three ragas in terms of information and hadn't even figured out if there were others, and what their names were, and what their ascending and descending scale might be. But today's emerging stars already have that information and that's what gets them even more excited about this art. Besides, I feel, today's musicians are even more connected to our traditional values than what we were in our days. In our younger days, we were inspired by the West; we wanted to go there, see the world. Today's generation already knows much of it. There is no mystery as to what Chicago is like, or what London has to offer. All the information is available here. So they can be much more focused on what's here.*

Q. There's also this reverse trend happening, the 'return home' attitude...

A. *That's a fact. Ten years ago there was hardly any book on musicians. Today, there are a dozen. There is no stigma attached to being an artiste anymore. The new generation can already see what awaits their pursuits. You are appreciated, honoured, revered, to the point of being worshipped! In our younger days, we did not enjoy such a scene. We were embarrassed at*

times, by people's attitude towards musicians.

Q. Did you personally experience this, ever?

A. *Oh yes! People were surprised that I spoke English! And I didn't smoke or drink, or chew paan...When I went to several cities to perform, I was ignored at the railway station by those who were sent to receive me! Nobody thought that a musician could look anything but a fat, dhoti-clad, paan-stained, middle aged man! (Laughs).*

Q. Tell me, as a tabla player, did you personally encounter a slightly demeaning attitude in comparison with the 'main' performer?

A. *Personally, no. Because I wasn't a master. If I were, say, Kishan Maharaj, I would surely have felt slighted. But I was just a young student who was happy to be even in the same room with those great maestros, in any capacity. Today's musicians, of course, are treated well even before they are famous. They are not ashamed, they don't feel looked down upon. They are sure and confident of their worth. So they are going to do much better than us.*

Q. Are you really so confident of the new generation musicians?

A. *I genuinely feel they are very good and have a really bright future!*

Q. Not all the stalwarts I have interviewed share this view...

A. *That may be because they perhaps don't interact so much. Take Pandit Jasraj or Pandit Shiv Kumar Sharma. They are constantly in touch with their students, and the other younger musicians of the world, watching, listening, travelling, interacting with other country's musicians. While there may be some other senior musicians who currently are not aware of what possibilities are being thrown up, what great talents are emerging. They also forget, that fifty or sixty years ago, say, a Vilayat Khan was a young master, a prodigy. Bismillah Khan was a young master. Just as, say, a Shahid Parvez or a Buddhaditya, or any other promising youngster is today. Not everyone thought that Vilayat Khan or Bismillah Khan would become such stalwarts in future! But look at them today: they are living legends of classical music! Likewise, there's nothing to stop today's young musicians from becoming as great in the future!*

Q. You are saying, this pessimism then is misplaced?

A. *This pessimism about Indian music's future, whoever has it, must be in relation to what it was; not what it is, or what it should be.*

Actually there's a loophole in the inherited concept of Indian classical music. It says, you must follow the tradition. But then, it also says, you must create spontaneously anew, afresh! It says that. But how are you going to do that if you are going to be stuck following tradition? It is very well and easy to say, there are millions of combinations possible in a raga! Well, name five hundred? (Laughs) You cannot! The old masters

were in their own Vrindavan, under their own banyan tree, practising in their own ashram, with their own students for decades...without actually hearing anything from anybody else! That is not true now. Today, you are going to be exposed to the world, you will imbibe, analyze, you are going to expand your vision, your impression of what music or what art is all about. It is the same for a musician, a writer, a painter, or any other artist.

You should be spontaneously improvising, creating something new. Raag Darbari played today should sound different from Raag Darbari played tomorrow. Why should anyone say that your music should be what it was fifty or hundred years ago? You do not even know what it was hundred years ago; there are no recordings available! You have no idea who played how!

Q. But people still try to cling to what they remember...

A. *It is your youth that you actually remember. Your first love. The first smile of a beautiful woman you saw. It's natural! It is gratifying as well to remember and maintain that high! Such people become compulsive keepers of a tradition. They are doing their job. While the others are going out and seeking and making changes as well! These others, when they are old, might complain that music is changing, they are not the same, and so on. So, you see, it is a cycle. Not to be taken as criticism, as if things are going awfully wrong. It is just a natural unfolding of life! There are people on both ends balancing it out. It perhaps happens in every generation, in every field and walk of life...*

Q. The unprecedented adulation you've received all over the world...have you ever tried to rationalize it?

A. *I cannot. Like I said, there are eight to ten tabla players today who are just as good. So how do I rationalize? Maybe, I was at the right place at the right time, that's all! And I do not believe that I necessarily deserve all this!*

Q.But there must be some very special abilities in you...

A. *My special ability might be that I am on the same wavelength as everybody else. I play the way I played thirty-five years ago; my sound is the same. It's just that after hammering it down everyone's throat and mine, for years, suddenly a window may have opened up! 'Ah, that's what he's saying!' It's as simple as that. Bhagwan Rajneesh didn't really say anything different. Nor did Swami Vivekananda or anyone else. There is really nothing that you do not know! What you are looking for is a confirmation of what you already know. When you hear it from somebody, and it makes sense to you, that somebody becomes important. That man appears to be a source of knowledge. But the fact of the matter is, that the same knowledge is already inside of you. I cannot say anything new. The world has existed millions of years before me; everything has been said and done. What I may do, however, is do something or say something in a manner that may appeal to someone who knows it, but hasn't understood it earlier...and suddenly we strike the same wavelength! That's what happens. We click!*

Q. From all the great masters you have accompanied over the years from an early age, is there any privileged, special learning you have acquired?

A. *Well, I have learnt to analyze and understand myself better. Where I am, what I am capable of. I know it is nothing extraordinary; it's just usual. A doctor, for instance, studies and gains experience and becomes proficient through a normal course of many years, as I have. He may not receive the same fame or adulation that I might receive as an artiste. Although I have been doing something very normal in my field, just as he, in his field.*

Q. You are being modest.

A. *No, I truly believe I have followed just a normal course. I grew up in this, it's just normal for me!*

Q. Tell us about your experience as a music composer in movies.

A. *Well, as you may have noticed, I don't do regular Bollywood kind of movies. I only do projects that I want to get involved in. Those, that I enjoy doing in terms of creative freedom and genuine contribution. When your musical interpretations of someone else's vision is given*

that much respect and importance, that's a challenge worth taking up!

Q. So, the movies that you have done...were they entirely satisfying?

A. *Yes. That's because I have done what I wanted to do! To me, that's the criterion of success! Success is not that it sold a million records. Success to me is to stand behind my work and say, 'this is exactly what I wanted to do!' Whether it is good or bad, that's not the issue. That's why I do projects that are independent, creative, and deal with subjects that allow you to be able to subtly and intelligently use your music to enhance the impact!*

Q. You have seen the world, known the world's music. Where would you place Indian classical music as against the rest?

A. *Why do I have to make such a placement? Why should there be a number one, or number two, or number five?*

Q. Well, I am not asking for a rating, but just a statement of distinction as to where you'd place your country's music in the global context?

A. *Okay, how important is family to you? How important is your home? Does that answer your question?*

Q. Yes, it does. Any intensely spiritual experience you remember?

A. *Making music itself is spiritual. Sometimes, when you are playing with a certain person, you connect with that person, and realize that he is thinking the same way at the same instant! This is an intensely spiritual experience. Say, with Pandit Shiv Kumar Sharma. Without overtly communicating, we get bonded by the same musical piece...we become one! With Pandit Jasraj...maybe I play something that complements his piece, and there's magic! We haven't rehearsed it; it just happened! He looks at me, I look at him. That's great! You are striving to get something out of your hands...your guru walks in and says, 'Yes, that's good! Now try this!' To me, even that is intensely spiritual!*

Q. Do you believe in rebirth?

A. *Do I believe in rebirth? Probably, yes. But while as a traditionalist, I may believe in rebirth and continuity, I am also a rationalist. I know that what I need to achieve I got to do it now, in this life! I cannot sit back and say, 'I'll do whatever I can, and then come back and take it from there'. I do not therefore dwell on rebirth issues, because I do not wish to save anything for a possible next life!*

Q. What about your past life?

A. *Well...I don't know. But yes, when you are barely six or seven, and you are producing something that generally takes years to master...then one wonders! Sometimes, people say, it's in the blood. But then, is it in your blood because you were doing this before you came here, or is it in your blood because it was the spirit of some master who was looking around, and decided to come back into this body? Who knows?*

Q. Have you ever done any thinking on this?

A. *Not really. Like I said, I don't want to rely on what was or what might be. I want to rely on what's here! And I want to be able to do the best I can, now! But yes, if I do come back again, fine! That'll be a bonus.*

Q. What would you then like to be born as?

A. *A tabla player, naturally! That's what I am.*

Q. But your musicality extends much beyond...

A. *I am still a tabla player. (Smiles mysteriously).*

Zia Fariduddin Dagar

Ensconced in the heart of IIT Mumbai, the renowned temple of science and technology, the seekers of truth might find an unexpected sanctum. Fanned by the cool breeze blowing across the picturesque Powai Lake, the greenery that forms a canopy around this sanctum is alive with much more than the chirping of the seasonal birds. The hermitage-like atmosphere actually resonates with some eternal music...emanating from human voices and handcrafted instruments.

Presiding over this daily festival of learning is the quiet presence of a saint-like guru. Ustad Zia Fariduddin Dagar. If the longish nomenclature sounds sacred, it enshrines an infinitely longer and sacrosanct musical heritage. Putting us in touch with the unpolluted Ganges of Indian music, the Dhrupad. Which may be regarded as the mother of all classical and light classical forms of music the world enjoys today. This chapter, without which this book would remain utterly incomplete, therefore belongs as much to Zia Fariduddin Dagar, as to the grand musical heritage he upholds: the Dhrupad.

Once you emerge out of the realms of mythology, you can mark the beginning of the unbroken ancestry of Indian music with the very first and archaic efforts of formalizing a musical structure, named the *Prabandha*. This was the music that rose like incense from burning lamps of devotion, at the myriad temples of ancient India. The words were those of temple rituals and the fervour was that of worship. From literary and poetic rhymes and metres in Sanskrit, the *Prabandha* gradually got set into some basic *ragas* and *talas*. With changing times, it began to embrace themes other than

Reflecting on music near the idyllic Powai lake

devotional, and entered the precincts of the king's courts. From serving a ritualistic purpose, it expanded its scope to become a performing art and cater to an elite audience and the demands of changing tastes and aesthetic sophistication.

Classical music thus found its first real formal expression and the term *Dhrupad* came into existence replacing the *Prabandh*. It continued to be sung in the temples of worship and it simultaneously established itself in the royal and aristocratic realms over centuries. The legendary Miyan Tansen in emperor Akbar's court, the fabled Sadarang and Adarang, sang Dhrupad of the highest order. And so did many saint poets who sang praises of the divine. A purist's language, the Dhrupad allowed very few liberties to the adventurous exponent. A recital had to begin with the delineation of the raga structure with some phonetic syllables. It would then spread itself over four stages or stanzas: the *Sthayi,* the *Antara,* the *Abhog,* and finally, the *Sanchari,* with continued emphasis on the text, which would generally be in praise of god, saint or king. Then, gradually, as music began to gain dominance over the words, Dhrupad began to acquire a different feel and character, with the tala aspect coming into prominence along with it.

Over two hundred years, the Dhrupad remained the highest and the most sublime form of music in India. During this long period it acquired different formal and stylistic variations, which came to be known as *bani-s*. Each of the bani-s, like *Shuddha, Bhinna, Goudi, Vegasura,* and *Sadharani,* attained distinction through their emphasis and specialization in various musical aspects, such as, *alapi, bol-baat, laykari*...Some of these distinctions were adopted by various musical gharanas that came into existence subsequently, after the inviolate rigidity of

Dhrupad began to allow the gradual advent of the more free, exploratory and imaginative *Khayal*.

Dagur Bani, with its distinctive emphasis on tonal nuances and elaborate *alapchari,* is the form of *Dhrupad* that Zia Fariduddin Dagar's family has been immersed in for the last eighteen generations. With religious steadfastness, the Dagars have not deviated from their music in this world of changing tastes and values. And that perhaps has as much to do with their pride in their distinctive musical lineage, as with their very deep realization of the fact that Dhrupad *is* after all, the mother of all classical music. And like the sound of the Vedic chants, like the resonance of the temple bell, the purity of Dhrupad is precious. It is to be cherished and kept alive till the next cycle of cosmic revolution touches us with a flood of light.

Baba Bairam Khan, Nana Vande Ali Khan, the legendary veena wizard, and then, his uncle Baba Gopal Das, the musical ustad of Jaipur *Maharana* and *Raja* Ranjit Singh are some of the great names that have embellished the illustrious lineage of the Dagars. They have influenced the ancestors of very many *gharanas* of today who do not even sing Dhrupad! More recently, Zia Fariduddin's father was not only the state musician of Udaipur, but also the musical ustad of its *Maharana,* Parvat Singh-ji.

Zia Fariduddin remembers growing up as a normal child in a natural but unimposing musical atmosphere. By the age of thirteen he began to be drawn towards music, and at eighteen he started to formally learn from his father. Later, the reins of his musical education were taken over by his elder brother Zia Mohiuddin Dagar.

Zia Mohiuddin was a celebrated exponent of the rudra veena. But that wasn't the reason why Fariduddin too had to learn the veena. It is believed in the Dagar family that pure sound emanates from the strings of the veena, and it helps the learner to understand the swaras or the notes much better. That's why traditionally the Dagars encourage even the aspiring vocalist to learn the veena first. Two fundamentals are always kept in view: the *tantra,* or technique, and the *gaana,* or practice. The swaras had to be felt alive, and then mastered. Rigorous voice training had to be adhered to every morning, as a *mantric* exercise! This made the voice produce effects like the sway, the swing, the tremour, the glide, the leap...all so that the divine music can flow through a cleansed and seasoned channel. Only then could a student grasp that the 'sa' is not the same every time you sing; the feel of the 'sa' is dictated by the raga you are about to explore. Different ragas not only have different swaras, or notes, they also employ the same notes differently! And this is something only your ears can detect and endorse, something only your *sadhana* can ensure.

The sadhana of teaching

Having begun his musical journey at a comparatively mature age, Fariduddin was already aware of his family's special place and reputation in the music world. Even the day-to-day interaction with the extended family circle of uncles and cousins was enriched with musical discussions and exchange of music notes. He understood and respected the stringent family philosophy and values that fuelled their musical fervour. Family elders used to say, that when a musician missed out on a single day's *riyaaz,* or practice, he would be set back by no less than a hundred days!

Since his elder brother Mohiuddin had a stronger passion for instruments, Fariduddin respected his father's wish that he should then take up vocal music. His voice had that deep resonance which could be honed further with the excellent voice training and discipline of the Dagar lineage. But the most powerful influence on Fariduddin was the basic philosophy of Dhrupad. The power of truth, the strength of

steadfastness, the joy and pride of knowing that by singing pure music, you are yourself becoming that music! You are invoking the raga as you would invoke the deity in a temple. You warm your voice with the first *swaras* just as you light the flame in preparation of worship. Then you add your heart's feelings and your knowledge of the rituals as you proceed to invoke the deity, stage after stage until it energizes, takes shape, and awakens. Similarly, through your singing, and your striking of the true notes, the raga takes shape, attains form, and comes alive. There's no bigger thrill and greater joy than to be able to do that every time you sit on the *aasan,* the seat of your *sadhana.*

That's why, in spite of acquiring remarkable proficiency as an accomplished performer, in spite of his innumerable recitals all over India, and his many concert tours to the appreciative West, Fariduddin's prime identity to himself has been that of an introspective and conscientious Dhrupadia. The reality that he has been seeing all around in the music world, where the genuine was being replaced by the fake, the pure, by the impure, and the profound, by the frivolous, has eventually made him realize his calling in life with a deep sense of responsibility. Both, towards his celebrated ancestry and towards his eternal art form. With time, he allowed the emerging preceptor, the teacher in him to take precedence over the performer. His scholastic grooming, his philosophical temperament, his divine calm, were just perfect for being the ideal guru...in a less than ideal situation. Because, apparently, the Dhrupad was being popularly regarded as passe, and was in need of revival. The musical river of Swami Haridas, Miyan Tansen and Baiju Bawra was seemingly running into a dry stretch of dreary desert...

That was the beginning of Zia Fariduddin Dagar's quiet crusade against the perceived injustice and misfortune of changing times. In his capacity of a blue-blooded Dagar, and a spirited worshipper of the purest art form in the world, he has been able to sublimate all the pain, hurt and despair born out of witnessing the obvious cultural erosion and moral slide of the era. And slowly, but surely he is affecting a change at the basic levels, he is working among the young, among the new generation of truth seekers, and creating a new breed of believers. After all, as the Dagars have always believed, if you can sing the Dhrupad with true devotion, you can turn the non-believing listeners into believers.

Today, institutes and universities are vying with one another to have Zia Fariduddin Dagar as an inspiring presence amidst their fresh young minds. As a living repository of the original source of Indian classical music, he is like the pitcher made of pure copper holding the water of the Ganges collected at Gomukh, the pristine source. And with the dignity and generosity of a high priest, he has been sprinkling his knowledge and understanding of the Dhrupad upon the faithful as a musical blessing.

Dhrupad stands for *Dhruva Pad* – the path of steadfastness. Regardless of who walks it and for how long, the path remains forever...like truth eternal. Waiting and willing, to connect the traveller with his destination.

Living Memories...

The venerated custodian of Dhrupad

Tuneful communion with God

Showing the dhrupad path. With nephew Baha'ud'din Dagar

Tuning a tanpura

Centre stage with other Dhrupadias

Making a poignant point

Invoking a raga

A rare glimpse from
the Dagar dynasty

Q. What difference do you notice in the concert situation today as compared to that of earlier times?

A. *Today's audience seems happy with showmanship, speed and volume. And today's performer is quick to wind up, collect his payment and disappear! Earlier, the best of artistes used to listen to others. I remember, learned ustads used to sit in the front rows, before the general public. The performer had to give off his best to measure up to the challenge of impressing the knowledgeable. And even ordinary listeners got the benefit of it! Today, everything is mercenary, there's no heart. Each one is busy trying to promote and project himself! Trying to get the media to acknowledge his dubious 'innovations'.*

Q. You mean the new ragas they create? Or is it the experimentations, like the fusion?

A. *Well, new ragas are virtually impossible to create. Everything already exists. There's no space for even a needle tip. It is out of ignorance that some feel they have 'created' something new. Our shastras refer to 5584 different ragas, does it leave any scope for anything else? And as for fusion, it is nothing but a farce! It is a manifestation of disrespect towards one's own music, one's own samskar, one's own distinction and sanctity!*

Q. Since when has all this dissatisfaction been bothering you?

A. *About thirty years ago, there were some musicians who were really great. Today there's hardly a vocalist who satisfies. Some good instrumentalists are still there, but they too are deviating from their path. There are no sadhaks today, there's no sadhana. Our classical character itself is in jeopardy. People approach me as well, to suggest populist performer's gimmicks, but I tell them I cannot do such things. I sing for myself, and my Eeshwar! Everyone knows what the Dagars stand for. My ancestors have built such a formidable reputation based on sincerity and dedication. I cannot even think of lowering that standard, or tarnishing that image.*

Q. But Dagar saheb, life has become so fast and complex...one has to move with the times?

A. *See, we too are moving with the times. But by taking our values with us; not by changing our colours. Wherever I go, in America or Europe, people throng to listen to my pure music, not a compromised or diluted version. They want to listen to Dhrupad more than any other form of Indian classical music. They are intrigued, riveted. Even here, at IIT, whenever we have a concert, the professors of science or engineering, and students from diverse disciplines listen with great attention.*

Q. But Dhrupad is losing popularity in a wider sense, because it is difficult to learn?

A. *Not really.*

Q. Doesn't one need greater lung-power to extend the breath?

A. *That's there. But the real deterrent might be that it is more serious, and deep. It doesn't have the romantic lightness and speed of the Khayal. Dhrupad does not bring out chirpy applause; it* *sends you deep inside, into a meditative, higher plane. But today's Khayal is also not what it used to be. It lacks feelings. It is too eager to impress.*

Q. With musical acrobatics?

A. *Exactly! The mantra today is to try to please the masses! But you see, people have different tastes, different attitudes. How many can you really please? The best thing is to truly immerse within yourself and please your own soul. The rest will all fall in line! In fact, you need not even look at the audience. Close your eyes and sing. I remember Pandit Nikhil Bannerjee, how he used to be immersed in himself on the concert stage. That is how it should be done. Not playing to the gallery or the lowest denominator.*

Q. Do you remember some of your own memorable concerts?

A. *I'll tell you. In Madhya Pradesh, there's a village called Chanderi, where there is the samadhi of the fabled Baiju Bawra. As a tribute to his memory, a concert was held there where a few artistes like me were invited to perform. The audience comprised some simple local villagers who made a living by rolling beedis. The organizers had warned me that I should try some popular 'kawwalis', at the most, and not anything 'heavy'. But when I took the stage, I asked the villagers as to whose samadhi was it where we had all gathered. When they said that it was some historic singer named Baiju Bawra, I asked them if they would like to hear the kind of music he used to sing. And thus, with this preamble, I began to sing Dhrupad. For two and a half hours the illiterate audience sat in rapt attention and enjoyed the performance! Then when I asked them if they would like to hear some light 'kawwali', they were unanimous in answering that nothing would make any sense after what they had heard. It was a memorable experience for me. And an eloquent pointer at what pure, profound music can do to simple honest people.*

Q. Amazing!

A. *Similarly, once at Chhattarpur, while I was singing, some armed dacoits came and joined*

Holding court at the Dhrupad Sansar of IIT, Mumbai

the audience. The organizers were very worried about my safety, because, some time ago the dacoits had abducted a Kathak dancer from such a performance, who was later returned, unharmed, after a few days of private and captive performances! My experience that day, although less dramatic, once again corroborated the dacoits' respect for the performing arts. They listened attentively for a long time and dispersed quietly without trouble.

Q. Tell us, have you ever performed along with anyone?

A. *On foreign tours, I have sung with my cousin Ustad Aminuddin Dagar. We also have cut an LP together...*

Q. Jugalbandi?

A. *Yes. When like-minded artistes perform together, they may sing individually, and also as a unit. Many times the ustad too may make his mature shagird sit and sing with him. Sometimes it is a combination of relatives, or blood brothers.*

Q. The Gundecha Brothers, for instance? They learnt from you, didn't they?

A. *Yes.*

Q. Why does Dhrupad embrace the pakhawaj and not the tabla?

A. *Pakhawaj creates that deep, weighty, gambhir sound...just right for Dhrupad.*

Q. What if the tabla is played in a deep, gambhir manner?

A. *(Smiles) No, that won't work. There are technical differences; the sound itself is different.*

Q. Do I detect a sense of austerity?

A. *Well, we use only the tanpura and the pakhawaj. No harmonium, no swarmandal, no other disturbances. Even the sarangi we generally avoid; it cannot play certain subtle notes...*

Q. Accompanists are utterly subservient?

A. *We often allow good pakhawaj players to improvise along with us. There's always a healthy give and take.*

Q. One finds pakhawaj players accompanying khayal exponents as well...

A. *If that is so, then the reason is, that such artistes wish to subtly suggest that they have a Dhrupad base. This is now becoming a sort of fashion for the showmen. But merely using a Pakhawaj player on the stage obviously is not enough. But yes, it does show how Dhrupad's glory is on the ascent.*

Q. Are there some cold vibes between the Khayal and the Dhrupad exponents?

A. *Shouldn't be. The Khayal is also a form of music; it has its own charm. Earlier, a 'Khayaliya' would make it a point to learn Dhrupad first. That's why their rendition of the ragas had that purity, that honesty. How to spread the swaras...how to present the alaap... first with the voice, the aakars, then with the words...then the taans...the bol-taans...people now have sadly deviated from the form itself! Where's all this today? A mere semblance of alaap, and there's this sudden switch to a bandish, whose words are often unclear. One must not think that just because you are singing classical music, you can ignore the words, the lyrics. The kavita too has as much right to be there as the swar. All the three elements should bond together: the swar, the taal, and the kavita! Then you have true music, true raagdari. Your challenge as a vocalist lies in how beautifully, how lovingly, how interestingly you bring out the beauty of the poetry by your sur sadhana, your singing skill. And how your chosen tala lends it further dynamism.*

Q. Is it necessary to be a good human being to be a good Dhrupad singer? Is it important to be a spiritual person?

A. *Very much so. You have to have faith in God. One who cannot keep faith in his God, he cannot keep faith in his guru.*

Q. How true!

A. *If you have faith in your God and guru, it will manifest in your soul, your music. The listener too will get a feel of what kind of a man you are, what are your values, and what's your character...*

Q. Do you believe you are going to be born again?

A. *Just as I feel I must have been a musician earlier too, I also pray to God that if he should bring me again, he should keep me in touch with music, with Dhrupad. For, it is from Dhrupad that I have acquired my peace, my joy, my values, my philosophy, my truth, my yearning for God. If these won't be there, then I would not like to be reborn. I believe that Dhrupad attracts only the truly fortunate ones! It opens up your ears, your consciousness. You can glimpse the entire cosmos, the Brahmand!*

Q. Coming back to the mundane, Dagar saheb, any message for the younger generations?

A. *Listen to good music, sing with sincerity, always dwell in good thoughts and values. But do embrace some art in life. That's what separates human beings from animals.*

E P I L O G U E

Fortune does favour the brave after all.

It did seem an act of rare bravery, even rarer in my case, to have sought close encounters with the living legends of Indian classical music, armed with merely a single musical qualification. That, of a 'music lover'.

And fortune did favour me with the most enriching treasure chest of human experiences. However, with all the words and pictures, all the art and craft at my disposal, I have been able to present only a fraction of these riches within the pages of this book. Many stories I heard have remained untold. Many photographs I took have remained unused. They shall keep me company, fading and ageing in oblivion.

It was not easy to chalk out an ideal constellation from the many stars that illuminate the firmament of Indian classical music. But providence, without whose design such a project is scarcely possible, seems to have lent subtle guidance, and has endorsed my own presumptuous subjectivity on whom to include.

Conspicuously, however, some deserving names are absent. Their fans and admirers might miss them dearly. My solace to them is that as a music lover, I do miss them as much. And hopefully, if and when there comes a subsequent volume, it could claim its share of some big names who have eluded this one.

Those who have finally appeared, present a colourful spectrum from many perspectives. Their profiles reflect and overlap the historic, cultural and social portrait of India itself over the last century. The list resonates with dramatic contrasts in character traits, life paths, and destinies. All united by the single string of their relationship with classical music.

I have found all the signs and shades of the zodiac in this gallery of maestros. We have birthdays here that coincide with those of Lord Krishna and Jesus Christ, not to mention Adolf Hitler! The maestros have spoken with warmth and candour in assorted Hindi, accented English, chaste Tamil, earthy Marathi, intimate Bengali, and have even broken into song. Some have bared their heart and soul in just one encounter; some have made me chase them for months. Some have refused to lift the phone or answer letters; some have invited me lovingly to their concerts and even inquired if I would be interested in writing their biography. Some have placed before me food cooked with their own hands. While they may all have responded from the depth of their hearts because of their commitment to classical music and its propagation, they have personally done me great honour. I shall forever cherish this sweet feeling of indebtedness.

Since I have tried to probe beyond the mere craft of music making, undercurrents of spirituality, devotion and destiny have surfaced on almost every page. That's because some have sought God through their music, and some have made music their God.

The maestros have not hesitated to acknowledge, in typical humility of great souls, their own ultimate status of a mere traveller on the eternal path of classical music. A path which, almost like the awakening kundalini, seems to spiral upwards into unknown realms of realization.

Finally, and not surprisingly, most of the accomplished, decorated, celebrated stalwarts have confessed to a secret resolve of being re-born. So they can come back and take their sadhana further. And perhaps grasp a little more of the divine essence of classical music, and become even better music makers.

That leaves me with a nagging question. Are we doing enough towards becoming better music lovers?

G L O S S A R Y

Aahat (ahat) : The Audible; The Audible part of the Naad is called 'Ahat' and the inaudible is ' Anahata'
Aai : Mother in Marathi
Aaroh-Avaroh : Ascending & descending order of the notes in a Raga. It forms the bare skeletal structure of the Raga
Alaap : Phrase in slow movement with which a melody is introduced
Alankar : lit. Decorations; Decorative figures that adorn a Raga
Alfaaz : Words (Urdu)
Ananda : Bliss, Happiness
Assar : Effect (Urdu)
Asthana Vidwan : Title for a resident maestro
Atmaa : Soul; Spirit

Ba-assar : With effect (Urdu)
Baanya : lit. Left; Dagga part of the tabla played with the left hand
Badhat : Orderly development of musical Ideas in a raga in the form of alaap
Bai : Lady; Female artiste
Bandish : The song text in khayal; Formal structure of construction of a musical composition
Bani : lit. Speech; Style of vocal music especially in Drupad singing are classified into different Bani's
Bansuri : Bamboo Flute
Beti : Daughter
Bhaisahab : Elder Brother
Bhajan : Devotional Song
Bhav : lit. Emotion; Emotional bed of the Raga
Bol : Syllable

Chaiti : Songs of Krishna Leela sung in the Hindu month of Chaitra (March-April)
Cheez : Song text of the Khayal
Chhota Khayal : The kind of bandish unlike vilambit Khayal has a tightness of phrase and structure. Its gait is swift (medium Madhya and fast Dhrut) and it extols the laya of the bandish.
Chittaswaram : Series of set swara-geometries usually sung at the end of a Kirti and after the Charanam in Carnatic music

Dadaji : Grandfather
Dadra : A light classical composition usually where the measures and stresses are equal
Dakshina : A gift or offering to a Priest or Guru given after the completion of religious rite or education.
Darbaar : Royal Courtroom
Darshan : Appearing; Vision
Deewana : Obsessed
Dharampatni : Wife

Gamak : A kind of musical embellishment produced by reiteration of notes giving the effect of forceful shake or trill
Gambhir : Deep and serious
Gandharva : A celestial singer who entertains gods, appears in Puranas and Indian mythology
Gayaki : Style of Singing; Denotes style specific to a Gharana
Gharana : lit. House or Family; family or lineage of musicians singing in a specific style
Ghazal : Originally a Persian form of love song
Ghee : Clarified butter
Ghungroo : Clutch of bells fitted on a belt tied on the ankles of a dancer
Guru : Teacher; 'Gu' means darkness and 'Ru' is light; Guru is the preceptor who takes the disciple from darkness to light
Gurukul : A residential teaching institution kept up by the tutor 'Guru'
Gurukulvasam : The act of residing in a Gurukul

Gopis : Cowherd's wives

Inaam : Reward
Ishtadev : One's tutelary deity; Guardian god to the family/race

Jaati Swaram : A composition without words but has divisions of Pallavi, Anupallavi and Charanam; Widely used for dance recitals
Jaatismar : Person who remembers past lives (Bengali)
Javali : A sensuous song
Jod : Stage of alaap when laya is brought into alaap
Jugalbandi : Performance of two artistes together

Kacheri : Tamil for Concert or Musical entertainment
Kamandalu : A water pot used by ascetics
Karmabhumi : The land you work on or perform religious rites
Kashtha Maunam : Keeping silent and fixed like a wooden log; a type of ritual penance
Kavita : Poetry
Kavya : Poetical composition
Khadj : Very low pitch
Khayal : lit. Idea; It is the dominant form of Hindustani Classical singing today. It affords great scope for improvisation and is subdivided into Bada and Chota Khayal
Khuda : Lord; God
Kinnar : Celestial musician accompanying Gandharvas
Kirtana : A recital of the glory (Kirti) of the Lord
Kriti : These form the bulk of the musical compositions in Carnatic music. It is a fully composed piece of music complete in its architecture and motion. The great Thyagraja and the other members of the trinity have given this form so much vitality that the sahitya (lyrics) have gathered a certain sacredness that the musician observes.
Kshetra : lit. Field; area
Kotha : lit. A mansion; usually a place where Female artiste used to entertain visitors with exclusive recitals
Kuldevi : The tutelary goddess; Guardian goddess to the family/race
Kundalini : The vital force (power) lying dormant within every individual, symbolized as a coiling serpent, until activated by the practice of Yoga
Kurta : Indian shirt
Kanjira : Tambourine

Laya : Principle of rhythm: Tempo of the song
Laykari : Play with the rhythm; Cross-Rhythmic play

Mahurat : Auspicious time according to Indian Astrology
Mala : Garland
ManoDharma Sangeet : Music sung extempore based on a skeletal architecture. Khayal gayaki is mostly manodharma
Mantric : Relating to Vedic hymn or sacred sanskrit prayer
Masjid : Mosque
Maulvi, Mulla : A learned Mohammedan priest
Meend : A graceful glide from an upper to a lower note in the process slightly touching the intermediate notes
Mehfil : A musical concert or gathering
Moksha : Liberation, Deliverance of the soul from rebirth

Naad : Emanation of life principle or Prana; it is subdivided into 'Ahata' Audible and 'Anhata' unheard
Naad Yoga : The work on the Swara as a kind of Yoga
Namaskaar : Hindu salutation
Namaz : Mohammedan form of praying to Allah, God
Natraj : King of dancers; The Dancing Lord Shiva
Natya : Indian Performing Art

Om : A Mantric word thought to be the complete expression of the Brahama. (It consists of 3 units of sound corresponding to the waking, dreaming and deep sleep as the 3 states of existence and followed by silence, which is fulfillment)

Paan : Betel leaf
Padam : A poetic composition with verses of lyrics
Pancham : lit. Fifth; the fifth note
Paran : Denotes mnemonic for the double, triple, thirds & fifth of a tempo in tala cycle
Parmatma : The supreme spirit or Brahaman
Patidev : Husband
Pitaji : Father
Pitamaha : Grandfather; and epithet of Bhishma from Mahabharat
Pranayam : Breathing exercise to control the life breath 'Pran'
Prasad : Part of the food offered to the God; Goods gift.
Pujari : Worshipper; Priest

Ragaswaroopa : The essential form of a Raga
Ragini : Conceived as female Ragas
Raj Purohit : Royal Priest
Ramta Jogi : Wandering mendicant
Rangoli : Decorative art created on the ground with rice paste, dry colours or flowers as a welcome for guest/god
Rasa : Creative emotion/essence
Rasik : Lover of music
Riyaaz : Practice

Sam : First and the most important point of stress in a tala cycle
Sachcha Sur : True note/tone
Sadhak : Man in dedicated pursuit
Sadhana : A creative endeavour through practice
Sadhu : An honorable, pious and virtuous man
Sadhavi : Woman in dedicated pursuit
Sahitya : Literary or rhetorical composition; the lyrics; Collection of material
Samadhi : Meditative state when the mind and the object of concentration merge into one another; It is the final and fifth stage of Yoga
Samraat : King of many kingdoms
Samskaar : Refinement; Upbringing; Training of the mind
Sam Veda : One of the four main Vedas
Sandhya arti : Evening prayers
Sangam : Meeting; union
Sangat : Musical accompaniment
Sangeet Martanda : The Sun of Music
Sangeet Sabha : Musical gathering
Sanyas : Renunciation of all worldly attachments
Sarvavyapi : All pervading
Satvik : Endowed with the quality of "Sattva' (Goodness and purity)
Sawa Lakha : 1.25 Lakh
Shadaj : The first note or the 'Tonic'
Shagird : Pupil; student
Shareer Veena : The human body as a metaphor of the Veena
Shastra : lit. Science or rule; A religious or sacred treatise
Shivalay : A Lord Shiva temple
Shloka : A Sanskrit term meaning poetry usually of four lines
Shravana : To listen and understand; To hear
Shringar : One of the navrasa's, indicating love and embellishment
Shruti : A sound that is audible; In Indian Classical music there are 22 Shrutis
Shuddha Shastriya Sangeet : Pure Indian classical music
Sindoor : Vermilion
Smashan : Cemetery
Sufiana : of the Sufi Philosophy
Swara : Tone; Note

Talim (Taleem) : Training
Taan : Rapid succession of notes; A fast passage
Tabalchi : Tabla Player
Tabla-Nawaz : One proficient in the art of playing the Tabla
Tahzeeb : Civilisation; Upbringing; etiquettes
Taiyari : Preparedness; maturity
Tala : Rhythm; particular time cycle ie. ek tala, teen tala etc.
Tameez : Good manners; Decorum
Tantrik : A follower of Tantra doctrine
Tapasya : Penance
Tappa : Form of music like khayal sung in frequent fast passages of notes
Teen Tala (Tri Tala): A tala of 16 beats
Teertha : A place of pilgrimage near a sacred water body; holy water
Tehai : A technique that repeats a phrase 3 times to the accented beat of a tala cycle
Thani Avartanam : A portion in a concert where the percussive instrument is given a free run to display the intricacies of the tala of the raga
Thillana : Carnatic Tarana tala configurations
Thumri : A light, mostly amorous song; a dominant form in light Indian music
Tukda : lit. A piece

Ustaad : Maestro; Mentor; Master; Guru

Vjra : Thunderbolt weapon of lord Indra
Varnam : Category or Colour
Vidushi : Learned Lady
Vidwan : Generic term for Scholar
Vidya Daan : Imparting knowledge
Vilambit Khayal : The slow tempo composition in the Khayal also called Bada Khayal
Vistaar : Elaborate; Expand

Wah Wah! : Bravo! A spontaneous expression of the listener's delight at the musical rendition it also acts as an encouragement to the artiste

Yagna Havan : The Sacred fire altar where a religious sacrifice, offering or oblation is made